MBI Publishing Company

The American Railroad

JOE WELSH

WITH JIM BOYD AND
WILLIAM F. HOWES JR.

To Katie and Kellie

Acknowledgments

I would like to give special thanks to Jim Boyd, who wrote the locomotive chapter, and to William F. Howes Jr., who wrote the chapters on stations and railroaders. I would also like to thank Mike Schafer of Andover Junction Publications, the producer of this book, for his assistance in writing several of the sidebars and for choosing illustrative material.

And, thank-yous to the following folks are in order for their assistance with THE AMERICAN RAILROAD: Chris Baer, Forrest L. Becht, Jim Beckwith, Seth Bramson, Suzanne Burris, Bill Caloroso, John Dziobko, Bill Connolly, Ed DeRouin, Ed Eckes, Ruth Eckes, Steve Esposito, Dan Frinfrock, Gordon Glattenberg, Sandy Goodrick, Barb Hall, Scott Hartley, Ellen Haltemann, Jim Hutzler, Paul Joslin, Tom Kline, Mitch Markovitz, Mike McBride, Mac McCarter, Dan Munson, Bill Middleton, Dave Oroszi, Howard Patrick, Elvis A. Presley, Jacki Pryor, Bob Schmidt, Jeff Schultz, Alvin Schultze, Steve Smedley, Brian Solomon, Richard Steinheimer, Peter Tilp, Bob Wayner, Tex Wilson, Doug Wornom.

Institutions, companies, and other organizations that also provided assistance include: Burlington Northern & Santa Fe Railway; the California State Railroad Museum Library, Sacramento; the Milwaukee Road Historical Association; Pixels, Your Image Place; the Railway & Locomotive Historical Society; and the St. Louis Mercantile Library.

First published in 1999 by MBI Publishing Company, 729 Prospect Avenue, Osceola, WI 54020 USA.

© Andover Junction Publications, 1999

Edited by Mike Schafer; book design and layout by Mike Schafer with Maureene D. Gulbrandsen, Andover Junction Publications, Lee, Illinois.

MBI Publishing Company books are also available at discounts in bulk quantity for industrial or sales-promotional use. For details, write to Special Sales Manager at Motorbooks International Wholesalers & Distributors, PO Box 1, Osceola, WI 54020-0001 USA.

Library of Congress Cataloging-in-Publication Data available
ISBN 0-7603-0512-9

On the front cover: Twin Electro-Motive diesels have a westbound Union Pacific manifest freight under control as they wind down from the summit of Tennessee Pass on tracks formerly belonging to the fabled Denver & Rio Grande Western near Mitchell, Colorado, in June 1997. It's a scene that embodies modern American railroading—modern diesel power on North America's largest railroad—and is a testament to the fascinating twists and turns of railroading's evolution since America's first common-carrier railroad, the Baltimore & Ohio, was established 170 years earlier. *Mark W. Bailey*

On the back cover: Main photo: The era of the steam locomotive in America is in its last decade as "double-headed" Norfolk & Western engines take a chartered passenger train through Virginia in September 1954. John Dziobko. Inset photo: Vintage diesel locomotives of the 1950s representing long-defunct railroads Delaware, Lackawanna & Western and Jersey Central stand on display at Steamtown, Scranton, Pennsylvania, in 1993. *Jim Boyd*

On the frontispiece: Just as railroads were integral to the America's growth and development, American railroads were involved in commemorating the nation's 200th anniversary in 1976. Many roads painted some of their locomotives in special Bicentennial paint schemes, as illustrated by Illinois Central Gulf's "American Eagle" locomotive, standing at Rockford, Illinois, during that city's fireworks presentation on July 4, 1976. *Mike Schafer*

On the title page: En route from Chicago to the Twin Cities of Minneapolis and St. Paul, Minnesota, a Burlington Northern freight is enveloped by the grandeur of the Mississippi River Palisades just north of Savanna, Illinois, in 1993. *Steve Smedley*

Acknowledgments photo: From inside the roundhouse, a young boy contemplates Central Vermont steam locomotive No. 501 outside on the turntable at CV's engine terminal at Brattleboro, Vermont, in 1953. *Philip R. Hastings Collection, California State Railroad Museum*

Table of contents photo: A Santa Fe freight flies over a Wisconsin Central freight, as viewed from the WC train's locomotives, in suburban Chicago. *Bill Beecher*

Printed in China

Contents

Foreword

I've been intrigued by trains and railroading for nearly all of my half century on this planet. My earliest railroad-related experiences date to about the time I was three years old, and I still clearly remember most of them from that time on. I still reminisce about my first train ride in 1953 on Illinois Central's *Hawkeye* between my hometown of Rockford, Illinois, and Chicago. And I recall walking home from a visit with a friend with my older sister circa 1958 and, upon crossing the IC tracks, hearing something in the distance. My sister asked, "Shall we wait?" I was thrilled at the sight of three IC diesels roaring into town with an inconceivably long Iowa-bound freight.

Perhaps my favorite recall of all occurred on March 27, 1964, when four of us high-school chums rode Milwaukee Road's *Arrow* to Chicago and then a bouncing, rocketing Rock Island Lines commuter train to Joliet, Illinois, for a day of train-watching. That was my first time out on my own in a new city to photograph and documenting railroad history in the making. (Little did I know that would someday be my career.)

The funny thing about those times is that we pretty much accepted railroading as it was. We took it for granted; it would always be the way it was. Santa Fe's *Super Chief* would always call at Joliet, right? And, of course, there would always be a Rock Island. After all, it seemed to us that day at Joliet that the Rock was dispatching a freight through town every 30 minutes or so. Lots of traffic; the Rock must be doing well.

But, alarm bells would shortly signal that nothing was forever. Later in 1964, almost overnight the Norfolk & Western swallowed up two legendary railroads: the Wabash and Nickel Plate. Suddenly, there was a new railroad in our midst—the closest that the N&W had come to Chicago before this was Cincinnati—but at the same time, two Chicago-based railroads I had been intrigued

by, but had only read about and never really seen, began to vaporize before I could even suitably document them on film.

In 1967 came a rather loud alarm bell. The summer of that year, our "hometown streamliner," Illinois Central's *Land O' Corn*—a train I had virtually grown up with—was discontinued. The disturbing trend of passenger-train discontinuances really began to accelerate. Shortly after, another merger occurred: the mighty Pennsylvania Railroad (another personal favorite) and the New York Central merged to form Penn Central.

Come 1971 I was teaching art to high-school students while, in my dwindling free time, also trying to continue documenting the American railroad scene—a scene that was changing more than ever. Penn Central had gone bankrupt, Amtrak arrived, and the Monon Railroad (yet another personal favorite) was merged out of existence. Change was accelerating, and I wasn't sure I could keep up with it—nor did I necessarily like it.

In 1971, too, I made a career move into publishing, in the field of railroading. I've been there ever since, and that career has been my window to

Tucked away in a remote area of Jamesburg, New Jersey, a surviving stretch of Camden & Amboy track, photographed in 1955, served as a silent reminder of the numerous chapters of railroad history that have unfolded since the track was laid in the early 1800s. *John Dziobko*

railroading of the 1970s, 1980s, and 1990s. Sometimes that window has been smudged, even broken. But the change I've seen through it has never been uninteresting.

I figure I've witnessed firsthand about 34 percent of railroading's span in American history. I feel pretty lucky about that (although I do sometimes wish I had been born just a few years earlier so that I could have witnessed the steam era; where I grew up, steam disappeared early), but that means I still missed about 66 percent of it.

And that's where this book comes in. The older I got and the more time I spent around railroads, observing, researching, and studying their operations and riding their trains, the more I realized how important it is to put it all in perspective. Sure, I think new General Electric's AC4400 diesels are impressive-looking locomotives (and one just went by my trackside house as I wrote this paragraph), but how did *that* locomotive evolve from a ponderous-looking creature called the *John Bull*?

More questions. How did a gleaming stainless-steel, two-story Amtrak passenger train descend from horse-drawn railcars? Why has the number of railroad depots dwindled from a peak of some 80,000 to less than 10,000? Even the track has changed dramatically. Check out the accompanying photo that photographer John Dziobko (JEB-ko) took of ancient track—with rails that still used stone blocks, not wood ties, for support.

This book will help answer those and other questions all of us have had regarding the fascinating and intriguing history of American railroading. The authors and photographers don't have answers to all the questions, but they'll certainly help put things into perspective. And that's what really counts. For knowing the past, you'll have a better understanding of the future.

—*Mike Schafer, Editorial & Art Director*
Andover Junction Publications

Introduction

This book traces the history of American railroads from inception to modern times. Like any single volume given to explaining a complex subject, it relies on its authors and editor to choose the images which summarize the topic and to find a story line in the millions of words of history already written about the subject. If there is a story line in THE AMERICAN RAILROAD, it's the "railroad as survivor"—companies reliant on change, sometimes inexorably slow and sometimes brutally swift, to stay alive. That's the written story line. But take a look at the pictures and you'll see an underlying storyline as well. . . a story of loss. For as gritty, costly, and labor-intensive as the railroad used to be, it was something with legitimate character.

Today, railroad schedules are planned on computers; trains are tracked by satellites while dispatchers thousands of miles away in sterile, space-aged facilities control train movement like Captain Kirk directing the starship *Enterprise*. On paper and at stockholders' meetings it all sounds pretty impressive. Railroading is, after all, a business, and one which must change and modernize to stay competitive. But the customs and character of railroading—once sacrosanct and still as much a part of the American fabric as baseball—have changed fundamentally. From a social standpoint, adjusting to those changes has been difficult.

Because of the previously labor-intensive nature of railroading, the industry was once an integral part of the communities through which it passed. Railroads maintained shops and yards in many towns to service locomotives and sort freight, employing hundreds of local people in the process—even for tasks as mundane as those of gate tenders, personally warning motorists of approaching trains.

The local depot, maintained in even the smallest of towns should the need arise for someone to ship a package or flag a train, was at one time a city's gateway—not to mention a social gathering place. Many a former young boy, standing awestruck on the station platform as a locomotive rolled to a stop, can remember with crystal clarity the first time the engineer crooked a finger at him to ask if he'd like to step up into the cab and have a look around. Likewise, the railroad tower, replaced by automation and now virtually a thing of the past, was a landmark and a beacon to every kid in the vicinity, many of whom got their edu-

Pondering railroading's future at Solitude, Utah, in 1997, photographer Brian Solomon records trains—and comets (Hale-Bopp in this case)—passing in the night.

cation on railroading under the wing of a kindly tower operator.

Chances are the depot, the tower, and even the train and the track are no longer there. The abandonment of rail lines and costly facilities under the banner of rationalization has been an alarming reality during the last half of the 20th century. On the cusp of a new millennium, the focus is on fast, point-to-point freight trains while passenger trains have been relegated to curiosity status—their full potential still awaiting rediscovery in an highway-obsessed nation. All of this has changed the way we encounter the railroad. Today the average kid knows a freight train only as an intermodal consist screaming through town at 60 mph. Finding a

safe and legal place to watch the railroad or talk to a railroader can be a real challenge.

This sweeping change is perhaps best symbolized by the demise of the railroad caboose in the 1990s. This classic icon of railroading, subject of children's books and full-length histories, once punctuated virtually every freight train. Its presence at the rear of the train was reassuring, and a wave from the railroader in its cupola or on the back platform was inevitable as it passed our vantage point. Now observers are surprised to find in its place a small electronics box attached to the last freight car's rear coupler. It not only flashes a warning, but it returns information on the train's condition to the engineer by radio. More cost-effective than a caboose and arguably just as safe, the EOTD (end of train device) saves well over 50 cents for each train-mile it is operated. It made eminent sense but replacing the caboose was like replacing the baseball pitcher with a machine because it was more cost-effective. Somehow it just doesn't feel right.

Nonetheless, there remains an aura of mystique and excitement to railroading, even in its sterilized form. Why else are there so many more people at trackside today than ever before simply to experience the pleasure of watching trains pass by. Witness what happened in Rochelle, Illinois. Situated at the crossroads of two busy railroad main lines belonging to Union Pacific and Burlington Northern & Santa Fe, this city of some 9,000 75 miles west of Chicago did what is surely an unprecedented undertaking: In 1998 the City of Rochelle opened a trackside park expressly for folks who simply like to watch trains. Today, the parking lot at Rochelle Railroad Park abounds with vehicles from all over the United States. In and around the park shelter are people of all shapes, sizes, and ages—male and female, toddlers and oldsters—enjoying the excitement and intrigue that railroading has brought to Americans for generations for well over 150 years.

The Railroad Saga

THE STORY OF THE AMERICAN RAILROAD is the story of America itself. Born of necessity, both the railroad and the country grew up together. Their successful partnership fostered America's transition from an isolated, post-Colonial, rural country to a leading nation. The railroad helped America improve its trade, settle its conflicts, and populate its frontier. The country we know today simply would not have been the same geographically and demographically had it not been for the railroad.

BIRTH OF THE AMERICAN RAILROAD

The growth of commerce in the Eastern United States made a quantum leap during the first half of the 1800s as a result of the fast, affordable transportation provided by railroads. In fact, railways were the midwife of the American industrial and commercial revolution of the day. Eastern manufacturers seeking raw materials and new markets found in the railroad a long-awaited partner. The railroads' speed and efficiency brought other improvements. Farmers could now ship perishable produce longer distances and still afford to sell it at market, and people could easily migrate to new frontiers to settle and build towns and cities.

It wasn't always that way. The extensive system of roads and canals that evolved in the period following the War of 1812 opened up the Eastern U.S. and paved the way for railroad construction. In New England, New York, and Pennsylvania, improved roads called turnpikes—named for the toll gates they employed—sprang up almost overnight, encouraged by the need to transport goods over land as a result of the recent wartime British naval blockade. The expansion of improved roads liberated the country from its dependence on nature. No longer would travelers have to wait for the mud to dry or the water level to change before they could travel. By the 1820s over 1,100 miles of paved road existed in Pennsylvania while neighbor New York State boasted over 4,000 miles of road. Authorized by Congress in 1806, the National Road—the longest turnpike of all—by 1833 had been extended as far west as Columbus, Ohio.

But despite the availability of a growing network of roadways, the cost of traveling on those roads—both monetarily and physically—could be prohibitive. All movement was by foot, horseback, or horse-powered wagon or stagecoach. Farm produce and many bulk goods were still rarely shipped over land; the cost in terms of time and money was simply too great. Passengers traveling in stagecoaches told harrowing tales of hard rides and sleepless nights on "improved" roads so poorly built that they were useless to all but those who had to travel them.

Other forms of transportation rose to fill the gap. Canals offered less-expensive and more-comfortable transport than early roads, though they were initially more costly and difficult to build than turnpikes. The greatest of all waterways of the day was a 364-mile watercourse from Albany to Buffalo, the Erie Canal. Begun in 1817 and completed in 1825 after a prodigious engineering effort, the state-sponsored Erie Canal proved a bargain to shippers and became an immediate success. By 1830 over 1,200 miles of canals had been built—the majority of them in Pennsylvania, Ohio, and New York—and many more miles were planned. Steamboat traffic increased too and rivers such as the Mississippi and Ohio hosted an expanding array of freight and passenger traffic. But river travel was dependent on water free of obstructions—including ice. Canals, too, froze in winter and were prohibitively expensive or impossible to build over mountain ranges. The stage was set for a newcomer to claim the mantle from these ambitious but flawed forms of transportation.

If the American railroad was born of necessity, the rivalry between America's cities helped it grow. Blessed with geographic advantages, New York City capitalized on its proximity to the Atlantic Ocean and the Hudson River. Already dominant in foreign trade, the city sought to expand its commerce to the interior by water, notably through the Delaware & Hudson Canal, opened in 1823, and the Erie Canal, both serving as feeders to the Hudson River. Concerned, rival Philadelphia supported a Pennsylvania state project to build a canal cross the Alleghenies to reach Pittsburgh and the Ohio River. The result was more than a canal. Completed in 1834, the 395-mile Main Line of Public Works was an integrated system of canals, inclined planes, and railways. Although it was enormously expensive to build and operate—it failed to turn a profit during its first decade—the MLofPW was critical to the future development of Pennsylvania—and for one of America's greatest institutions, the Pennsylvania Railroad, early segments of which incorporated portions of the MLof PW.

To the south, another port city, Baltimore, Maryland, took a more progressive approach. Disdainful of the Chesapeake & Ohio Canal which

FACING PAGE: The Union Pacific is an elder statesman of American railroading, having been in existence since 1862. Its patriotism is evident in this scene at the UP facilities in south suburban Chicago at Dolton, Illinois, in 1986. *Mike Schafer* ABOVE: Sunset on Southern Pacific's Tucumcari, New Mexico, line. Steel rails form part of the tapestry of transportation arteries that bind together the United States. Without those rails, America would have been a decidedly different place—had it survived at all. *Brian Solomon*

city fathers felt was better positioned to serve Washington, Baltimore put its money and spirit behind a newfangled transportation technology that had emigrated to America from England—the railway. City fathers chartered the Baltimore & Ohio Railroad in 1827 and commenced construction in 1828, becoming the nation's first common-carrier railroad. By 1830, the railroad had completed 13 miles of track, from Baltimore to Ellicott City.

Initially, railways caught on less quickly than roadways and canals. Though they provided a superior ride, construction was more complex and costly than roads, and the proven locomotion technology at the time was the horse—with all its limitations. This rapidly changed following the introduction of the steam locomotive on U.S. soil in 1829, when the *Stourbridge Lion* became the first locomotive to haul an American train, on tracks belonging to the Delaware & Hudson Canal Company.

In 1830 in South Carolina, the *Best Friend of Charleston* steam locomotive pulled 141 passengers on the first scheduled steam-powered passenger

LEFT: The earliest English and American railways were horse powered. Skeptics viewed the infant steam locomotive as a curiosity, a feeling fortified when Peter Cooper's *Tom Thumb* locomotive lost a race to a horse-drawn train, as depicted in this re-enactment at the Baltimore & Ohio Railroad Museum in Baltimore in 1977. The skepticism faded as locomotive technology quickly evolved, proving that "iron horses" were more than a match for the real thing. *Jim Boyd.*

BELOW: Manufactured in England but assembled in America in 1831, Camden & Amboy No. 1—a.k.a. the *John Bull*—was a portend of basic steam-locomotive design and technology that would endure until the end of the steam era after World War II. The *John Bull* still exists (along with a replica built from scratch by the Pennsylvania Railroad in 1924), and, thanks to major restoration work by the Smithsonian Institution, is operable, as demonstrated in this 1981 scene, with Smithsonian curator John H. White serving as engineer. *Jim Boyd.*

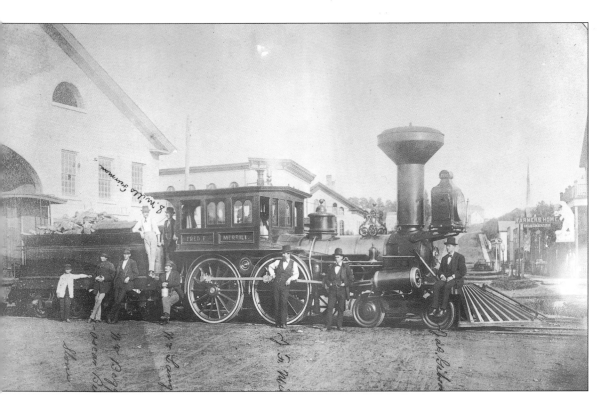

Locomotive *Fred F. Merrill* of the Milwaukee & St. Paul was a 4-4-0 (four pilot wheels, four drivers, and no trailing wheels) built in 1848 as engine No. 37 for M&StP predecessor Milwaukee & Mississippi. Like most steam locomotives of the period, the *Merrill* was wood-burning—coal would not come into wide acceptance until America's railway network had developed enough so that the "black diamonds" could be distributed in large quantities from the mining regions of Pennsylvania, the Virginias, and Kentucky. Note the *Merrill*'s large kerosene headlight—about four feet tall—in this scene at the stone depot at Waukesha, Wisconsin, circa 1870. *Milwaukee Road Historical Association Archives*

About That Light at the End of the Tunnel . . .

Railways revolutionized the way people and goods moved about the country, but without sub-technologies, railway development would have been hamstrung. One was the locomotive headlight. Headlights today, be they for autos, trucks, or railroad locomotives, are taken for granted. But in the wild youth of railways, train travel came to an abrupt halt when night fell—and with it a clear vision of the perilous path ahead.

The first "headlight" is said to have appeared on New Jersey's Camden & Amboy in the 1830s. As traffic grew on the C&A, so did the need to run trains around the clock. The railroad's solution for safe night travel? Push a flatcar of burning timber ahead of the locomotive. For obvious reasons, this was a stopgap measure: the ongoing possibility of leaving a path of destruction in a dry forest or field limited the popularity of the open flame as headlight.

Oil lanterns mounted on the locomotive were far more successful. A metal shield mounted behind the flame focused light forward into the darkness rather than in the engine crew's eyes. Lanterns weren't particularly bright, but then trains only moved at 15-20 mph. The more-powerful kerosene headlight provided more lumens. They were bulky appliances, but necessary for the faster trains being run in the mid-nineteenth century.

Railroads were one of the first major industries to apply new electric technologies, and the headlight was first electrified in 1883—and none too soon. Locomotives were now capable of 50-60 mph—speeds which outdistanced the range of a kerosene headlight. Electric headlights were more efficient, required less maintenance, and were far more powerful. Well over a century later, electric headlights protect trains that now speed along at well over 100 mph.

train in the United States, and during that same year Peter Cooper's *Tom Thumb* hauled a train over the fledgling B&O. By 1833, for three dollars, passengers on the Camden & Amboy Railroad & Transportation Company could travel the 80-odd miles between the New York area and Philadelphia in just seven hours behind the *John Bull* steam locomotive. The new "iron horse" quickly ascended to prominence, replacing the four-legged variety.

Another development—the iron "T"-shaped rail, which replaced wooden track—helped speed the spread of the new form of transportation. The new track was more durable and could carry heavier loads than its wooden counterpart. Even simple inventions, such as the locomotive headlight, revolutionized the new transportation king, allowing railroads to operate 24 hours a day.

With technology on its side, the American railroad expanded significantly during the 1830s. By 1840 22 of the nation's 26 states had seen track laid. By far the majority of trackage served the Eastern seaboard; only 250 miles of the 3,000

miles of track laid to date was west of the Appalachians. Nonetheless, railroad mileage now equaled that of canals.

The 1840s and 1850s saw continued growth of the rail network as well as the birth of some the country's most important future railroads. The Pennsylvania Railroad was incorporated by Philadelphia businessmen in 1846 to connect Philadelphia to Pittsburgh and the Ohio River via an all-rail route. The impetus for the project was dissatisfaction with the state's canal system—including the Main Line of Public Works—as well as the threat to trade posed by B&O's efforts to reach the Pittsburgh and the Ohio River. In New York State, too, things were happening. Benjamin Loder's New York & Erie Railroad, chartered in 1832, was finally being built through New York's Southern Tier to the shores of Lake Erie, which it would reach in 1851. The birth of what was destined to become the Erie Railroad encouraged the 1853 formation of the New York Central Railroad, born from the union of ten individual railroads, including the

Immigration and land grants fueled the growth of railroads which in turn grew America. The mid-nineteenth century saw railroads expand at fever pitch in what would become known as America's Middle West, with Chicago at the base of Lake Michigan serving as the region's (and eventually the whole nation's) rail hub. One of the most prominent, aggressive railroads of the region would be the Chicago, Milwaukee & St. Paul, later popularly known as the Milwaukee Road. Pulled by a Civil War-era 4-4-0, a CM&StP train poses high above the Wisconsin River at Kilbourn (now Wisconsin Dells). Note the brakeman riding the roof of the first car. *Milwaukee Road Historical Association Archives*

Mohawk & Hudson, the nation's first chartered (in 1826) railroad to be built. The NYC soon siphoned traffic from the paralleling Erie Canal.

Southern and western frontier states saw significant growth as well. In the South, Georgia could claim 450 miles of new track in the 1850s, achieving prominence as the South's rail hub. In Ohio a patchwork quilt of lines now tenuously linked Cleveland, Sandusky, Columbus, Dayton, and Cincinnati. By 1850 the national rail network contained 9,000 miles of track, a 300 percent increase in just ten years. By mid-century the railroads had eclipsed the turnpike and canal. The goal of moving large volumes of freight and people quickly, for less money, had been met. The railroad was here to stay.

PROLIFERATION AND CIVIL WAR

The railroads' numerous advantages made them more appealing than other modes, and their prolific expansion continued in the 1850s aided by Americans' insatiable desire to push ever westward. The rail network grew from 9,000 miles in 1850 to over 30,000 miles by 1860. Rail systems from the East tamed the mountains and reached the "West" (future Midwest). Baltimore, New York, Philadelphia, and Boston all achieved rail links to the Ohio River and beyond, assuring continued competition.

Chicago became a new rail hub for budding rail lines expanding westward, as well as a destination for railroads from the East. In 1848, the Galena &

Chicago Union—a future marriage partner of the Chicago & North Western—operated the first train ever out of Chicago. Formed in 1851, the Illinois Central Railroad built south to the Gulf of Mexico. Formed in 1855, the Chicago, Burlington & Quincy stretched west to the shores of the Mississippi while the St. Louis, Alton & Chicago reached St. Louis. The Chicago & Rock Island Railroad extended to Rock Island, Illinois, and built the first railroad bridge across the Mississippi River there in 1856. Meanwhile, the Milwaukee & St. Paul was feverishly acquiring numerous smaller railroads in the upper Midwest to build an empire that would become known as the Milwaukee Road.

By the end of the 1850s, the Northeast, Middle West, and South had roughly equal mileage. Though expanding, America's rail "system" was hardly an integrated one. At least eleven different track gauges were in use in the North. Other barriers existed, such as the many major rivers that had yet to be bridged. The transfer of goods and people between railroads was hardly seamless. It took determination—and often several changes of trains and railroads—to get to some destinations by rail.

Despite these challenges, by the eve of the Civil War in 1861 America's rail network extended through a large part of the country as far west as the frontier. Railroads played a vital role in that extraordinarily tragic war. The disparity in quantity and quality between Northern and Southern rolling stock, motive power, and trackage was one of the deciding factors in the North's ultimate victory. Less industrialized, the South's lower capital investment in infrastructure and its inability to replace trackage and equipment destroyed by the Union Army contributed to its defeat.

Railroads on both sides of the Mason-Dixon line experienced significant increases in everyday demand as a result of the war. In addition, the railroads for the first time were used for the rapid deployment of troops. Fighting war on a broad front with inferior numbers of soldiers, the Confederacy often used the railroad to its advantage to shift troops from one theater to another. Confederate General Robert E. Lee, for example, divided his army to reinforce Stonewall Jackson in the Shenandoah Valley and used the railroad to do it. The result was a Confederate victory on both fronts. General Braxton Bragg once moved his entire army of 30,000 troops from Mississippi to Tennessee in less than a week by train.

Understanding the importance of the railroads, the North sent General William Tecumseh Sherman's army on a devastating sweep through the South in 1864. Arcing in a great crescent through the heart of the Confederacy, Sherman's veteran troops used the railroads as a vital supply line on their march—while annihilating the rail lines in their wake. Iron rails heated by bonfires and twisted to prevent their reuse came to be known by the troops as "Sherman's neckties."

The Civil War destroyed over half the South's railroad resources. Conversely, the war strengthened the North's transportation infrastructure. Once highly individual entities, the railroads had been forced to cooperate effectively with each other. In the peace that followed the end of the war in 1865, the railroads stood poised to open an incredible new chapter in American history.

THE OPENING OF THE AMERICAN WEST

In the period before the Civil War, American railroads had been developed to serve the commercial and passenger needs of the East. After the Civil War, the focus was primarily on westward expansion through a largely uninhabited land. The Great Plains lacked extensive, deepwater rivers necessary for navigation, so the railroad became the natural tool to open the West.

Penetrating the frontier, the iron horse brought "civilization" in its wake. Where free-roaming herds of Buffalo and tribes of Native Americans had wandered the plains, farmers and ranchers stayed put, firmly rooted to the railroad—their lifeline. Between 1865 and 1915 railroad mileage in the Great Plains, Rocky Mountain states, and Southwest deserts expanded from a paltry 950 miles to over 90,000 miles.

The railroad's principal advantage was its ability to eclipse the West's formidable distances. And no destination was farther away or more appealing than the Pacific Coast. Prompted by the acquisition of California and the discovery of gold there in 1849, Congress appropriated funding for the survey of possible rail routes to the Pacific. The depression of 1857 distracted attention from the goal but even in the midst of the Civil War, the Republican Party stuck to its platform, calling for a "Pacific Railroad." On July 1, 1862, President Abraham Lincoln signed the Pacific Railway Bill authorizing the *Union Pacific Railroad* to build west from the Missouri River and the Central Pacific Railroad to build east

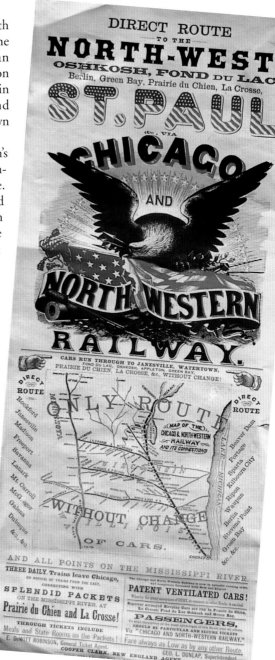

As quickly as rail lines were completed, railroad companies extolled their virtues. This poster issued circa 1860 by the new Chicago & North-Western Railway hyped travel to St. Paul and other growing cities of the upper Midwest as well as to the Mississippi River where travelers could board packet boats to reach cities up and down the river. *Mike McBride Collection*

ABOVE: The wedding of the rails—at 80 miles per hour! As part of the 1969 celebrations commemorating the 100-year anniversary of the completion of America's first transcontinental railroad, Union Pacific dressed up two elderly 4-4-0s to represent Central Pacific's *Jupiter* and UP's No. 119, the two locomotives in attendance at the original Golden Spike ceremony (the real *Jupiter* and 119 had not survived the ensuing century) and ushered them about the UP system as part of a special Golden Spike Centennial display train. The *Jupiter* and 119 "actors" are shown in the familiar nose-to-nose position that was a signature of the original 1869 ceremony, only here they are speeding across Nebraska rather than standing stationary at Promontory, Utah. The date is July 1969 and the Centennial display cars are attached to the rear of UP mail train No. 6 en route to Omaha. *Jim Boyd*

RIGHT: This postcard shows the 1869 ceremony as viewed from the nose of the *Jupiter* looking east toward the 119 before the two locomotives advanced to touch pilots. *Mike Schafer collection*

DRIVING THE LAST SPIKE, PROMONTORY POINT, UTAH, MAY 10, 1869

5A-H834

from Sacramento, California. UP started from Omaha, Nebraska, on December 2, 1863. Led by Grenville Dodge, a small army of 10,000 men, including veterans and ex-convicts, built the UP west. By the end of 1866 the railroad had reached North Platte, Nebraska, 293 miles from Omaha.

On January 8, 1864, the Central Pacific commenced construction east from Sacramento. Largely comprising imported Chinese labor, the CP construction gangs conquered the formidable Sierra Nevada mountains then raced east across Nevada. Prompted by greed, both railroads had actually passed each other in their haste to lay more government-subsidized track. It took Congress to arbitrate and set Promontory, Utah, as the official meeting site. On Monday May 10, 1869, at 12:47 P.M., a 17.6-carat golden spike was "driven"* into a solid laurel wood tie joining the two railroads. America now had its first transcontinental railroad.

Within 30 years of the Civil War, five transcontinental railroads had been built to the Pacific. They included the Northern Pacific and the Great

---

*A spike made of real gold would have been too soft to drive into a tie with a mallet, thus the golden spike was set into a pre-driven hole in the final, laurel-wood tie as part of the ceremony. Central Pacific president Leland Stanford used a regular mallet to drive a regular iron spike; both were wired such that the contact of the mallet with the spike sent a signal over the telegraph lines that triggered fire bells in Chicago and a lowered a ball above the Capitol dome in Washington.

Northern from the upper Midwest to the Pacific Northwest, the Union Pacific/Central Pacific (the latter would become part of Southern Pacific) across the plains to Northern California, the Santa Fe to Southern California from the Midwest, and the Southern Pacific to California from the Gulf.

Four of the five transcontinental railroads and all of the Plains railroads—principally the Chicago & North Western, the Chicago, Burlington & Quincy, the Chicago, Rock Island & Pacific, and the Chicago, Milwaukee & St. Paul—received significant grants of land from the government which used grants to encourage railroad expansion and the establishment of newly settled territory.

The concept had been initiated in 1850 when Illinois Senator Stephen Douglas and a counterpart from Alabama had secured land grants for the Illinois Central and Mobile & Ohio railroads. By the time the practice ended in 1871, 170 million acres had been granted by the federal government to 80 or so railroads. The total value of the land was estimated at $500 million; today it would be worth billions. Contrary to popular belief, this was not a massive giveaway on behalf of the government. In exchange for the land, the federal government reserved the right to use the railroads at greatly reduced rates—and it did so whenever possible and especially at wartime. To the railroads,

the grants provided a source of credit to fund their growth. But, as intended, the land grant also assisted the domestication of the West by allowing the railroads to sell the land to settlers. Railroad representatives haunted Eastern seaports in search of newly arrived immigrants and produced elaborate brochures extolling the virtues of the frontier. Some railroads even promoted agricultural research to pioneer new farming techniques that could be used in the West as a way of encouraging settlement. It worked. Between 1870 and 1890, for example, the population of the Dakotas rose from 14,000 to over 500,000. The West was tamed.

THE RAIL BARONS AND ECONOMIC REGULATION

The lusty expansion of the post-Civil War period gave rise to corruption. Northern carpetbaggers took money from Southern state treasuries to reconstruct railroads destroyed by war, then did little or nothing with it. North Carolina, for example, issued $17 million in state bonds to rebuild its shattered railroads. Only 93 miles of track were built. Most of the money ended up in the pockets of the confidence men and the officials they bribed.

But the efforts of the carpetbaggers in the South amounted to small change when compared to the antics of Northern and Eastern railroad financiers

---

George Westinghouse's Air Brake

In the primitive days of railroading, stopping a train was a pretty straightforward procedure: When the locomotive was braked to a stop, so was the train—but with a jolt as the still-rolling cars banged against the now-stopped locomotive. However, as rolling stock grew heavier and trains ran faster, such inertias became dangerous. The solution was to add a set of brakes to each car which could be operated manually through a brakewheel mounted atop the car. A "brakeman" turned the brakewheel which in turn tightened the brakeshoes against the wheels, and the car came to a stop.

This was a profound advancement in train operation, but it required a lot of dexterity on the part of the already-dangerous job held by brakemen (see also the sidebar on couplers). When the engineer (or train schedule) determined that the train had to be stopped, the brakeman or brakemen had to run along the roofs of the cars to activate the brakes—regardless of weather conditions. Hopefully, the whole train could be brought to a halt in a timely manner, stopping precisely in front of the depot—or short of whatever might be obstructing the tracks. Obviously, this technology limited train length, as did the availability of daring brakemen.

This all changed following the 1869 introduction of the air brake. George Westinghouse's invention allowed the train's engineer to activate, from a single control in the cab of the locomotive, the brakes on the locomotive and every car of the train via air pressure applied through a flexible brake line strung through every car (the air-brake lines were manually linked by brakemen as cars were coupled together). The system was soon modified to be "fail safe"—or nearly so. Each car had its own air cylinder which was connected to the car's brake rigging. These cylinders were in turn activated by changes in pressure in the main air-brake line as controlled by the locomotive engineer or by the conductor in the caboose or rear passenger car if the train were backing up. Rather than to activate the brakes, air pressure was applied to *release* the brake shoes, which were sprung. Thus if the air-brake line became disconnected or severed during train operation and the air escaped from the line, all brakes would activate and automatically stop the train. Though improvements have been made to the Westinghouse air-brake system over the years, the basic principles remain unchanged and today are used to bring even 125-mph Amtrak passenger trains to a safe stop.

Getting Hitched, Then and Now

Early railway cars were simply linked together by chains—which didn't make for very comfortable starts and stops. As the locomotive started to move, it yanked the first car behind into motion ("slack action"), which in turn lurched the second car into motion. . . and so on. And when the train came to a stop—hold on to your seat!

A more formal system of coupling cars—that of the link-and-pin coupler—proved a great leap forward for traveling mankind and freight. A simple affair, link-and-pin coupling systems featured an iron housing mounted on the car frame. The housing had two holes that allowed a heavy iron pin to be dropped into it. A hefty iron link was used to connect two cars, with the pins dropped through the holes to hold the links in place. To uncouple the cars, the brakeman "pulled the pin" (a term still used today) as the cars were parted by the locomotive.

Now limited by the length of the link rather than the length of chains separating cars, slack action was reduced considerably—though far from completely. The main drawback of the link-and-pin coupler was that it was extraordinarily dangerous for brakemen to deal with. The brakeman had to hold the link in position as the locomotive shoved cars close enough together so that the pins could be dropped into place. One not-quick-enough withdrawal of the hand could result in it getting caught between the two coupler housings and

Modern couplers such as these two photographed in 1992 trace their ancestry to the Janney coupler of 1873. The hose passing under the couplers is the air-brake line. *Tom Kline*

smashed—or instantly amputated.

A letter from a Chicago & North Western conductor to a friend dated August 29, 1875, graphically portrays the danger:

"Friend George, I thought I would drop you a few lines to see if you were still alive. My partner—that is, the man that brakes with me—got his right hand cut off last week making a coupling. I tell you it bled pretty hard. It took it clear off. . ."

Finally in 1873, Eli Janney introduced the automatic coupler. The Janney coupler mimicked two clasping hands. When two open couplers were pushed together, the "glad hands" closed, allowing a pin to drop into place to lock them shut.

Though Janney's invention reduced slack action considerably and was much safer, it did not catch on quickly. Railroads were not interested in investing in such a massive upgrade, which would have involved thousands of locomotives and huge fleets of rolling stock. Their stubborn refusal was finally overthrown by labor unions, and in 1893 a new federal law mandated that all locomotives and rolling stock in interchange service be equipped with automatic couplers.

Today's couplers reflect many improvements—for example, they can be released by a lever from the side of the car—but the basics of the Janney system are still there.

such as Cornelius Vanderbilt, Daniel Drew, and Jay Gould. These men of influence and their minions watered stock, fueled rate wars, and otherwise cheated and swindled their way to fortune. When Cornelius "Commodore" Vanderbilt entered the railroad business in 1862 by acquiring the New York & Harlem and New York & Hudson railroads he already possessed an $11 million estate earned in the steamship trade. When he passed his inheritance to his son, it included the New York Central Railroad as well. Son William parlayed this into a $200 million fortune in just eight years.

The elder Vanderbilt figured in an episode which personified the swashbuckling attitude and abuse of law common to some rail barons. In an attempt to gain control of the rival Erie Railroad, Vanderbilt had begun buying stock in that company. Sensing the moment was right, Erie managers Daniel Drew, Jim Fisk, and Jay Gould unloaded 100,000 worthless shares on the Commodore, who responded by convincing a New York City judge to issue an arrest warrant for the three swindlers. The Erie men skedaddled across the Hudson River, holing up in regal splendor in a Jersey City hotel. Surrounded by millions of dollars, a host of security men, and issuing statements to the press, the three fugitives took an expedient course to solving the problem—they bought off the New York State legislature with the help of $500,000 in cash and a New York fixer, Senator "Boss" Tweed.

As spectacular as the affair was, more damage was being done to the average man on the street. The wholesale abuses of shippers by railroad management gave rise to a ground swell of opinion in favor of tightly regulating the industry. Caught in the grip of high rates, or discriminated against by rebates paid by the railroads to richer competitors, the average shipper became disgusted. He was joined by the farmer who suffered income losses due to the now-high cost of shipping crops to market. Labor unrest and its brutal repression by railroad management added to the railroads' growing unsavory image. Prodded by the Grange, a powerful social and political movement in the farm states, several rural states enacted Granger laws to fix railroad rates in the 1870s. This was followed by the establishment of the Interstate Commerce Commission in 1887—a regulatory body that would rule for over 100 years. At first a relatively low-key organization, the ICC's power was enhanced significantly early in the twentieth century in response to the growing corporate power (and abuses) of the railroads. As rail systems consolidated at the turn of the century, they began to acquire enormous influence. By the early 1900s nearly two thirds of the country's rail mileage was controlled by just seven groups. The scramble to acquire that control had been characterized by antics that would have made Jim Fisk blush. And it caught the attention of a formidable foe.

With the arrival in office of President Theodore Roosevelt, the railroads had met their match. Roosevelt devoted his considerable energies to strengthening the ICC and establishing a system of controls. The practice was continued by his successors with the result that the railroads' destructive behavior was largely curbed by the early 1900s. But it left a lasting legacy. The railroads would remain a heavily regulated industry for most of the twentieth century.

PEAK YEARS OF PROSPERITY

The suppression of the railroads' excesses initially had a positive effect that led to a period of rational growth, consolidation, and standardization as the industry matured. In the 30-year period between 1880 and 1910, America's total rail mileage nearly tripled from 93,000 miles to 240,000 miles. Most of the major, "classic" railroad companies that would dominate the twentieth century were now in place (Chapter 2), many of them the result of a frenzy of mergers during that period.

In the densely populated, industrialized Northeast and in the agriculturally rich Midwest, a colorful variety of railroads—some industry analysts will say too many—competed for freight and passengers. Because of the great expanse of the West, the longer distances between major cities, and less population density, Western railroads tended to be larger and fewer in number. Southeastern railroads may have been in the best position: the devastation of the Civil War and the Southeast's late bloom as an industrial power resulted in a more rational network of railroads that would better weather the hard times that would follow World War II.

Major operating efficiencies were introduced following the Civil War, chief among them the adoption of a standard track gauge, 4 feet 8½ inches. Other new developments likewise had a profound

ABOVE: A stock certificate from the New York, Ontario & Western, a company more or less isolated from surrounding giants like New York Central and Erie, both of which gained notoriety through the questionable actions of their leaders. Railroad stock transactions in the late nineteenth century were fraught with fraud, politics, and pure greed, and rail barons of the period earned a shady reputation that would taint the railroad industries for decades. *Mike Schafer collection*

RIGHT: The railroads' powerful presence in the closing years of the nineteenth century was often reflected in their structures, particularly depots. In 1881 in the heart of Philadelphia, the Pennsylvania Railroad—for years the most powerful railroad in America—opened Broad Street Station, an imposing Victorian pile that served PRR patrons until 1952. *Mike Schafer collection*

The start of a new century is at hand as the new *20th Century Limited,* inaugurated in 1902, races along the Lake Shore & Michigan Southern—a component railroad of the New York Central System—on a finely manicured, double-track main line protected by new automatic block signals. Block signals kept following trains spaced safely apart and at the same time permitted high-speed operation. By the eve of the twentieth century, American railroads had achieved an importance that towered above most other American industries. The period bracketed by the 1880s and World War I is considered by some historians to be railroading's "classic" period in terms of locomotive styling, ornate and plush passenger trains, and an unparalleled sense of pride among railroaders (replete with handlebar mustaches and bib overalls, of course) doing their job. *New York Central System, Cal's Classics*

effect on the safety and evolution of the American railroad, in particular the air brake (1869), automatic coupler (1873), and automatic-block-signal train control (1890s). Advances in motive-power and rolling-stock technology allowed for larger, faster, and yet safer trains—and more of them to haul still more passengers and freight. As a result, major freight and passenger terminals rose on once-empty lands to handle the burgeoning traffic.

As the railroads evolved into a national network, it became apparent that the practice of running trains on local "sun" times would have to end. Today, the practice seems ludicrous, but until after the Civil War it was commonly accepted. The depot in Buffalo, New York, for example, had three clocks, each showing a different time to match the schedules of the different trains operating out of the facility. It was once estimated that there were 27 local times in use in Illinois alone. The railroads united to establish four national time zones by the turn of the century—time zones still in use.

Operating practices and strategies also evolved. Trains themselves became more specialized. Instead of sending out one train after another full of freight, passengers, and mail, the passenger and freight traffic was largely separated and then scheduled to meet market needs. Railroad companies that could benefit one another allied themselves against other amalgamations, with the net result being improved flow of freight and passenger traffic and an increased spirit of competition—which of course resulted in overall improved service quality and lower rates. It should be remembered that, unlike the second half of the twentieth century, the bulk of competition was between railroads themselves rather than between railroads and other forms of transportation. The railroad had become king.

Freight traffic grew astronomically and passenger traffic also expanded, though at a slower pace. The railroads had helped America make the transition from an agrarian economy to one based largely on industry. By 1916 American railroads would

Variations on a Theme

American railroads evolved into a standardized network following the Civil War, but there were exceptions. Two of note were interurban and narrow-gauge railways.

Spurred by the application of electricity to propulsion, interurban lines quickly sprang up beginning around the turn of the century along with their close cousins, streetcar systems—the latter providing service *within* major cities. Interurbans, on the other hand, provided badly needed local passenger service *between* towns and cities in an era when mud roads were the norm and "steam railroads" offered only limited schedules and stops. Major interurban lines—nearly all of which were electric powered—were owned by utility companies, and many eventually developed freight and express service as well, making them an "enemy" of the steam railroads.

The rise of the automobile and improved roads began to wipe out interurbans in the 1920s almost as quickly as they had risen in popularity. The Depression took care of nearly all the rest, but a few soldiered on into the postwar era, some of them refocusing on freight transportation. Only one true interurban survives, the Chicago SouthShore & South Bend, whose electric-powered trains still speed passengers between its namesake cities.

In the face of track-gauge standardization, a few American lines still were built to narrow-gauge standards. Why? Narrow-gauge trackage could easier penetrate rugged mountain territory, and they were

An Illinois Terminal interurban train bound from Peoria to St. Louis invades the streets of Morton, Illinois, in 1953. IT got out of the passenger business in 1958 but lasted as a diesel freight-hauler until acquired by Norfolk & Western in 1981. *Sandy Goodrick*

simply cheaper to build, requiring smaller locomotives and cars. The most notable of America's narrow-gauge railways was a network of lines that flourished quite late in the Colorado Rockies, including several branches of the otherwise standard-gauge Denver & Rio Grande Western.

Other late-surviving narrow-gauge lines could be found in Pennsylvania, Maine, and Tennessee.

Alas, the advantages of narrow gauge were outweighed by the disadvantages, mainly the need to transfer freight and passengers at interchange points, and narrow-gauge railways all but vanished following World War II—if they hadn't already been done in by the Depression. Interestingly, D&RGW in 1967 still offered narrow-gauge freight and passenger service, but the freight service was phased out that year while the passenger service was experiencing a boom—it had been discovered by tourists! Rio Grande sold its remaining narrow-gauge lines to private operators in 1979. Another significant narrow-gauge operation, the East Broad Top in Pennsylvania, likewise survives by hauling tourists.

Nineteenth century technology and narrow-gauge track survive today on the Durango & Silverton, a private operator which took over some Rio Grande operations. The popular tourist run is at Beaver Creek Canyon in southern Colorado in September 1995. *Tom Kline*

ABOVE: Railroads received a rude awakening with the onset of World War I when it became clear they were not up to the (admittedly daunting) task of moving unprecedented numbers of passengers and tons of freight. As a result, the United States Railroad Administration was formed to oversee the operation of most companies as well as to standardize certain procedures and equipment specifications. The initials on the tenders of these Chicago, Milwaukee & St. Paul locomotives at Milwaukee, Wisconsin, in May 1919 testify as to who's really in charge. *Milwaukee Road Historical Association Archives*

RIGHT: In the 1920s, American transportation still very much centered on the hometown railroad station, regardless of what was being moved—people, mail, or freight—or in this case the remains of a deceased U.S. president. The date is August 6, 1923, and President Warren G. Harding's funeral train is arriving at De Kalb, Illinois, on the Chicago & North Western. In those days, everyone in town knew where the depot was, and on this day it appears everyone in town was there. *Mike McBride collection*

reach the peak of their influence. A national network of 254,000 miles of track was in place employing 1.7 million workers. Impressive edifices like New York's Grand Central Depot—opened early in the 1870s and then in 1913 replaced by the gleaming secular temple that is today's Grand Central Terminal—and Washington (D.C.) Union Station (1910) stood in mute testimony to the importance of the railroad in America.

But disturbing trends lurked behind the outward signs of progress. In 1916 the most important federal highway construction legislation in decades went into effect. That same year, the Ford Motor Company made a $60 million profit, mainly by selling the Model T automobile it had introduced in 1908. Railroad operating costs were increasing faster than revenues, thanks in part to tight government control of railroad tariffs (rates) and in part to the establishment of labor unions. New challenges lay ahead.

WORLD WAR I AND TRANSITIONS

America's entry into World War I resulted in an incredible increase in traffic—and in decrease in available work force as workers went off to war. The industry's inability to manage the demand prompted the federal government, under President Woodrow Wilson, to take control of the railroads in December 1917 through the formation of the United States Railroad Administration (USRA). The USRA in essence rented the U.S. railroads and made many of the decisions that had been the job of the railroads' presidents. In addition, the USRA raised wages, eliminated competition by setting standardized rates, and established standards for new equipment, of which more than 2,000 locomotives and some 100,000 cars were built to USRA specification.

But when government control finally ended in 1920, the railroads were left with significantly higher wages to pay. To its credit, the industry refused to dwell on the past and focused on the future. Expending $6.7 billion for capital improvements like motive power, equipment, track and signaling, the railroads enhanced their efficiency

dramatically, and many of the physical plant improvements of the period—such as bridges and track relocations—are today still evident. Several railroads continued to abide by some of the standards set forth by the USRA long after it had been dissolved. This revitalization period ushered in by

Few people—and businesses—escaped the despair wrought by the Great Depression. This interesting poster from the 1930s hints at the magnitude of the Depression, when children were often sent to trackside to gather spilt coal to take back home for heating and cooking. *Mike McBride collection*

the "Roaring Twenties" would help the industry weather the Great Depression and prepare it for World War II; the capital to do this would not have been available during the Depression.

The Depression was as unkind to railroads as it was to other industries. Freight and passenger

traffic plummeted to alarmingly low levels. Several railroads went bankrupt, while others went out of business completely, their remains picked up by surviving companies who were more financially stable. But it was a case of "natural selection"—only the strong survive—as applied to industry. Arguably the single most important positive outcome of the Depression for the railroad industry was the transition of the diesel locomotive from that of a curiosity to an extraordinarily viable form of motive power that would vastly lower operating costs and revolutionize railroading.

WORLD WAR II AND DECLINE

In contrast to the Great War, World War II was the American railroad's finest hour. Self-managed but under the guidance of the Office of Defense Transportation, the railroads performed Herculean efforts. When German submarines forced traffic off the sea-lanes, the railroads stepped in to deliver the goods. With a total capacity no greater than that of World War I, the railroads moved 50 percent more freight traffic. Rationing of gasoline and rubber at home forced people to travel by rail, and the railroads met the demand. From 1943 through 1945, passenger traffic was the highest it had ever been and double that of 1918. The railroads' strategic value was immeasurable. Passenger and special troop trains carried 97 percent of all domestic troop movements, and 90 percent of all military freight traffic moved by rail. Increased operating efficiencies—thanks in part to the USRA and the effects of the Depression—were the principal reason the railroads had been able to absorb the phenomenal demand.

But victory came at a price. With the conflict behind them, the railroads faced a number of challenges—some new, some old. The demands of war had prematurely worn out their equipment and physical plant, and the booming growth of other forms of transportation continued to cause problems. Despite increased freight efficiencies and the widespread acceptance of diesel power and streamlined passenger trains, the railroads lost business. The

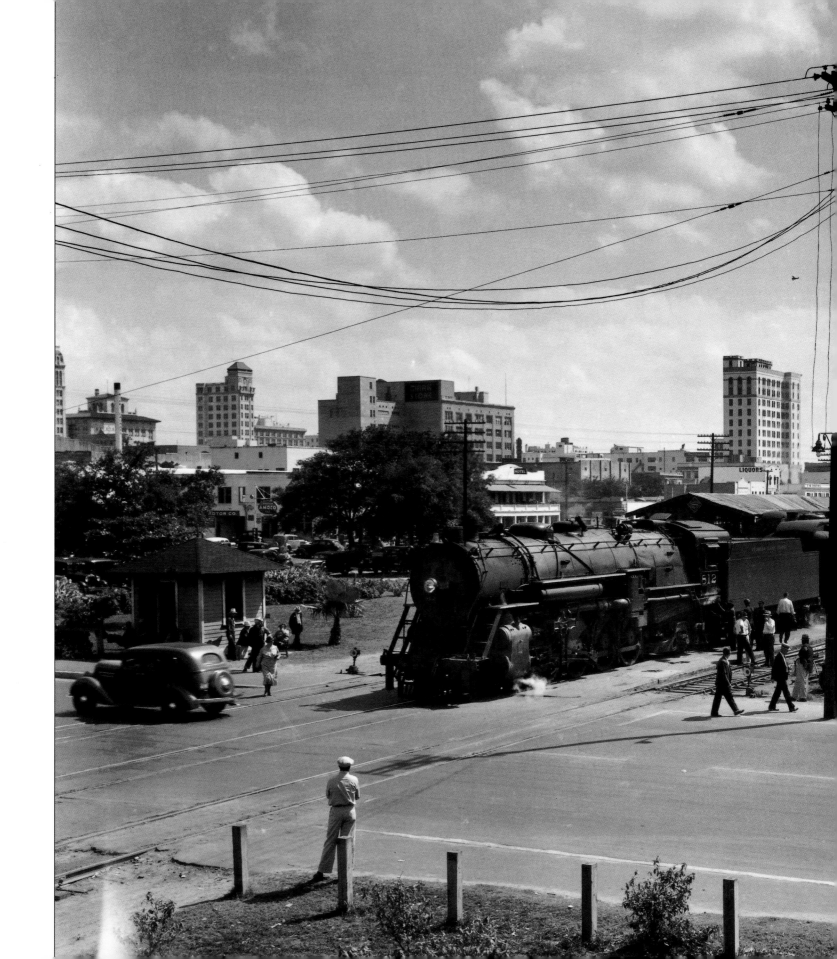

With most of the Depression behind them, Miamians bustle about the Florida East Coast Railway station on a sun-filled afternoon in 1937. Steam still reigned as two of FEC's 4-8-2 Mountain-type locomotives head up trains bound for Jacksonville and points north. Diesels and streamliners are still two years away for the Miami-Jacksonville carrier, which in 1999 was still an independent company. Though suggestive of being the FEC depot, the handsome pinnacled building is the Dade County Courthouse. *Harry Wolf/FEC, South Florida Rail Sales*

decline could be traced to the 1920s when the nation began to widely embrace the automobile and the truck. Unregulated until the mid 1930s and operating over a system of roads provided by taxpayers, the trucking industry rose to prominence garnering entire freight markets from the railroads. For example, less-than-carload (LCL) rail freight dropped from over 50 million tons in 1919 to just over 4 million tons by 1958. The airplane blossomed as a passenger carrier after World War II, with a meteoric rise following the introduction of the jet airliner in the late 1950s. Controlling only 3 percent of the intercity passenger market in 1945, the airliner had captured 35 percent of all intercity traffic by 1957. Another competitor, the automobile, received a huge boost in 1956 when the federal government launched construction of the 42,000-mile Defense Highway System—the Interstate. As the railroads continued to pay taxes on their facilities, they watched local communities build new facilities for their competitors—in part using tax monies paid by railroads. Likewise, federal taxes on tickets purchased by rail passengers went in the General Fund, which in part was used to bankroll highway projects. Meanwhile, government regulations kept a tight rein on the railroad industry.

The inroads of competition led to the abandonment of superfluous trackage and services and spurred the development of further efficiencies. By the late 1950s, well over 90 percent of freight, passenger, and yard work was being handled by diesel-electric locomotives. The steam locomotive, king of the rails for over a century, had largely vanished. Fast, streamlined passenger trains flashed to and fro across the country, but they were fighting a losing battle with the automobile and airliner, and passenger-service abandonment accelerated as the 1950s drew to a close. Larger, more efficient classification yards and improved signaling sped freight on its way. "Piggyback" service, carrying truck trailers on railroad flat cars, revolutionized the movement of freight. In spite of improvements, rail traffic continued to decline. Despite the growth in freight traffic overall on all modes after World War I, between 1916 and 1957 the total percentage of that freight hauled by rail dropped from 77 to 46 percent.

The passenger train was particularly hard hit, and the problem had been brewing for years. In 1936 the ICC estimated that the national net loss from passenger operations was $233 million annually. By 1951, fueled by postwar inflation, rising operating costs, and the impact of the auto and the

Modern "MOHAWKS" on the Warpath

New Dual-Purpose Locomotives Speed War Traffic on the Water Level Route

THERE'S a roar from her stubby stack as "Mohawk 3112" rolls west with a string of troop-filled Pullmans. There's an answering roar from her twin locomotive, eastbound with a train of war freight.

Two engines of a kind. Two of New York Central's versatile "Mohawks"... with big, six-foot drivers... able to haul heavy freight on the Water Level Route or speed the 20th Century Limited on schedule.

Made possible by this almost gradeless route, "Mohawks" are newest among Central's fleet of steam, electric and Diesel locomotives. And their adaptability to freight or passenger service means much to wartime efficiency on this vital link in America's railroad supply line.

Today, thundering through valleys where Mohawk braves once fought, these "Mohawks" too are on the warpath. And even as they speed the Victory traffic ...their performance guides Central designers in planning the finer locomotives of tomorrow.

MODERN MOTIVE POWER
Latest New York Central locomotive weighs only 198½ tons, yet develops 5,400 h.p. ... ample for heavy freight on Water Level Route.

LEVER OPENS FIREBOX DOORS

AIR BRAKES

STOKER CONTROLS

WHISTLE VALVE

TRACK PAN SUPPLIES WATER

POWER-OPERATED REVERSE GEAR

SIX-FOOT DRIVERS

AUTOMATIC STOKER

"GREEN OVER GREEN." Fireman shouts readings of signals to engineer as a safety check. It's also part of his training as a future engineer.

15,500-GALLON WATER TANK

EXPERT THROTTLE HAND. Though New York Central engineers average 20 years' experience, each takes frequent tests for fitness and knowledge of operating rules.

600 MILES ON A TENDERFUL. The "Mohawk" of today pulls a passenger train 600 miles on one tender of coal. Gets ⅓ more power per ton than World War I engines.

AUTOMATIC TRAIN CONTROL. Electric control on right of tender would stop train automatically if a caution or red signal were passed.

New York Central

NEW YORK CENTRAL SYSTEM

One of America's Railroads All United for Victory

LET YOUR DOLLARS FIGHT INFANTILE PARALYSIS

PENNSYLVANIA RAILROAD

They come first!

BUY UNITED STATES WAR BONDS & STAMPS *for Victory!*

During World War II American railroads—and railroaders—exhibited astonishing patriotism, not only in their all-out efforts at moving freight and goods, but also in their advertising.

LEFT: Throughout the 1940s and 1950s, New York Central ran numerous magazine ads touting its passenger trains as well as an interesting ad series that explained to the public the workings of a railroad. This ad from February 1944 trumpeted the latest in NYC steam power and how the new locomotives were helping win the war.

ABOVE: This Pennsylvania Railroad timetable from April 1944 reminded civilians that troop travelers were priority. *Both, Mike Schafer Collection*

Few events had as much impact on railroad history as the coming-of-age of the diesel-electric locomotive. Diesel-powered streamlined passenger trains caught on quickly as the 1930s progressed, but not until the end of the decade did diesels finally prove their worth in heavy-duty mainline freight application. Electro-Motive Corporation's introduction of the FT-series diesel-electric locomotive (at right in photo) in 1939 and the FTs' subsequent success during wartime duties eventually convinced American railroads that diesel-electric power could do the work of steam and then some—and at a fraction of operating costs. The FT spawned upgraded F-series models after World War II, such as the Santa Fe F7A at left in photo, while other builders scrambled to introduce their own line of diesel-electric mainline locomotives. The Santa Fe locomotive set in this 1989 scene has been preserved at the California State Railroad Museum in Sacramento; the FT belongs to the Museum of Transport at Kirkwood, Missouri. *Jim Boyd*

airliner, the loss had tripled to $681 million. Throughout the next two decades, passenger services would be consistently reduced in the face of continued deficits.

Since World War II, the railroads had poured tens of billions of dollars into their operations and facilities, but the return on the investment had been dismal. Alarm bells went off when, in 1957, the 541-mile New York, Ontario & Western became the first major railroad to abandon all operations.

The economics of the situation fueled another wave of mergers, one which began with a ripple and ultimately reached tidal-wave proportions in the twilight years of the twentieth century. The scenario was not unlike the merger sweep of 100 years earlier: choose your partner—or partners—and eliminate duplicate facilities and operations in favor of a leaner, more efficient system. The difference was the competition. In the 1800s it had been railroad versus railroad; now it was railroad versus highway and air.

The first major postwar merger of note was the 1947 union of the Gulf, Mobile & Ohio with the Alton Railroad. Except for its handsome red-and-maroon paint scheme, the Alton's identity vanished and GM&O suddenly stretched beyond St. Louis to Chicago and Kansas City. Things remained quiet until 1957 when Louisville & Nashville acquired the Nashville, Chattanooga & St. Louis. That same year, industry watchers were stunned by the announcement that the Pennsylvania and New York Central—two huge rival railroads—intended to merge.

That merger stalled, but the pace quickened elsewhere. In 1959 Norfolk & Western united with one-time competitor Virginian Railway, and

Life in the 1950s wasn't quite the utopia for railroads that it may have been for the average American. As this 1952 scene at Elizabeth, New Jersey, depicts, automobiles were proliferating—as was highway transport in general—and would soon prove fatal to the extensive passenger-train network that once moved Americans to nearly all nooks and crannies of the nation. The postwar period thus represented a new era of freedom for citizens, for whom the automobile would become a necessity more than a luxury. For railroads, however, the government would continue its stronghold on railroad regulation, nearly suffocating the industry. *John Dziobko*

in 1960 the Delaware, Lackawanna & Western and Erie merged as did Chicago & North Western and Minneapolis & St. Louis. In some cases, whole new railroads resulted—for example, Erie and DL&W became Erie-Lackawanna—while in others the name of the controlling railroad remained as it swallowed up its acquisitions.

One of the biggest unions of the period happened in 1964 when the 2,700-plus-mile Norfolk & Western leased (and later merged) the 2,400-mile Wabash Railway and merged with the 2,170-mile New York, Chicago & St. Louis (Nickel Plate Road), thus nearly tripling parent N&W's size. In 1967, two highly regarded Southeastern carriers, Atlantic Coast Line and Seaboard Air Line, united as Seaboard Coast Line. NYC and PRR finally merged in 1968 to form the Penn Central. Then in 1970 came the most massive merger to date: Chicago,

Burlington & Quincy + Great Northern + Northern Pacific + Spokane, Portland & Seattle. The result was an all-new, 24,000-mile railroad, Burlington Northern.

Following this came another merger of sorts. In 1970 President Richard Nixon signed a bill which formed a new "railroad"—the National Railroad Passenger Corporation—comprised of railroads wishing to be relieved of the financial burden of running intercity passenger trains. Amtrak, as NRPC is more popularly known, was in effect the merger of selected intercity (versus commuter) passenger operations of the various railroads that existed at the time, forming a 21,000-mile coast-to-coast system whose losses were underwritten by taxpayers. As the first scenario in which government—for better or worse—began subsidizing rail operations in a major way (if you don't count

LEFT: A new Fairbanks-Morse road-switcher diesel belonging to the Virginian Railway effortlessly tows a freight through Roanoke, Virginia, in August 1956. Dieselization was the hallmark of railroading in the 1950s. *John Dziobko*

BELOW: By the late 1960s, the passenger train was on its deathbed. The two coaches trailing the joint Rock Island-Burlington *Zephyr Rocket* at Cedar Falls, Iowa, in April 1967 would more than suffice the few passengers using this Twin Cities–St. Louis run. Shortly, the mail would disappear, too, and this and numerous other passenger trains throughout the country would vanish. *Philip R. Hastings Collection, California State Railroad Museum*

Amtrak's *North Coast Hiawatha* arrows its way through the Minnesota countryside near La Crescent in the summer of 1975. With stock owned by "member" railroads—carriers that turned their passenger operations over to the newly formed company—Amtrak set about the daunting task of reversing the slide in rail passenger patronage and revenues. This it did, and with a skeletal system, no less. More passengers rode Amtrak trains in 1998 than rode pre-Amtrak U.S. railroads intercity trains in 1970. *Mike Schafer*

the land-grant arrangements of yore, which did not involve monies from taxpayers), Amtrak signaled a turning point for the whole industry. The reasoning of this new era ushered in by the 1970s was that government was already subsidizing other forms of transportation—albeit indirectly—so why not the railroads?

Industry challenges continued. After suffering from disastrous operating problems for more than two years, the ill-planned Penn Central, which now included the New Haven Railroad, collapsed in bankruptcy in June 1970—at that time the largest corporate failure in American history. The event triggered a chain reaction of railroad failures in the Northeast and threw cold water on the

merger movement in general. Fearing economic upheaval in the Northeast and a disruption of interstate commerce, the federal government intervened, establishing the Consolidated Rail Corporation (Conrail), which began operation on April 1, 1976. Conrail was a private for-profit carrier whose stock was held by the creditors of the bankrupt railroads in the Conrail system: Penn Central, Erie Lackawanna, Lehigh Valley, Reading Company, Jersey Central, Lehigh & Hudson River, and Pennsylvania-Reading Seashore Lines. Federal financial support got the company back on its feet.

Despite the setbacks, the industry in general continued to become more productive and innovative. Unit trains—trains dedicated to hauling a single commodity—sped shipments of coal, grain, ore, and chemicals to market. "Piggyback" or trailer-on-flat-car (TOFC) service expanded dramatically in the 1970s, and eventually in the 1980s containerized freight took on new importance. New technology like computerization enhanced the industry's efficiency by increasing productivity with a reduced work force—labor being the single most costly aspect of a railroad's operation.

FREE AT LAST: DEREGULATION AND A NEW BOOM

Despite the severe competition of the 1950s, 1960s, and 1970s, the railroads remained shackled by heavy regulation—a throwback to the late 1800s. That changed in 1980 when President Jimmy Carter signed the Staggers Act into law, relaxing the ICC's regulation of mergers and rate-making while freeing the railroads to bid for the traffic of their choice. An industry which had suffered for the sins of its forefathers was now free to respond to the market. It did so with a vengeance.

Merger mania resumed. CSX Corporation was formed in 1980 and its rail division grew to 18,300 miles, incorporating the former lines of Chesapeake & Ohio, Baltimore & Ohio, Western Maryland, Clinchfield, Georgia Railroad Group, Seaboard Air Line, Atlantic Coast Line, Louisville & Nashville, Monon, Richmond, Fredericksburg & Potomac, Pittsburgh & Lake Erie and others. Burlington Northern merged with the Frisco in 1980 and then with fabled Atchison, Topeka & Santa Fe in 1995. The Norfolk & Western and the Southern Railway joined under the new Norfolk Southern banner in 1982. Union Pacific, dating from 1862, became the goliath of them all, absorbing the Missouri Pacific and Western Pacific railroads in 1982, the

Text continued on page 32

Surrounded by the grandeur of Glacier National Park, a Burlington Northern grain train heads westward near Belton, Montana, in 1993. The first of the postwar "mega-mergers" was arguably that which spawned the Burlington Northern Railroad (the Norfolk & Western/Nickel Plate/Wabash merger of 1964 could probably be termed "mega," though it did not create a new railroad per se and did not result in a railroad that was larger than any existing company). The 1970 result of the combining of Chicago, Burlington & Quincy, Northern Pacific, Great Northern, and Spokane, Portland & Seattle, BN would further expand in 1980 with the absorption of the St. Louis-San Francisco Railway–the Frisco. *Phil Gosney*

LEFT: Buffalo-bound, a Conrail train out of northern New Jersey drifts across the Delaware River at Millrift, Pennsylvania, in February 1987. The train is riding the former Erie Railroad main line. In the 1990s, profitable Conrail would become the subject of an intense bidding war between Norfolk Southern and CSX. *Jim Boyd* TOP: With a set of locomotives that happened to illustrate the merger arrangement of NS, an NS freight flies high above the Virginia countryside at Lynchburg in 1988. *Dan Munson* ABOVE: A CSX freight ducks through a tunnel on the ex-L&N main line between Cincinnati and Louisville in 1997. CSX and NS are modern-day rivals. *Mike Schafer*

Deregulation resulted in many railroads spinning off lines that to them were of marginal value, resulting in the proliferation of numerous new railroads, mostly shortlines or operations that were regional in nature, to operate orphaned lines. Illustrating the classic modern-day regional is this scene of two Wisconsin Central trains south of Fond du Lac, Wisconsin in 1994. WC was formed in 1987 to acquire most of the Soo Line's Wisconsin trackage after SOO deemed it surplus following its 1985 purchase of the Milwaukee Road. The new WC quickly rose to prominence and by the end of the century was one of the leading regional railroads in the U.S. *Mike Schafer*

The ample assignment of locomotives to this eastbound Union Pacific train near Cedar Rapids, Iowa, tells a bit of the story of UP's rise to becoming the world's largest railroad. The two leading locomotives still wear the livery of Chicago & North Western and Southern Pacific—two key additions to UP's empire during the 1990s. *Mike Schafer*

Text continued from page 29

Missouri-Kansas-Texas (Katy) Railroad in 1988, Chicago & North Western in 1995, and finally merging with giant and one-time rival Southern Pacific (itself owned by Denver & Rio Grande Western interests) in 1996. The UP of 1999 boasted over 40,000 route-miles and is one of the last surviving major U.S. railroads whose name has never changed.

As a ward of the government, Conrail became profitable by rationalizing its routes, revamping its infrastructure, targeting new freight markets, and reducing costs. In 1987 it was sold to the public on the New York Stock Exchange. Conrail's profitability made it a desirable marriage partner—so much so that two major suitors, CSX and Norfolk Southern, vied for its acquisition in the mid-1990s. The near-vicious bidding war prompted the Surface Transportation Board (the skeletal remains of the ICC) to mediate, the result being that Conrail was split up and sold to both companies in the spring of 1999.

Even non-U.S. railroads got into the act, with Canadian Pacific absorbing the Soo Line—SOO having grown substantially through its 1986 acquisition of the Milwaukee Road—and gaining control of the Delaware & Hudson. In 1999, Canadian National was to acquire Illinois Central—and therefore a route to the Gulf of Mexico.

Perhaps most important, the Staggers Act freed the railroads to dispose of lines with low productivity by selling them to other parties without having to provide labor-protection guarantees. The large railroads were thus free to reshape themselves as high-volume trunk lines. Lower-volume and/or surplus lines were spun off to new operators or existing small carriers, resulting in a whole new legion of shortline and regional railroads throughout the country, carriers like Wisconsin Central and Montana Rail Link. Unburdened by certain labor-law restrictions that had dogged major railroads, some of the new upstarts could provide improved, personal service to smaller customers.

The new merger boom did have its negative ramifications. Overzealous abandonment of supposedly redundant trackage left some railroads unable to respond to increasing demand. Hasty mergers sometimes caused major headaches for railroads wallowing in the complexities of managing huge systems, and the question remains, "Is there such as thing as too big?" Further, the focus on high-profit, low-maintenance traffic left gaps in service for shippers who didn't fit the railroads' ideal customer profile. Unions rightly pointed out that the quality of life of railroaders has deteriorated in the face of increasing demand.

Nevertheless, the big picture is one of success. In 1995 American railroad freight traffic reached 1.3 billion ton-miles, an all-time high at the time and almost twice the volume carried at the height of World War II—and it was done using only about half the number of locomotives, cars, and-trains on a significantly shrunked rail network, clearly reflecting vast improvements in efficiency and productivity.

Even the passenger market has had its bright spots. Although Amtrak continues to rely on a modest amount of federal support as the century closes, its revenues cover more of its costs than any other major rail passenger system in the industrialized world. Further, Amtrak is targeting 2003 as the year it will finally break even.

On another passenger front, the U.S. has seen a remarkable resurgence in commuter and other rail transit developments. For example, car-crammed Los Angeles—devoid of rail transit since the 1950s—once again enjoys the benefits of commuter-train, subway, and trolley service. As the millennium approaches, most major American cities have either revamped their existing rail-transit systems or built new ones, proving that rail transport, though nearly 200 years old, is hardly outmoded.

THE FUTURE

For some time, rail industry analysts have wistfully predicted that one day the nation would be served by as few as two "super railroads." Recent events seem to indicate those predictions will come true sooner rather than later. In the west, Burlington Northern & Santa Fe and Union Pacific dominate the landscape. In the East, CSX and Norfolk Southern are the big two. These four railroads control almost 80 percent of the Class I railroad assets in America. Depending on whom you believe, the future result will be undreamed efficiencies or less responsiveness to the shipper and the public.

Whatever the outcome, the railroad, like America, is a survivor. Constantly evolving and improving with time, this industry, so steeped in tradition, stands ready to meet the challenges of the future.

Born of merger between the Burlington Northern and Atchison, Topeka & Santa Fe, the new Burlington Northern & Santa Fe Railroad has become one of the industry giants of the new millennium. In this 1998 scene, a BNSF freight led by three locomotives—the lead wearing the new company colors with the trailing two still clad in their heritage-railroad livery—departs the modern skyline of Kansas City, Missouri. *Dan Munson*

2 *The Railroad* Classics

Generally, American railroads grew in three different ways. They could grow in the traditional manner of building track and physical plant and acquiring locomotives and rolling stock; they could grow by either merging with or purchasing outright other railroad companies; and, of course, they could choose both approaches.

The railroad-building boom of the mid and late nineteenth century spawned an astonishing number of railroad companies. Many were truly independent concerns while others were "paper" railroads formed by a regular railroad for purposes of construction and expansion. The paper railroads helped insulate the parent railroad in the event the offspring failed financially during its formative years.

Like a fish that swallows a smaller fish and then itself gets gulped by a larger fish, American railroads grew markedly in size but dwindled in number in a merger/acquisition mania that swept the nation in the late 1800s. The result was the emergence of the "classic" carriers that would dominate the twentieth century—companies whose names today still ring familiar as icons of American railroading. As of the mid twentieth century, there were more than 130 Class 1 carriers (i.e., a railroad grossing more than $1 million per year). But even most of these companies had a finite life span, their longtime identities having been eradicated during the industry's second major merger era, that of the late twentieth century.

Herewith is a sampler of some of those classics of yore—and a few that are still around ("born" dates indicate first appearance of a railroad's name and not when its first predecessor emerged; route mileage is approximate for mid-twentieth century):

Atchison, Topeka & Santa (1859–1996; mileage: 13,000): Stretching from Chicago to the West Coast, with branch lines poking into all corners of Texas, Kansas, and Oklahoma to gather the nation's grain, Santa Fe was among the largest of U.S. railroads and also laid claim to one of the most famous passenger trains in the world, the *Super Chief.* The tradition of "Santa Fe All the Way" ended with the 1996 merger of Santa Fe and Burlington Northern into Burlington Northern & Santa Fe.

Atlantic Coast Line (1893–1967; mileage: 5,500): ACL's 100-mph, double-track main line south from Virginia was *the* artery for freight and passenger traffic between the Northeast and Florida—the latter being dominated by the railroad. Best known for its New York–Florida *Champion* streamliners, ACL merged with competitor Seaboard Air Line in 1967 to form Seaboard Coast Line. SCL would last until its 1982 merger with Louisville & Nashville, forming Seaboard System.

Baltimore & Ohio (1827–1987; mileage: 10,000): America's first common-carrier railroad, B&O linked the East Coast with the Midwest and in the early years was a despised adversary of the Pennsylvania Railroad. In the 1960s, B&O became allied with Chesapeake & Ohio and later Western Maryland, all three collectively marketed as the Chessie System since 1973. Forever remembered for its fine *Capitol Limited* between Chicago and the East Coast, B&O was formally merged into C&O (under CSX Corporation) in 1987.

Bangor & Aroostook (1891–present; mileage: 600): An important connection for Maine Central, BAR serves northern Maine from Bangor north to the Canadian border, hauling forest products and, in an earlier era, potatoes.

Boston & Maine (1835–present; mileage: 1,700): Once a quaint New England institution, B&M—"Route of the Minute Man"—fanned out from Boston, Massachusetts, to New York State, Vermont, New Hampshire, and Maine. Since 1983, B&M has been operated by Guilford Industries.

Chesapeake & Ohio (1868–1987; mileage 5,300): Coal was the lifeline commodity of this Tidewater-to-the-Midwest carrier serving Virginia, West Virginia, Ohio, Kentucky, Indiana, and Illinois. In 1947 C&O merged the Pere Marquette Railway, extending its reach throughout Michigan, through southern Ontario to Buffalo, New York, and even to Wisconsin via Great Lakes carferries. C&O acquired ownership of the B&O in 1962 and itself was acquired by CSX Corporation in 1980. C&O was formally merged into CSX in 1987.

Chicago & Eastern Illinois (1877–1976; mileage: 900). A speedway for traffic bound for the Southeast via Evansville, Indiana, C&EI was also the sometimes forgotten contender for Chicago–St. Louis traffic. Missouri Pacific merged the C&EI in 1976, having sold a portion of it to Louisville & Nashville in 1969.

Chicago & North Western (1859–1995; mileage: 9,700): C&NW's three principal routes were anchored in Chicago and reached west for

FACING PAGE: Atlantic Coast Line diesels head up the Chicago–Florida *City of Miami* near Waycross, Georgia, in 1965. ACL handled the train between Albany, Georgia, and Jacksonville, Florida, where associate Florida East Coast took over for the trip to Miami. *Mike Schafer* ABOVE: Classics large (Santa Fe) and small (Monon) populate Chicago's Dearborn Station in 1957. It's just after 8:45 a.m. and Monon's *Tippecanoe* is easing away from the station at the start of its journey down "The Hoosier Line" to Indianapolis, Indiana. In about 25 more minutes, Santa Fe's *Chief* will depart for Los Angeles. *John Dziobko*

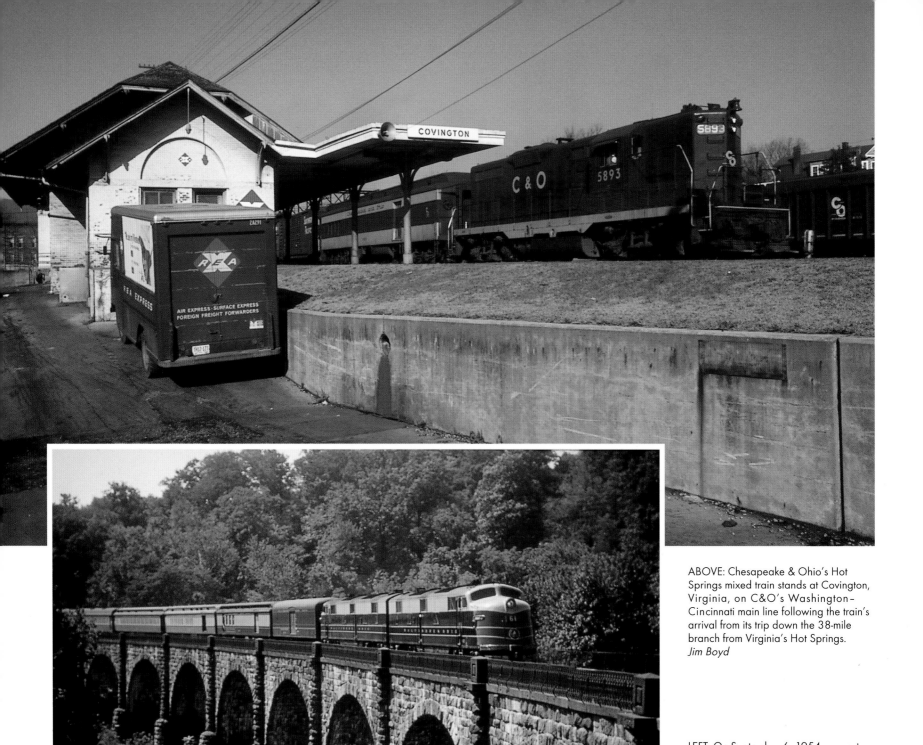

ABOVE: Chesapeake & Ohio's Hot Springs mixed train stands at Covington, Virginia, on C&O's Washington–Cincinnati main line following the train's arrival from its trip down the 38-mile branch from Virginia's Hot Springs. *Jim Boyd*

LEFT: On September 6, 1954, an eastbound Baltimore & Ohio passenger train sweeps across landmark Thomas Viaduct at Relay, Maryland. B&O's route between Jersey City (New York City) and Chicago was the most circuitous and rugged of all roads in that east-west market, so B&O made up for those shortcomings with superior-quality passenger and freight service. For many years, B&O was affiliated with neighbor Chesapeake & Ohio. *John Dziobko*

Nebraska, northwest to Minneapolis/St. Paul, Minnesota, and north to Upper Michigan. Less well known was the railroad's main line south to St. Louis. Famous for its fleet of *"400"* streamliners, C&NW's real livelihood was agricultural transport and as an artery for east-west traffic to and from the Union Pacific, which acquired C&NW in 1995.

Chicago, Burlington & Quincy (1855–1970; mileage: 11,000): A high-class operation all the way, Burlington Route was among the most innovative yet pragmatic railroads of the post-Depression era. In 1934 it pioneered streamlined passenger trains and mainline diesel power in the form of its famous *Zephyr* 9900, a little train which propagated a whole fleet of *Zephyr* streamliners. Linking Chicago with Denver, Kansas City, Omaha, and Minneapolis/St. Paul, Burlington was a classic granger road. In 1970, the "Q" merged with Great Northern, Northern Pacific, and Spokane, Portland & Seattle to form Burlington Northern.

Chicago Great Western (1892–1968; mileage: 1,400): Another "X"-shaped railroad, the CGW stretched from Chicago to Omaha and from the Twin Cities to Kansas City, crossing at little Oelwein, Iowa. Great Western's modest size compared to surrounding railroads made it easy pickin's as a merger partner—which it was for C&NW in 1968.

Chicago, Milwaukee, St. Paul & Pacific (1909–1986; mileage: 10,600): The Milwaukee Road was one of the all-time great Midwest institutions, made legendary by its fleet of high-speed *Hiawatha* passenger trains. The Milwaukee held a marked presence in Wisconsin, Iowa, Minnesota, South Dakota, Illinois, Indiana, Missouri, and Upper Michigan, but it also reached the West

Coast via its Pacific Extension, opened in 1909. Milwaukee downsized drastically in 1980 and was merged away into the Soo Line in 1986.

Chicago, Rock Island & Pacific (1866–1980; mileage: 7,500): A railroad of song and lore, this railroad nearly achieved the goal of its name, stopping instead at Tucumcari, New Mexico. Iowa was the Rock's strong suit, but the carrier also had a commanding presence in Oklahoma, Kansas and Arkansas and reached the Gulf of Mexico via the

A westbound Chicago Great Western freight bound from Chicago to the unlikely terminal city of Oelwein, Iowa, breaks the stillness of Stillman Valley, Illinois, in 1965. Oelwein was CGW's hub where traffic was sorted and forwarded on other trains to Omaha, Minneapolis/St. Paul, and Kansas City. Some industry analysts insist there were too many railroads between those points, and therefore supported Chicago & North Western's takeover of the mystique-filled CGW in 1968. Others insist it was merely a ploy on behalf of North Western to reduce competition. *Jim Boyd*

heart of Texas. Financial stability, alas, was *not* Rock's strong suit, and in 1980 it became the largest U.S. railroad to abandon operations.

Clinchfield (1924–1983; mileage: 300): This spunky north-south carrier hauled coal and bridge traffic over a scenic, five-state (Kentucky, Virginia, Tennessee, North and South Carolina) main line that burrowed through the Appalachian Mountains. The "Clinch" merged into Seaboard System in 1983.

Delaware & Hudson (1851–present; mileage: 700): Currently the oldest surviving transportation company in America, the D&H originally was a

coal-hauler. The railroad's role in Northeast rail operations evolved to that of "bridge line," acting as middle man for freight moving between Canada and Northeast points to the west. As a condition of Conrail's 1976 startup, D&H's reach was extended to Buffalo, New York, and Washington, D.C., through trackage rights on Conrail and Amtrak. Canadian Pacific now controls the D&H.

Delaware, Lackawanna & Western (1853–1960; mileage: 900): The Lackawanna's scenic, well-engineered route between metropolitan New York City and Buffalo via New Jersey, Pennsylvania, and southern New York State was also the shortest. Among the railroad's notable legacies was massive Tunkhannock Viaduct in northeast Pennsylvania, now used by D&H. In 1960, DL&W merged with Erie to form Erie-Lackawanna.

Denver & Rio Grande Western (1921–1996; mileage: 2,400): A relative latecomer in U.S. railroading, Rio Grande was the middle link in an alternative transcontinental route that included Burlington and Western Pacific. While UP skirted the Rockies to the north, Rio Grande—which called Denver, Colorado, its home—penetrated America's most rugged mountain range to reach Salt Lake City and the Western Pacific. In a case of tail wagging the dog, Rio Grande interests acquired control of the Southern Pacific in 1988, dropping the Rio Grande name. In 1996 SP was merged into UP.

Erie Railroad (1859–1960; mileage: 2,300): Reaching from Atlantic shores to Chicago with branches to Buffalo, Cleveland, and Cincinnati and a strong presence in northern New Jersey and western New York State, Erie spent most of its life beset by financial woes. One of Erie's positive claims to fame was that it was first to employ train dispatching via telegraph. Erie merged with the DL&W in 1960.

Florida East Coast (1885–present; mileage: 700): The railroad of Henry M. Flagler—the visionary who in the late 1800s set Florida on its course to becoming prime travel destination—is basically a straight-shot main line from Jacksonville south along Florida's Gold Coast to Miami (and at one time all the way to Key West). FEC in 1963 suffered a vicious labor strike that was not settled until the 1970s. During the strife, FEC eliminated passenger service, went to two-man crews (thereby eliminating cabooses), and rebuilt the railroad which to this day remains a feisty independent.

Georgia Railroad group (1833–1983; mileage: 550): This amalgamation included the Atlanta & West Point and Western Railway of Alabama, all three roads being leased to ACL and L&N. Together the trio cut a swath through Georgia and Alabama that provided a handy link for traffic off of ACL destined for Atlanta and Gulf points on the L&N. The Georgia Group roads were merged into Seaboard System in 1983.

Great Northern (1889–1970; mileage: 8,200): GN was built by good-guy rail mogul James J. Hill. GN's principal route linked the upper Midwest with Seattle, Washington, and the railroad was a financial success from start to finish. Its most famous passenger train, the *Empire Builder* (adopting Hill's nickname), still runs, now under Amtrak. Joint ownership (with rival NP) of the Burlington Route and SP&S led to the 1970 merger of all those lines into Burlington Northern.

Grand Trunk Western (1928–present; mileage: 1,000): GTW essentially was (and is) parent Canadian National's American arm, serving numerous cities in Michigan and reaching Chicago via South Bend, Indiana. At one time the railroad also served Wisconsin via Lake Michigan carferries. In 1983, GTW merged the Detroit, Toledo & Ironton, thereby extending its reach to the Ohio River.

Gulf, Mobile & Ohio (1940–1972; mileage: 2,900): As the result of the combining of the Mobile & Ohio and Gulf, Mobile & Northern railroads in 1940, GM&O was a pioneer in the modern merger movement. The union made for a strong, innovative St. Louis-to-the-Gulf carrier, which early on embraced diesels and streamliners. In 1947 "Gee-Mo" extended itself to Chicago and Kansas City by acquiring the Alton Railroad. Far less successful was GM&O's 1972 merger with Illinois Central forming Illinois Central Gulf.

Illinois Central (1851–1972 and 1988–present; mileage: 4,800): Serving Chicago, Omaha, St. Louis, Memphis, Birmingham, and New Orleans, IC has been a spit-and-polish operation

Clad in the road's famous "barber-shop pole" paint scheme, a Rock Island Alco road-switcher toddles into the Englewood station in south suburban Chicago with a commuter train in August 1956. The railroad is perhaps best remembered for its extensive fleet of *Rocket* streamliners—fancy cousins to this lowly suburban run. *John Dziobko*

Great Northern was held in high esteem by the industry, as well as by passengers who used its famous *Empire Builder* passenger train, gracing this 1947 postcard. *Mike Schafer collection*

THE *Empire Builder* — GREAT NORTHERN RAILWAY STREAMLINER

ALONG PUGET SOUND NORTH OF SEATTLE, WASH.

Recreating a famous publicity scene dating from the 1940s when Kansas City Southern's *Southern Belle* streamliner was new, KCS's executive train poses at Blue Parkway viaduct near Kansas City, Missouri, in 1996. The train carries the same elegant black livery KCS streamliners wore more than a half century earlier. The modern-day KCS is closely aligned with Illinois Central and Canadian National interests as well as those of Mexico's railroads. *Dan Munson*

for most of its life. It operated one of the finest passenger trains in the country, the *Panama Limited*, as well as one of the earliest streamliners, the *Green Diamond*. Its high-speed banana trains between the Gulf and Chicago were legendary, but the "Main Line of Mid-America" also hauled much coal, grain, and meat. IC may be the only major railroad to "come back from the dead." In 1972 IC vanished into the Illinois Central Gulf merger. A reorganization in 1988 resulted in the return of its original name—and its pride.

Kansas City Southern (1900–present; mileage: 1,000): Though largely off the beaten path, KCS's main line between Kansas City and New Orleans was an ideal short cut to the Gulf for railroads feeding Kansas City—one of America's great railroad hubs. A modern-day maverick, KCS purchased MidSouth Rail (former ICG lines) in 1994 and the Gateway Western Railway in 1997; the latter got KCS to Louis.

Lehigh Valley (1853–1976; mileage: 1,300): Born and raised as a coal-hauler, the Valley was yet another link between New Jersey ports and Upstate New York, making it a competitor to the Lackawanna, Erie, and New York Central. LV's star passenger train was appropriately named the *Black Diamond* (a nickname for coal). The Valley went bankrupt in 1970 and was folded into Conrail in 1976.

Louisville & Nashville (1850–1982; mileage: 4,800): Aside from linking its namesake cities, L&N also reached Cincinnati, New Orleans, Memphis, Atlanta, and Birmingham. In 1957 "Old Reliable" expanded to Atlanta by merging the Nashville, Chattanooga & St. Louis. In 1969 the L&N arrived at Chicago by buying a portion of the Chicago & Eastern Illinois—and again in 1971 by merging with the Monon Railroad. L&N lost its identity under the umbrella of "Family Lines," a cooperative network formed in the mid

1970s by L&N, Seaboard Coast Line, the Georgia Railroad group, and the Clinchfield. In 1982 the L&N (and the Family Lines name) disappeared forever into the new Seaboard System.

Maine Central (1862–present; mileage: 800): Maine Central (MEC) held a virtual rail monopoly on the southern half of its namesake state, connecting Maine's two largest cities, Portland and Bangor. Numerous branch lines served paper and lumber mills. Today, MEC is a ward of Guilford Transportation Industries, which bought "The Pine Tree Route" in 1981.

Missouri-Kansas-Texas (1923–1988; mileage: 2,200): "Katy" was the underdog among Midwest–Texas roads, periodically skirting financial ruin. The railroad's final rejuvenation in the 1970s, however, made it a attractive associate for MP and later a merger partner for Union Pacific in 1988.

Missouri Pacific (1870–1997; mileage: 9,000): A conglomeration of several subsidiaries, Missouri

Pacific Lines played prominent in south central U.S. "Mop's" fleet of *Eagle* streamliners delivered passengers to Omaha, Denver, Kansas City, St. Louis, Dallas, Houston, and San Antonio, among other locales. MP expanded in 1976 by acquiring long-time affiliate Texas & Pacific as well as the Chicago & Eastern Illinois, which got MP to Chicago. Following a 15-year "engagement" with Union Pacific, MP was formally merged into that company in 1997.

Monon (1882-1971; mileage: 600): The 1882 date refers to the first use of this railroad's nickname (pronounced MOE-non), which actually did not become its official title until 1957. Monon, Indiana, was where Chicago, Indianapolis & Louisville's two major routes—Chicago–Indianapolis and Michigan City–Louisville—crossed. Monon merged into L&N in 1971.

New York Central (1853–1968; mileage: 10,700): An industry powerhouse, NYC was long the nemesis of the Pennsylvania Railroad. Central's four-track "Water Level Route" main line (because it followed major rivers and the Great Lakes) was a pipeline for trains—including its world-class *20th Century Limited* and its *Pacemaker* freights—moving

ABOVE: A Missouri Pacific mail and express train departs the massive train shed of St. Louis Union Station (see chapter 6) in August 1966. Destination: Kansas City Union Station, on the other side of the railroad's namesake state. *Mike Schafer*

LEFT: Its years as a passenger locomotive mostly behind it, Louisville & Nashville 4-6-2 No. 85 has been relegated to local freight service in this 1952 scene at Barbourville, Kentucky. *Railroad Avenue Enterprises, Andover Junction Publications collection*

ABOVE: Being entrenched in the most populous regions of the U.S., New York Central operated extensive freight and passenger services. Though known best for its *20th Century Limited*, most NYC passenger trains were work-a-day runs such as this at Dayton, Ohio, in the late 1950s. *Alvin Schultze*

RIGHT: Although very much a regional railroad, the New Haven was widely known thanks in part to the A. C. Gilbert Company, until 1967 the Connecticut-based manufacturer of American Flyer toy electric trains, many of which featured New Haven markings. In this 1952 scene at New Haven, Connecticut, a New York-bound NH run has just exchanged its Alco diesels (in background) for a box-cab electric locomotive for the trip into New York's Pennsylvania Station. *John Dziobko.*

between New York and Boston and major Midwestern cities, including Chicago, Detroit, St. Louis, Cincinnati, and Cleveland. NYC's 1968 merger with "the enemy"—the Pennsy—resulted in the ill-fated Penn Central Railroad whose failure prompted the formation of Conrail in 1976.

New York, Chicago & St. Louis (1881–1964; mileage: 2,200): The Nickel Plate Road, as it was better known, was a modest-size Midwest carrier sandwiched by giants PRR and NYC. Linking Buffalo and Cleveland with Chicago and St. Louis and blanketing Ohio and Indiana with branch lines, NKP held its own thanks to reliable, high-speed freight service. Acquisition of the Wheeling & Lake Erie in 1949 brought the Nickel Plate to Pittsburgh,

Text continued on page 44

ABOVE: Two Alco PA-type locomotives and an Electro-Motive E-series passenger diesel sweep through Santa Susana Pass near Chatsworth, California, with train 98, Southern Pacific's famous *Coast Daylight*, en route from San Francisco to Los Angeles in the late 1950s. *Robert Hale photo, M. D. McCarter collection*

LEFT: All the might and brawn of the Pennsylvania Railroad seems to be summed up in this stirring scene of double-headed locomotives (a Class L-1s 2-8-2 and one of the road's omnipresent K-4s Pacifics) storming upgrade through Horseshoe Curve west of Altoona, Pennsylvania, with train No. 13, the *Day Express*. The date is November 20, 1947. World War II is but a chilling memory, but a new era awaits the "P Company," though not necessarily a good one. In 1946, PRR experienced its first financial loss in decades, a sign of problems for the entire industry. *Bruce D. Fales, Jay Williams collection*

Continued from page 41

Pennsylvania, and Wheeling, West Virginia. In 1964, NKP disappeared into Norfolk & Western.

New York, New Haven & Hartford (1872–1969; mileage: 1,800): For all of its financially frail life, Connecticut-based New Haven was a high-profile passenger carrier, operating a dense network of trains that fed New York City with both commuters and intercity travelers. In 1969 the Interstate Commerce Commission forced the bankrupt NH onto newly formed and very doomed Penn Central—and the rest is history. Interestingly, NH's principal main line—New York–Boston—is now a high speed, all-electric showcase route for Amtrak.

Norfolk & Western (1881–present; mileage: 2,100): Coal was the name of the game for the N&W, whose name summed up its territory and future. Coal mined in West Virginia and Virginia was trafficked east to Norfolk, Virginia, west to Ohio, and northward to ally Pennsylvania Railroad. N&W's 1964 acquisition of the Nickel Plate, Wabash, and Pittsburgh & West Virginia virtually tripled N&W's size, bringing it to Pittsburgh, Chicago, St. Louis, Cleveland, and Kansas City (the "Norfolk & Very Western" some now called it). In 1990, N&W became a subsidiary of the Southern Railway which at the same time changed its name to Norfolk Southern.

Northern Pacific (1864–1970; mileage: 6,700): Its line completed to Seattle in 1863, NP was the first of upper Midwest–Puget Sound transcons, but lived in the shadow of its stronger neighbor, the Great Northern. Regardless, NP's *North Coast Limited* was a highly respected passenger train for all its 71-year tenure in the Chicago–Seattle market. On March 1, 1970, NP, GN, CB&Q, and SP&S merged into Burlington Northern.

Pennsylvania Railroad (1846–1968; mileage: 10,000): Though gone for over 30 years, the Pennsylvania Railroad has consistently ranked as one of the all-time popular lines among railroad aficionados. At one time one of the most powerful companies in the U.S., the PRR served nearly half the country's population—despite the fact its trackage did not go west of the Mississippi River. Among Pennsy's multitude of passenger liners, the *Broadway Limited* became its signature train. PRR also boasted one of the greatest feats of railway engineering: Horseshoe Curve. "The Standard Railroad of the World" moved huge quantities of freight and millions of passengers between New York, Philadelphia, Chicago, St. Louis, Pittsburgh, Cleveland, Indianapolis, Cincinnati, and many other industrial centers. Alas, in 1968 PRR did the unthinkable, merging with arch-enemy New York Central.

Reading Company (1896–1976; mileage: 1,300): The railroad made famous by the board game Monopoly© was based in its namesake city in eastern Pennsylvania. Coal was its principal commodity, but it also operated extensive passenger service out of Philadelphia. Reading (pronounced RED-ding) and ally Jersey Central were merged into Conrail in 1976.

St. Louis–San Francisco (1876–1980; mileage: 5,000): The "Frisco's" X-shaped system crossed at Springfield, Missouri, reaching northeast to St. Louis, northwest to Kansas City, southwest to Texas, and southeast to Florida. Though dogged by financial woes in its earlier years, Frisco's twilight years—the 1970s—revealed the line at its dynamic best, which made SLSF a choice acquisition by Burlington Northern in 1970.

Seaboard Air Line (1900–1967; mileage: 4,100): The railroad with the odd name (in railroading, "air line" meant a direct route between two points) did a commendable job competing with the Atlantic Coast Line throughout the Southeast. Indeed, the two became merger partners in 1967, forming Seaboard Coast Line.

Soo Line (1888–present; mileage: 4,200): Originally the Minneapolis, St. Paul & Sault Ste. Marie, the Soo is, like Monon, another instance

Union Pacific has called Omaha home for the entire life of the railroad. Locomotives in various states of maintenance swarm the Omaha shop complex in the mid 1980s. *Jeff Schultz*

ABOVE: Wabash's *Banner Blue* passenger train departing Chicago for St. Louis in 1963 meets Chicago & Eastern Illinois' combined *Humming Bird/Georgian* streamliners from New Orleans and Atlanta. Wabash's slogan was "Follow the Flag," referring to its banner logo. *Jim Boyd* RIGHT: Western Pacific avoided the treacherous crossing of the Sierra Range that was the foil of parallel Southern Pacific by approaching Sacramento from the northeast through the beautiful Feather River Canyon. This Electro-Motive F-series diesel, preserved at the California State Railroad Museum, made that scenic trip countless times. *Mike Schafer*

where the railroad's nickname became its official name late in life (1961 in this case). Soo Line is a gateway between Chicago and the Twin Cities and Canada, where connection is made with its parent road, Canadian Pacific.

Southern Pacific (1884–1997; mileage: 15,000): One of the giants of U.S. railroading until merger into Union Pacific in 1996, "Espee" was a California institution that reached all the way north to Portland, Oregon, and east to Texas and New Orleans. Its *Daylight* streamliners were among the most beautiful trains anywhere, and its freights moved a huge amount of produce out of California. SP's sphere of influence included the St. Louis Southwestern (Cotton Belt), D&RGW, and Northwestern Pacific.

Southern Railway (1894–1990; mileage: 6,300): SR webbed the Southeast with lines, tapping the Midwest at St. Louis, Louisville, and Cincinnati and the North at Washington, D.C. Southern was yet another carrier whose corporate structure involved numerous subsidiaries, including Central of Georgia, an independent railroad until merged into SR in 1971. SR had a long history

of being a heads-up operation, so its union with Norfolk & Western—another company of high reputation—in 1990 to form Norfolk Southern was a match made in heaven.

Spokane, Portland & Seattle (1908–1970; mileage: 6,700): SP&S was jointly owned by rivals GN and NP, assuring both a connection to Portland, Oregon, out of Spokane and Pasco, Washington. SP&S was swallowed into the 1970 Burlington Northern merger.

Union Pacific (1862–present; mileage: 9,700): The UP was how the West was won. From its shaky beginnings as a railroad pushing west from the Missouri River, the UP grew into what is today the world's largest railroad with some 40,000 route-miles. The "classic" UP of yore stretched from Omaha to Ogden, Utah—the "Overland Route"—with a main line northwest from there to the Pacific Northwest and southwest to California. Today, the UP goes just about everywhere West, thanks to its 1981 merger with Western Pacific, the 1995 merger with Chicago & North Western, the 1996 mergers with SP, Cotton Belt, and Rio Grande, and its 1997 merger with Missouri Pacific.

Wabash (1889–1964; mileage: 2,400): Wabash spanned the "heart of America" with main lines that stretched from Buffalo to Kansas City and Chicago to St. Louis, with several secondary mains filling the gaps. The *Wabash Cannonball* of song fame was a real train, running on Wabash's Detroit–St. Louis route until 1971, seven years after Wabash's disappearance into N&W.

Western Maryland (1853–1983; mileage: 850): WM—the "Fast Freight Line"—competed directly with B&O between Baltimore and western Pennsylvania in earlier years, networking with the likes of the PRR, Reading Lines, and Pittsburgh & West Virginia. Nonetheless, B&O merged WM in 1983 after several years of close affiliation under the Chessie System banner.

Western Pacific (1903–1981; mileage: 1,100): Coordinating with the Rio Grande and Burlington, Western Pacific, reaching west from Salt Lake City, Utah, was the final link in an alternative route (to SP and UP) in the "central corridor" between Chicago and Oakland/San Francisco. Interestingly, UP wound up with WP in 1981 and Rio Grande trackage in 1996.

3 The Railroad Freight Train

Without question, the most important commodity the railroads have ever hauled was freight. The glamorous passenger train may have captured the public's fancy, but the unremarkable freight train paid the bills. From the turn of the century through the 1960s, well over 100,000 freight cars were loaded each day in North America. Even during the heyday of private railroad operation in the early twentieth century, passenger business comprised only a fraction of the railroads' revenues and expenses. Today, with intercity passenger rail services provided by Amtrak, and suburban passenger operations largely handled by local government agencies, the majority of railroads earn nearly 100 percent of their business hauling freight. Further, modern American railroads are, tonnage-wise, hauling more freight than ever before in their history—with about half the number of trains and cars. (How is this possible? Today's freight cars are larger than ever and trains are longer.)

The earliest railroads were built to carry freight—primarily lumber, coal, and iron ore—but the industry rapidly expanded its influence by hauling an ever-expanding range of commodities from produce to grain to livestock. The longer the distance or the heavier the load, the greater the railroads' advantage over the wagon and road. By the late 1830s, railroad shipping rates were only a fourth to a third of the cost of wagon transport.

Although canals still enjoyed an advantage in hauling bulk goods at an even lower cost than the railroad, they suffered from inherent flaws. The Erie Canal, for example, regularly froze solid for up to five months a year while competing railroads kept rolling in all but the worst winter weather. Speed was also a primary consideration. The railroads were the fastest method of transport, moving goods in less than a third the time of the average

Pacemaker Freight Fans Out to Serve New England!

NEW
Mile a Minute
Merchandise
between New England
and New York and key
Midwest cities

BOSTON & ALBANY ROUTE
of the
NEW YORK CENTRAL SYSTEM

canal. Accessibility was another issue; the railroads could go to places that waterways could not.

Despite imperfections like a lack of standardization in track gauge or schedules, the inherent advantages of rail transportation fostered rapid expansion. The railroads' position as the nation's preeminent freight hauler was ensured by the mid-nineteenth century. At its zenith in 1916, a standardized 254,000-mile network of track reached every populated nook and cranny of the continent. Rail freight traffic expanded from 10 billion ton-miles (a ton of freight moved one mile) shipped per year in 1865 to 366 billion in 1916.

MOVING THE GOODS—FROM TOMATOES TO IRON ORE

The extensive rail network that had developed by the early twentieth century allowed America to take advantage of its regional strengths. Vast

amounts of raw materials were moved by rail between regions to produce products, then those products were shipped all over the country, again by rail. The railroads excelled—and still do—in the movement of bulky and heavy materials. Ore mined in Lake Superior iron-ore country was carried by rail to Great Lakes boats for the run to steel mills at the base of the lakes. From the other direction, coal mined in the Appalachian states of Pennsylvania, West Virginia, and Kentucky was shipped to the same shores for use in the mills. Steel forged at the mills was transported by rail to automobile plants and other manufacturers that, in turn, shipped their gleaming finished products nationwide by rail.

Bulk farm products from all over the country also traveled by rail. Perhaps the greatest example of this was the movement of grain from the golden fields of the West and Midwest to mills and then as a multitude of food products to the nation's dinner tables. Thousands of miles of granger branch-line track sprang to life as this phenomenon began with the autumn harvest. Great fleets of cars were marshaled to handle the swell in traffic which often lasted through much of the winter. The traffic tapered as spring approached, only to swell again as the winter wheat was harvested. Twenty to thirty thousand cars were loaded at rural grain elevators in small farming communities located on main lines as well as on a spider's web of lightly used rail that fanned out into the more remote corners of farm country. These cars then converged on grain storage elevators at terminals like Kansas City, Missouri, Wichita, Kansas, and Fort Worth, Texas. From here the grain was shipped to mills for refinement and processing.

But man does not live by bread alone. The shipment of livestock, now handled largely by truck, was once nearly the exclusive province of the railroad.

FACING PAGE: Reflecting an era when railroads actively pursued potential customers through widely distributed litera-
ture, a New York Central brochure from the 1950s banners the expansion of the railroad's famous *Pacemaker* freight service. *C. W. Newton* ABOVE: Grand Trunk Western freights pass one another on former Ann Arbor Railroad trackage at
Toledo, Ohio, in the summer of 1988. *Mike Schafer*

Railroads are ideal for moving bulk commodities cheaply such as coal, iron ore, and grain. At Ashtabula, Ohio, in 1994, mountains of coal and ore await transfer between Conrail trains and Great Lakes boats on Lake Erie (background). *Brian Solomon*

With the center of livestock production over a thousand miles west of the center of meat processing, the railroads were a natural method of shipment for meat on the hoof. Replacing the storied cattle drives, which had once taken up to two months, railroads could transport livestock to market in less than 28 hours. Handled in specially equipped stock cars, animals traveled up to 1,600 miles between Montana, for example, and the major stockyard and meat-packing centers such as Sioux City and Cedar Rapids, Iowa, and Chicago and Kansas City. In turn, processed meats moved from those areas to all points of the country in refrigerator cars. (The decentralization of meat processing has significantly reduced travel distances for livestock, hence the switch to trucks.)

Other, non-animal perishables were once the domain of rail as well, and still are to a degree. In 1872, a bulk shipment of strawberries from the South to Chicago marked the first successful carload shipment of farm products by rail under refrigeration. By the 1880s the cold storage and shipment of dairy products, fruits, and vegetables by rail in refrigerator cars or "reefers" had become an established service of the railroads. The availability of that service changed the way Americans farmed and lived. Southern perimeter states like Florida and Texas were developed for agricultural production, with railroads distributing the produce throughout America. The bounty on America's table now included not just regional specialties but citrus and other fruits and vegetables—including the import of such exotic fruits as bananas from South America, a huge number of which moved in solid banana trains on priority schedules on the Illinois Central from New Orleans to Chicago.

There was a time in America when tall, belching smokestacks were synonymous with industrial might, and in the thick of those industrial complexes were the railroads. Together, industry and railroads helped forge a nation that is still bound by boulevards of steel.

LEFT: The Bethlehem Steel plant at Bethlehem, Pennsylvania, in 1976. The plant is closed now, but the Lehigh Valley Railroad main line in the foreground remains an artery of rail freight transportation. *Mike Schafer*

ABOVE: Erie Railroad map brochure from 1953. *Mike Schafer Collection*

The perfection of the shipment of perishables owed its success largely to technical advances in refrigeration and insulation. Cooling the fleet of reefers was perhaps the biggest job of all. At its zenith, the refrigerator-car fleet required 13 million tons of ice on any given day. As perishable trains arrived at icing stations along their routes, an army of workers descended upon the trains to re-ice and inspect the cars. The boom in frozen foods following World War II severely impacted ice reefer transportation. Ice cooling was in fact not very effective in maintaining the below-zero temperatures required by frozen foods. By the end of the 1960s this and the problem of labor-intensive icing stations were solved by mechanical refrigeration in which new, well-insulated refrigerator cars carried their own compact diesel engine to operate cooling equipment.

More challenging than a method of cooling the produce was the movement of the product itself. Great numbers of refrigerator cars had to be assembled at the right time and at the right place to move crops to market as they ripened. For the most part organized into regional car operations like Pacific Fruit Express (PFE), the vast fleet of refrigerator cars moved on tight schedules which required advance planning and close monitoring of car movement. One of the most interesting aspects of much of these shipments was the fact that, although the produce was dispatched in the general direction of a market, neither the shipper nor the railroad always knew where the car would finally come to rest . . . for the product had yet to be sold! Keeping track of products on the move, shippers and brokers feverishly sought out buyers for the produce and wired instructions ahead as to where the cars should finally go once the deal was closed. In this situation, a freight train was in fact a rolling warehouse. It was all part of highly efficient, specialized operation which the railroads had perfected —changing the way America lived in the process.

As intriguing as the special movements were, the carriage of everyday goods comprised the bread-and-butter of the railroads' operations in the heyday of their operation. At mid-twentieth century, up to 45 million freight-car movements occurred during an average year in the U.S. The majority of those cars carried general merchandise (versus perishables and bulk commodities) in predictable patterns. Shipments of everything from schoolbooks to furniture to canned goods moved back and forth between shipper and consignee (receiver) with the railroad acting as the go-between, ensuring the product arrived in a timely manner.

TYPES OF FREIGHT TRAINS

To understand rail freight transportation, it is important to realize that there are different basic types of freight *trains* as well as different types of freight *traffic*. Some of these types—merchandise and general freights for example—were far more prevalent in early to mid twentieth century railroading than today while unit and intermodal trains are the stuff of contemporary railroading:

General freight train: A "general" freight train (sometimes referred to as a "mixed" freight or irreverently as a "junk" freight) comprises a variety

A mixed-bag of car types identifies this Southern Pacific train cruising through the Nevada desert near Golconda in October 1964 as a general freight. Five Electro-Motive F-series diesels are in charge of this Overland Route train. *Gordon Glattenberg*

Advertised Freight Schedules

In 1931 the St. Louis Southwestern Railway—The Cotton Belt Route— established the *Blue Streak Merchandise*, the first fast overnight merchandise freight guaranteed to carry package freight picked up the after the close of business and deliver it 400 miles away by morning or 600 miles away by noon. By the advent of World War II, over a hundred trains of this type on several railroads connected most of major distribution centers with hundreds of smaller stations across the country. Coupled with expedited handling methods for unloading and loading freight cars and coordinated rail-

truck delivery services, the concept revolutionized an industry where freight-delivery schedules had previously been figured in several days and even weeks. Such trains were marketed not unlike passenger trains, as illustrated by the brochure that leads this chapter.

Although the package-freight aspect has all but been replaced by intermodal freight on the nation's rails, high-priority freight trains still exist, operating on fast (in terms of overall point-to-point scheduling, not necessarily in higher speeds), scheduled times much like passenger trains. With the exception of passenger

trains, which generally have higher operating status, scheduled freight trains usually have the highest priority on the railroad.

Greater in number during railroading's classic period, regular or general freights also often operated on schedules and were the backbone of the system. Although it did not necessarily operate on as tight a time schedule as high-priority freights, the general freight was still marketed with estimated arrival periods (e.g., "morning" or "by noon" rather than specific clock times) at major destinations. The general-freight network was the advertised service the railroad

offered and the one which the majority of customers used. Unlike fast, high-priority trains, which usually catered to the high-speed, point-to-point market, advertised freight trains were generally designed with connectivity (at major junction points) in mind to offer the customer as many options as possible, and the railroads closely plotted the connections available between their own trains as well as with those of connecting railroads. The network of advertised freight trains and their connections allowed a freight car to travel anywhere on the system and beyond in a relatively short time.

of individual cars—boxcars, gondolas, hoppers, and so forth—each loaded with just about any type of freight, including general merchandise and bulk commodities like grain or coal. Each car is perhaps chartered by a different shipper and each has a unique final destination. Shipments moving in traditional freights are often less time-sensitive than those in other types of freights. In addition, empty cars migrating back to their home railroads often ride in these freights.

Merchandise trains: These trains—a close cousin of the traditional freight—primarily carry time-sensitive manufactured products, are made up largely of boxcars, and often run on advertised schedules; no empty cars are handled. These trains are usually closely tied in with trucking distribution and warehousing at at least one end of the shipment.

Auto-parts trains: Auto-assembly plants are high-volume users of materials, so much so that whole trains can be dedicated to hauling parts and supplies to auto-assembly plants found in Detroit, Kansas City, St. Paul, and other auto-producing centers. Often these trains are scheduled in a "just in time" manner—the parts arrive just as the factory needs them. This reduces warehousing costs for auto manufacturers.

Unit trains: Railroads have always handled large-scale movements of products. At the same time, largely as a result of past abuses in rate-making and unfair kickbacks to large shippers, the railroads were for many decades prohibited from offering "quantity" discounts for those movements. Gradually, the government relaxed regulations and the railroads were freed to pursue the market—with the unit train as the ultimate result. Comprised entirely of the same cars, carrying a single product for a single customer, and moving between origin and final destination without switching of cars en route, the unit train is incredibly cost effective, hence the justification for the lower shipping rates.

Quickly loaded or unloaded upon arrival—sometimes by fully automated systems which can load the commodity into moving trains or unload it by rotating an entire railroad car (equipped with special couplers that allow it to be rotated without being uncoupled from adjacent cars) upside down like a child's toy—the unit train is ready to return within hours. It is not uncommon to see unit trains complete a 2,000-mile round trip in 96 hours. In an industry where a regular train could take weeks to do the same thing, the concept was revolutionary. The principal commodity carried by unit train

ABOVE: The advent of cooling technology in the 1800s helped revolutionize rail transportation—and how Americans were fed. For the better part of a century, refrigerator cars were cooled with ice at icing stations such as this at Pennsylvania Railroad's Grogan Yard in Columbus, Ohio, shown in 1956. Blocks of ice were moved by a chain conveyor along the platform as men slid the ice blocks with poles over to the open roof hatches of the refrigerator cars. *John Dziobko*

RIGHT: Laden with reefers belonging to Wilson and other Iowa and Nebraska meat packers, the hottest freight on Illinois Central's Iowa Division—perishable train No. 76—hotfoots it through Rockford, Illinois, at noon on a late summer's day in 1965. Like many freights of the period, No. 76 was also assigned a symbol—in this case "CC-6"—by the railroad as part of an overall freight-marketing scheme. CC-6 stood for "<u>C</u>ouncil Bluffs [Iowa]–<u>C</u>hicago, train 7<u>6</u>." *Mike Schafer*

is coal. As of the end of the twentieth century, unit coal-train traffic comprised approximately 40 percent of the tonnage moved on Class I railroads and brought in over 20 percent of the revenues.

Intermodal and stack trains: As the railroads evolved, so did the way the world shipped freight. Many goods that once were unloaded from or transferred between ships, trucks, or railroad cars item by item now move in containers or truck trailers. Containers and trailers are "intermodal"— which means the they can move between modes of transportation (sea, rail, and truck) without ever being unloaded and reloaded—a huge savings in labor and time.

Although intermodal rail transport is often bannered as a new concept, it's not. Containerization dates from the late 1700s in England, and in the late 1880s wagons were carried by rail on New York's Long Island Rail Road. Truck trailers were handled by rail as early as the 1920s, but the concept really didn't take off until the 1950s when the Pennsylvania Railroad and New York Central greatly expanded the carriage of truck trailers on flatcars. The impetus was a desire to maintain a share of the LCL (less-than-carload) business being rapidly lost to the trucking industry. For the truckers, the motive for cooperating with the railroads was the inherent cost effectiveness of shipping a large number of truck trailers great distances for a fraction of the fuel and labor cost.

A fairly recent development that has met with reasonable success is the "RoadRailer" concept whereby the railroad flatcar is eliminated from the haulage of truck trailers. Rather, the trailers themselves are set upon flanged-wheel "bogies" at the point where they enter the rail mode of their journey and are coupled together and run as a train. The result is a freight train of very light weight (thereby requiring less fuel and horsepower) and smooth operation.

Containers—today's preferred intermodal conveyance—are basically steel or aluminum boxes that carry freight. Unlike truck trailers, they lack wheels until they are put on a truck chassis or a railcar. The absence of permanent wheels on a container is actually an advantage. Hauling the entire truck trailer is more costly as it involves the extra weight of the

Graphically illustrating the modern-day unit train is this Union Pacific coal train at Bonner Springs, Kansas, in 1996. The train is empty and heading west from Kansas City back to the Wyoming coal country for another load of low-sulphur coal. *Dan Munson*

ABOVE: Two Conrail piggyback trains converge briefly at Sugar Run Gap on the former Pennsylvania Railroad Harrisburg–Pittsburgh main line near Gallitzin, Pennsylvania, in 1994. Instances of TOFC (Trailer On Flat Car) transport date back to pre-World War II days on roads like the Long Island Rail Road and interurban Chicago North Shore & Milwaukee, but the Pennsylvania Railroad is credited to popularizing piggyback when in 1954 it launched its "TrucTrain" service and in 1956 incorporated TrailerTrain Company (today TTX Company) to provide a pool of flatcars designed especially for piggyback operation. *Tom Kline*

RIGHT: A radical variation on piggyback is the RoadRailer. This truck-trailer-on-rail-wheels concept was pioneered by Chesapeake & Ohio in the 1960s when for a short time it operated specially equipped truck trailers attached to the the last car of selected passenger runs. The concept went dormant for several years, re-emerging in the 1980s when Norfolk Southern and trucking affiliate Triple Crown began operating an integrated network of fast, scheduled RoadRailer trains—such as NS RoadRailer train No. 244 at Parkers Lake, Kentucky, in 1989—and trucks using specially designed trailers and rail wheel bogies. *F. L. Becht*

wheel assembly. Containers can also be stacked more easily. On ships they are transported stacked several high. On the railroads, newly designed container cars carry a "double stack" of two containers on top of each other. Some modern double-stack cars are comprised of five articulated units which can carry up to ten containers. New York Central pioneered container trains in the 1950s and 1960s, with a few other railroads—notably Illinois Central and Milwaukee Road—utilizing containers to move mail on passenger trains. Interestingly, container transport was slow to catch on; hindsight proves that NYC was 20 years ahead of its time.

Perishable trains: These carry food products that are temperature sensitive and must arrive at their destination in a very timely manner. The trains can be made up of varying cars with varying destinations, or they can be unit trains, such as the famous juice train—made up entirely of mechanical reefers painted in the bright orange scheme of their owner, Tropicana—that ran between Florida and the Northeast.

Local freights and switch jobs: Local freights follow a specified routing to gather and deliver cars at on-line shippers and receivers. The local funnels these cars through a freight yard or some other staging point for transfer to or from higher-priority freights. In days past, many local freights handled a limited number passengers who rode with the crew either in a passenger car (usually a combination baggage-coach) or the caboose. These were referred to as "mixed" trains (not to be confused with mixed-freight trains), the last of which disappeared on U.S. soil in 1983. Local trains took on a variety of nicknames. On the Milwaukee Road, they were known as "patrols," and on numerous other lines they were known as "way freights."

A close relative of the local freight, switch jobs are usually confined to working a large complex of industries and trackage. They "pull" emptied and loaded cars from industries and "spot" inbound cars, grouping outbound cars for pickup by local freights. Like the local train, switch jobs had their nicknames as well. On Eastern lines, for example, they are often referred to as "drills."

Text continued on page 61

A Conrail stack train bound for northern New Jersey ports is but a few miles from its destination as it rolls southward along former New York Central "West Shore" trackage along the Hudson River at Bear Mountain, New York, in 1991. *Richard Steinheimer*

Two local freights—a diesel-powered Boston & Maine run (right) and a steam-powered local of the Central Vermont Railway—pass on joint CV-B&M trackage in southeastern Vermont. It's the 1950s, and local freights are still commonplace on the nation's railroads. During the ensuring two decades, railroads would relinquish a large amount of such local service to trucks and instead concentrate on handling bulk commodities and less labor-intensive freight. *Philip R. Hastings Collection, California State Railroad Museum*

A Freight Car Primer

The ubiquitous boxcar was once the jack-of-all-trades conveyance for most freight, and it came in a wide assortment of sizes and styles, from the basic 40-foot single-door boxcar that dominated most of the twentieth century to 50-foot cars as illustrated above in 1985 (these Santa Fe cars have "Shock Control" coupling arrangements to lessen the jolts of starting and stopping) to mammoth 85-foot "Hi-Cube" boxcars for handling auto parts. *David P. Oroszi*

In the primordial years of American railroading, most freight was shipped either in boxcars or on flatcars, the two most basic of all freight cars. Over time, railroads and car-building companies refined the boxcar and flatcar and developed other types of cars tailored to the transport of specific kinds of freight. Today, virtually anything can be shipped by rail, including airplanes (albeit disassembled), monster electric generators, and all types of liquid products. Some basic car types. . .

Boxcars: Once the most common of all freight cars, boxcars essentially are empty boxes on wheels. As such they can carry a variety of products like furniture, paper, certain food products, and anything else that requires dry transport and protection from the elements but where temperature is not critical. In the 1960s, well over 300,000 boxcars, either plain or specially outfitted to handle special loads, roamed American rails every day. For decades the standard boxcar length was 40 feet, but 50-foot cars gained popularity in the mid-twentieth century and longer cars followed, with mammoth 85-foot "Hi-Cube" boxcars appearing early in the 1960s.

Refrigerator cars: A close cousin to the boxcar, "reefers," as refrigerator cars are more commonly called, are basically heavily insulated boxcars that are cooled—earlier by ice and now by mechanical means—to keep contents chilled, if not frozen. Mechanical reefers with diesel-electric powered refrigeration are capable of keeping products frozen or refrigerated for up to two weeks on one tank of fuel. During the 1960s, over 100,000 refrigerator cars roamed the rails carrying 28 million tons of food every year.

Stock cars: Add wide air vents all along the sides of a boxcar and you have a rolling cattle or pig pen, in both single- and double-deck varieties. Stock cars have virtually vanished from American rails, thanks to trucking and the decentralization of meat-processing plants.

Flatcars: The lowly, simple flatcar is in fact a multi-talented conveyance. In its simplest form, the flatcar is perfect for carrying large, bulky items such as farm tractors, transformers, road-building equipment, and other heavy machinery. In slightly modified form, they provide a "parking lot" for truck trailers moving piggyback style, and further modified with a steel center divider, the flatcar handles stacks of pulpwood and lumber.

Hoppers: These cars transport loose bulk that can be unloaded via gravity through funneled openings in the car bottoms. Material relatively unaffected by moisture—coal, crushed stone, ore pellets—can move in open-top hopper cars,

but materials like grain, potash (a type of fertilizer), and cement must move in covered hoppers to be protected from rain and snow. The open hopper, of which there were over 350,000 cars in the U.S. in the 1960s, came in a variety of shapes and sizes designed to carry different types of products. Metal ores, for example, traveled in hopper cars of relatively small cubic capacity—known as "ore jennies"—due to the high density of the product. Today, over 4.5 million carloads of coal per year—more tonnage than any other commodity—travel in open hoppers, making coal the most common commodity shipped by rail.

Covered hoppers are a relatively recent development, popularized only after World War II, prior to which grain and such was moved in boxcars outfitted with temporary special side doors. Each year close to a million and half carloads of grain, averaging nearly 90 tons per car, travel across the country, but covered gons also handle such commodities as plastic pellets and silica sand, both used in manufacturing. Many newer covered hoppers are cylindrical shaped for

added capacity and strength.

Gondolas: The traditional gondola is basically a flatcar with sides so as to be able to carry loads of loose items, from steel piping to scrap metal. Open-top "gons" abound, but covered gons are employed, too, often in the transport of coiled steel or sheet metal which needs to be protected from the rusting effects of moisture. Over 35 million tons of scrap metal and 60 million tons of new metal products were shipped by rail in an average year, primarily in the nation's fleet of over 180,000 gondolas. A newer type of gon is often mistaken for a hopper. Unit coal trains that feature cars which are emptied by being rotated upside down rather than through car-bottom openings are technically high-sided gons, not hoppers.

Sulphur-laden tank cars as far as the eye can see roll east on the Santa Fe out of Clovis, New Mexico, in March 1974. The locomotives are "mid-train helpers," operated by the crew in the lead locomotive set (out of photo); they will assist the train over the lead locomotives in moving the train over heavy grades. *Forrest L. Becht*

Tank cars: Liquid chemicals and food products as well as gaseous chemicals travel by rail in tank cars. Crude oil was once a common commodity carried in rail tank cars, moving from sea ports or Texas and Oklahoma oil country to refineries. During the first half of the twentieth century, milk was commonly carried on trains (usually in local passenger trains known as "milk" runs) in special glass-lined tank cars from farms to dairies, and finished dairy products from there to stores. Some types of petroleum products such as liquefied petroleum gas are carried under pressure in specialized tank cars. Dangerous chemicals such as chlorine gas and sulfuric acid also travel in tank cars, in part because the railroads provide one of the safest and most efficient methods of transporting the product, removing it from public highways. The nation's fleet of over 170,000 tanks cars is largely owned by private shippers.

Auto-rack cars: The auto carrier railcar so common on contemporary railroads evolved from a boxcar. Auto-carrying boxcars had end doors for easier loading and interior ramps that allowed cars to be doubled up, and these concepts were in part transferred to what was essentially an open, double-tiered flatcar. Today's auto-racks are double and triple level and can carry 12 to 18 automobiles; some of the very newest cars are articulated for maximum capacity—that is, the car is in two sections joined by a common center truck (wheel) assembly.

Stack (well) cars: The containerization boom spurred the development of a car that could carry containers in stack formation. The result: a car that is in essence a cross between a flatcar and a gondola. The main portion of the car rides lower than the bolsters (the pivot points at which the carbody rests on the trucks) to lower the center of gravity—even when the car is stacked with containers—and provide a smoother, more stable ride. A standard stack car carries two containers, one atop the other. Articulated stack cars usually have five permanently coupled sections (holding ten containers), with adjacent sections sharing common trucks, and the end sections having standard couplers. Although articulated stack cars appear to be five cars long, they are, for accounting purposes, considered to be a single car.

Autos destined for showroom floors move along Penn Central's former Pennsylvania Railroad main line between Altoona and Gallitzin, Pennsylvania, in 1968. Today's auto-rack cars feature covered sides to thwart vandalism. *Mike Schafer*

At one time owned by Henry Ford interests, the Detroit, Toledo & Ironton Railroad, merged into Grand Trunk Western in 1983, was a pipeline for auto-parts traffic moving to and between auto manufacturer plants at Detroit and Toledo. This southbound DT&I run crossing the Chesapeake & Ohio at Carleton, Michigan, in 1979 is a classic auto-parts train, laden with Hi-Cube boxcars and a few auto racks. *Mike Schafer*

Continued from page 56

Transfer freights: Found primarily in large cities, transfer freights move blocks of cars between major terminal yards. These freights can be operated by the regular railroads themselves or by a terminal railroad, such as the Belt Railway of Chicago, whose primary reason for existence is to transfer cars from one railroad to another.

The distinction between freight-train types isn't always clear cut. Quite often piggyback and stack (container) cars can be found together on a single train, or mixed in with regular freight cars on a general freight. The volume of perishables moving by rail today is considerably less than that during the first half of the twentieth century, so mechanical reefers tend to be mixed in on traditional freight trains rather than moved in solid reefer trains.

TYPES OF FREIGHT TRAFFIC

Aside from freight-train types, there are three basic types of freight traffic:

On-line traffic both originates and terminates on the "home" railroad and never leaves the home railroad—although it might travel 15 miles or hundreds of miles over different lines on that railroad.

Interline traffic originates on one railroad and terminates on another. A boxcar of merchandise shipped from Cucamonga, California, on the Burlington Northern & Santa Fe to Wapakoneta, Ohio, on CSX is an interline movement.

"Overhead" or "bridge" traffic. Here, a railroad serves as a "bridge" for traffic moving between off-line points of origin and destination. That boxcar of merchandise moving from Cucamonga to

ABOVE: Two Alton & Southern Alco road-switchers have a transfer freight under way in the East St. Louis area early in the 1960s. Located mostly on the Illinois side of the Mississippi River across from St. Louis, Missouri, the A&S is a belt line linking the major railroads that converge on East St. Louis. *Jim Boyd*

RIGHT: Little railroad, big freight: A former Northern Pacific Z6-class Mallet now in the employment of the Spokane, Portland & Seattle is shaking the ground at Marshall, Washington, on April 21, 1951, with a general freight that trails out of view. A better portrait of big steam doing what it was built to do—move the nation's freight—would be hard to come by. *Philip R. Hastings Collection, California State Railroad Museum*

Wapakoneta may have moved over the Gateway Western Railroad between Kansas City and St. Louis, so for the GWRR that car represented bridge traffic.

There are two basic ways that traffic moves, by the carload or by less-than-carload (LCL). In the first, a shipper is assigned an entire car to collect, ship, and deliver a product between one point of origin and one destination. Usually this involves major shippers—an appliance factory, for example—and receivers (often warehouses) which have their own rail siding(s). A carload of washers and driers can be shipped directly from the factory to a warehouse where they are stored until redistributed by truck to local stores.

With LCL shipping, a shipper with less than a carload of freight would share a freight car—almost always a box car specifically assigned to LCL service—with other shippers. For example, it would not make economic sense for a bicycle dealer to use an entire boxcar to move a dozen Schwinns. LCL freight usually moved through freight stations. The shipper trucked the goods to the freight depot of the railroad of choice; the railroad loaded it onto the appropriate car assigned to LCL service on selected scheduled freight trains.

The freight was off-loaded at the appropriate destination and held at the depot for pickup by the consignee. By the 1940s LCL comprised about 2 percent of the tonnage carried by the railroad, but since it was in a sense a "premium" service, LCL yielded about 7 percent of the revenues. The amount of LCL freight moved via rail dropped from over 50 million tons in 1919 to just over 4 million tons by 1958. Since then, virtually all railroad-operated LCL traffic has been relinquished to the trucking industry as railroads refocused on what they do best: moving bulk commodities and intermodal freight. Nonetheless, some LCL traffic has in a sense returned in the form of that intermodal freight. Numerous truck trailers and containers hauled on railcars today carry . . . LCL traffic!

FREIGHT DISTRIBUTION

Larger railroads are organized into "divisions." In earlier days, the length of a division was generally the distance a freight train could travel during the course of a work day, usually between 100 and 150 miles. At each division point was a major yard and engine-servicing facility as well as a hostelry for crews laying over away from home.

Well into the twentieth century, freight trains were usually yard-to-yard operations and carried cars bound for all sorts of destinations. At each division-point yard, the cars were reshuffled and put onto new trains to continue to the next division-point yard, where they were shuffled again or handed over to a connecting railroad where the yard-to-yard process might be repeated. At last, the cars would be put onto local freights to be delivered to their final destinations. This was a very economical way to move freight, but it could take days—or weeks—for a car to move just a few hundred miles from shipper to receiver.

The rise of the trucking industry in the 1920s forced railroads to rethink this cumbersome way to move freight. Eventually, railroads developed different types and priorities of freight trains—the perishable train, the coal train, the merchandise express, and other trains likewise tailored to the needs of customers through predictable, faster schedules and specific routings. This is still true today. Intermodal trains run on expeditious schedules to compete with trucks on cross-country runs. Unit coal trains maintain a consistent supply of black diamonds to power plants. Stack trains connect at ocean ports with ships.

To illustrate a typical freight movement, we'll make a hypothetical freight shipment as it would

Maine Central's Lewiston Lower switch job spots and pulls cars at industries in Lewiston Lower, Maine, in 1981. Gathered cars will be forwarded along MEC's Lewiston Lower branch to the yard at Brunswick, Maine. There, cars will be placed on MEC mainline trains headed east to Bangor or west to Portland. *Jim Boyd*

have happened in the middle part of the twentieth century. The process began when the shipper contacted the freight agent of the local railroad of choice and requested an empty car to ship its products. The car selected would not necessarily belong to the home railroad (unless the shipment was on-line); rather, it might be an empty car of a foreign-line road migrating back to its home base near the ultimate destination of the product being shipped.

Our freight car gets "spotted" (positioned) for loading. This might be at the loading dock at the shipper's factory or at a "team" (public) track where shippers who did not have their own sidings could still access cars. After the car was loaded, the agent or shipper filled out a "bill of lading"—a contract between the railroad and shipper—and a "waybill" detailing the car's contents, destination, shipper, and receiver, among other things. The waybill accompanied the car on its journey.

The shipment's actual journey began when the local switch job arrived to collect the car. Depending on the location of the shipper, the car may be picked up by a locomotive and crew that exclusively performed switching in an urban switching

district, or it might be collected by a local freight that gathered and distributed cars along a branch or main line. Regardless, the car would be brought to a yard for sorting and placement in the appropriate train. A car might pass through more than one yard. For example, if the shipper were in a smaller city, the car might first be brought to the city yard to be placed on a semi-local train headed for the nearest major terminal classification yard. There, the car is again reclassified into yet another, higher-priority train going a longer distance.

Let's suppose our car left one of Chicago's major classification facilities, Corwith Yard, in one of Santa Fe's scheduled general-merchandise trains bound for Los Angeles. It was one of 76 cars organized into "blocks" (groups) bound for selected intermediate points as well as the L.A. area. There might be a block of 5 cars together for Fort Madison, Iowa, 26 for Kansas City, 8 for Amarillo, Texas, 17 for Belen, New Mexico (a major Santa Fe junction point), and 20 for L.A. including our car. The blocks are "set out" at these locations and other blocks picked up; at Kansas City, for example, our train may pick up an addition 40 L.A.-bound cars to add to the existing L.A. block.

The Freight Yard

Railroad yards are a "necessary evil" to the railroad industry. Yards can take up enormous amounts of valuable real estate, they are easily clogged due to unexpected traffic conditions (or weather), and, as the railroad's giant chessboard, they can be a headache to operate for even the most skilled of yardmasters.

Nonetheless, yards are necessary for breaking down inbound trains, sorting cars, and making up new trains. A good yard is relatively empty yard, for it means that traffic has been fluid through its maze of tracks.

Major yard complexes encompassed a number of different sections. Often, major yard complexes include locomotive-servicing facilities as well as a car repair area. The main component of a yard, of course, are the tracks, each one with an assigned purpose. Arrival tracks hold inbound trains awaiting reclassification or through trains that are undergoing inspection, as required by law. Departure tracks hold made-up trains awaiting their crews. Some tracks are for temporary storage of cars being sorted, while others hold blocks of cars destined for a single location.

Railroads use two basic types of yards to sort, or classify, cars:

Flat yards: In a flat yard (which, as the name implies, is level), cars are organized into blocks or whole trains by a switching crew using a locomotive—usually a switcher—to pull and shove the cars into the appropriate tracks and, in larger flat yards at major terminal points, organize the

Milwaukee Road's principal Chicago-area classification yard at suburban Bensenville was a hump yard. This eastward view from the yard's control tower shows a string of freight cars being slowly pushed over the hump by a switcher (out of photo behind the photographer). As each car crests the hump, a switchman at trackside uncouples it and it begins its freewheeling ride down hill. The retarders (seen between the C&EI boxcar and the flat car already rolling) automatically kick in while the control-tower operator(s) align the switches. Milwaukee Road's successors, the Soo Line and Canadian Pacific, have since converted Bensenville back to a flat-switching yard, the result of a growing fleet of run-through and unit trains, which require little or no enroute switching. *Ed DeRouin*

resulting blocks into trains. Some yards may comprise no more than two or three sorting tracks.

Although experienced switching crews can efficiently assemble what is essentially a huge puzzle with many wheeled pieces, the "flat switching" method of assembling and un-assembling trains can be time-consuming and therefore expensive. So, where feasible, railroads can allow Mother Nature help in sorting cars. . .

Gravity or "hump" yards: The beauty of a gravity yard is that it lets physics do the work. The basic concept is to shove a whole string of cars being sorted over a man-made hill or hump and let gravity pull them downhill into the appropriate track. An operator in a nearby control tower remotely aligns switches so that the car rolls by itself into the appropriate track. In early hump-yard installations, the speed of the car was controlled by a brakeman riding the car over the hump and setting the car's hand-brake. Later a mechanical "retarder" pinched the wheels as they rolled down from the hump, slowing the car to the appropriate speed. Using this method, a switch engine and crew had much less work to do and the cars could be sorted more quickly since numerous back-and-forth movements in and out of each track were eliminated. Gravity yards are best-suited for major classification yards.

Major yard complexes may actually be made up of several smaller yards, some flat, some hump, and there may be more than one hump facility in a yard.

Upon the train's arrival at Santa Fe's major L.A.-area classification yard at San Bernardino, our car went through much the same process it experienced at the beginning of its travels—but this time in reverse. As the arriving merchandise freight was broken apart, our car was pulled from the train and switched onto a track to await other cars destined for the same local area. The final act in the process was played out when the crew of the local freight containing our car delivered it to a track accessible by the recipient.

MOVING FREIGHT BY RAIL TODAY

As part of the evolution of the American railroad, the industry as a whole continues to become increasingly efficient in handling freight. Ironically this has resulted from markets having been taken away from the railroads by aggressive competition. The movement of railroad-originated LCL freight has vanished. Refrigerated transport has dwindled too. But if these more labor-intensive services have been reduced, that change, coupled with government deregulation in the 1980s, has enabled the railroads to focus on handling more cost-effective freight. And, reducing the amount of effort expended in handling each car has yielded a significant increase in productivity. Between 1980 and 1995 the amount of freight hauled per railroad worker increased an astounding 250 percent.

In the past, the majority of freight trains were general freights and merchandise trains carrying a variety of cars that were switched in and out of those trains at various points. Though these types of freights still reign, they no longer reign supreme. In the 1950s, general and merchandise freights began to be supplanted by piggyback trains. Growth in this traffic rose slowly but steadily until the 1970s when it accounted for nearly 9 percent of the revenues of the Class 1 railroads. Since then, the intermodal industry has evolved and expanded more rapidly and now includes containerization. The flexibility and cost effectiveness of containerization have resulted in an amazing increase in container traffic, which doubled between the mid 1980s and late 1990s.

Today the movement of bulk commodities in unit trains and merchandise in intermodal trains serves as the foundation of the industry.

A Santa Fe stack train climbing through Southern California's Tehachapi Mountains crosses over itself at Tehachapi Loop in 1991. *Jeff Schultz*

4

The Railroad
Passenger Train

If the freight train was a blue-collar worker, the passenger train was the company spokesperson. There was a time when millions of Americans, from school children to important shippers, judged the railroads by the passenger trains each provided. Although each train had its own agenda, the thousands of passenger trains operated between 1830 and the present defy easy compartmentalization. Some trains connected destinations more than 2,000 miles apart while others barely ran 20 miles. The distances they covered or the places they went often had little relationship to the services offered on board. Western Pacific's no-frills, one-car *Zephyrette* traveled over 921 miles on its daily run between Oakland, California, and Salt Lake City, Utah, while the Reading Railroad's sleek stainless-steel streamliner, the *Crusader*, complete with dining/tavern service and observation cars, covered only 90 miles on its journey between Philadelphia and Jersey City, New Jersey. Santa Fe's swank *Super Chief* made a household name for itself connecting important cities like Chicago and Los Angeles while few remember Chicago & Eastern Illinois Railroad's inviting streamliner, the *Meadowlark*, which ran south from Chicago to terminate at the obscure outpost of Cypress, Illinois, population 300.

Passenger trains were as different from each other as the accent of their passengers, and at one time they were virtually omnipresent. Passenger trains could be found skirting the Pacific Ocean, the canyons of Colorado, the Mississippi River, the hollows of West Virginia, the woods of Cape Cod, and virtually anywhere else there were two rails and a modest potential for income. Trains with names as famous as the *20th Century Limited* or as obscure as the *Egyptian Zipper* poked their way into almost every corner of the U.S.

From the 1830s to 1971 the privately operated passenger train was a fixture on the American transportation scene. For much of the nineteenth century and a majority of the twentieth century, it provided an absolutely essential service linking cities and towns in the absence of a safer, more convenient or faster method of travel. In addition to providing intercity service, local commuter trains carried millions to work and home every day. But beginning in the 1920s and with the exception of World War II when high ridership guaranteed increased revenues, the passenger train declined in profitability as growing forms of competition skimmed the cream of the railroad's trade. By the 1960s the privately operated passenger train was in desperate straits. Unable to recover their operating expenses in the face of rising costs, unable to compete with growing air and highway transport—both government sponsored to at least some degree—and unwilling (or unable) to invest significant capital to keep up with changing travel tastes, American railroads sought relief.

These difficult financial times coupled with the recognition of the importance of maintaining a passenger rail option prompted a significant change. Since 1971 Amtrak, the National Railroad Passenger Corporation, which receives government assistance, has operated the vast majority of long-distance passenger trains in the U.S. Today, as private bus and airlines withdraw service from unprofitable markets or weather conspires to close airports and roads, residents can still rely on the safety net of rail service. In many regions, policymakers are gradually coming to the realization that they cannot build their way out of the congestion encouraged by several decades of focus on the single-occupant vehicle. High-speed intercity rail has come of age in the Northeast Corridor (Boston–New York–Washington, D.C.) and in the Pacific Northwest between Seattle and Portland. Commuter railroads, now customarily administered by public agencies, are taking on increasing importance as urban areas struggle under the burden of growing traffic congestion.

EARLY PASSENGER TRAINS

On Christmas Day 1830 in Charleston, South Carolina, the *Best Friend of Charleston* locomotive pulled a train carrying 141 passengers on a six-mile section of track. It was the first steam-powered scheduled passenger run in America. Passenger service initially proved more alluring than freight service. Traveling at the unheard of speed of 20 mph, the first passenger trains carried as many people who rode out of curiosity as necessity. The Baltimore & Ohio, which charged the first passenger fare in America, carried almost 100,000 paying passengers in its fourth year of operation. Passenger income comprised up to a third of the revenues of the average railroad before the Civil War.

FACING PAGE: This huge mosaic once greeted passengers at Cincinnati Union Terminal, opened in 1933. When the concourse section of this stunning depot was razed, the mosaic was rescued and stored. *Mike Schafer* ABOVE: With the Chicago skyline receding in the distance, the Milwaukee Road-Union Pacific *City of Denver/City of Portland* is into the first few moments of its overnight journey to Denver, Colorado, and three-day trek to Portland, Oregon, in 1969. The Milwaukee will hand the train over to the UP at Omaha, Nebraska, late this same evening. *Mike Schafer*

It may have been a novel way to go but the comfort of riding the rails was still questionable. The earliest railroad passenger cars more closely resembled the horse carriages and stagecoaches they were modeled after rather than the traditional railway car. Later models usually featured center aisles in which the traveler could move about, stretch his legs, or suffer the attention of vendors. Poorly heated or not heated at all, they were sweltering in the summer as riders prudently avoided opening windows to avoid the cinders from the stack of the steam locomotive (a problem which plagued passengers until the advent of air-conditioning in the 1920s). American improvements enhanced basic European designs. Two "trucks" (wheel assemblies) each containing two axles and four wheels appeared under the ends of American passenger cars by the late 1830s predating the same design in Europe by 40 years where much shorter cars rode on two-axles and four wheels total. By the 1850s, American cars were being equipped with springs to cushion their ride over rough track—of which there was plenty.

Passenger car design improved gradually in the 1800s in a number of other areas. As the railroads consolidated and grew, travel distances expanded, and the need for sleeping cars developed. The sleeping car made its debut in 1838 on the Cumberland Valley Railroad. The first sleepers were crude contraptions equipped with wooden shelves on which hardy travelers could recline. George Pullman, known as the father of the modern sleeping car, built a dynasty for himself by catering to the increasing need for sleeping accommodations—and the need for comfortable, reliable sleeping-car service.

A cabinetmaker by trade, Pullman along with partner Benjamin Field converted two Chicago, Alton & St. Louis coaches into crude sleeping cars complete with berths and bedding but not linens—male passengers of the era not being accustomed to removing their boots en route before retiring.

Pullman's first sleeping car built as such was the *Pioneer* completed in 1865. The car was also notable for a number of other reasons. It was longer, higher, and wider than other cars—so large

in fact that it couldn't run on many of the railroads of its day because it couldn't clear structures and other impediments close to the tracks. Costing an exorbitant $20,000, the *Pioneer* nearly ruined George Pullman—until, as rumor had it, the car was drafted to carry the body of martyred President Lincoln on part of its journey home to Illinois. To accommodate the car, the Chicago &

Early passenger cars were based on horse-drawn carriages or stagecoaches, as evidenced by this special display assembled by the Baltimore & Ohio in 1956. Sitting on a modern 40-foot flatcar, the ancient passenger car appears miniscule compared to modern-day equipment. However, note the pioneering bilevel concept! *John Dziobko*

Alton Railroad changed its clearances to allow the sleeper to operate over its line—and the *Pioneer* had found a home and Pullman developed a market. Pullman boasted that the *Pioneer* was bigger and better than any of its contemporaries. In truth, the *Pioneer* was barely comparable to the excellent works of other contemporary sleeping-car builders such as Woodruff and Wagner.

Eventually, thanks to savvy marketing and business management, Pullman would become the most important passenger-car builder and sleeping-car operator in the nation. It swallowed up the competition or forced it out of business, and by 1899 Pullman's Palace Car Company had a virtual

monopoly in the sleeping-car business aside from a handful of railroads such as the Milwaukee Road which operated their own sleeping cars. In the same year, the company changed its name to, simply, the Pullman Company.

As a separate company operating its fleet under contract to the railroads, Pullman's cars could be found on railroads and in trains serving virtually every region of America. At its zenith, Pullman carried over 35 million customers annually. Its fleet once rostered over 9,800 cars, mostly sleepers, but also parlor cars, lounge cars, and a small number of cars held for private lease.

Eating on the rails was also important. For a number of years in the 1800s, the railroad passenger had taken meals when and where he or she could. Prior to the arrival of dining cars, a box lunch brought on board or a meal stop at a depot restaurant were considered an acceptable means of eating en route. But, with the exception of the Harvey Houses along the Santa Fe and a handful of others, few lineside restaurants provided good food. Further, the stress of being one of 300 customers—all of whom needed to eat and run in the space of a 20-minute stop—made the experience less than inviting.

By contrast, dining by rail was (and is) a positively serene experience. There is something completely enchanting about dining on good food as the scenery passes by outside the window. Despite its appeal, the dining car didn't become a major part of the American railroad passenger scene until the mid to late 1800s. But once accepted, the concept expanded dramatically. At the zenith of rail passenger service in the 1920s, over 1,700 dining cars roamed the country.

In addition to sleeping and eating accommodations, other creature comforts were added. Evenly distributed steam heat provided via a line from the locomotive replaced the potbelly stove at the end of each car. Indoor plumbing improved life aboard the cars too. Electric lighting, a major improvement over gas and oil lamps, appeared in 1888. Introduced on Atlantic Coast Line's crack *Florida Special*, it was powered by a large dynamo in the baggage car. The later development of a smaller generator on each car that could provide current, and batteries that could store sufficient energy made the use of electricity on the cars more practical, and electric lighting became a standard.

Car design in the 1800s was notable for more than technical improvements. Ornate interiors and rich furnishings evolved as design approached an art form. The transition in little over half a century was amazing. From the crude, poor-riding cars with wooden bench seats of the 1830s, passenger cars of the late 1800s, especially cars built for new luxury trains, resembled something fit for royalty.

With notable exceptions, exterior colors had actually become more sedate as the 1800s progressed. Passenger cars of the early to mid 1800s had sometimes carried beautiful or garish hand-painted murals on their flanks. Transportation wasn't the only theme. Landscapes, battle scenes, and even reproductions of the great masters graced the sides of railroad cars. The predominant exterior color scheme prior to the Civil War was yellow. After the war exterior colors became more sedate and exterior artwork on the cars became rare. In its place were more somber colors such as olive green or chocolate brown. Gold leaf pinstriping which extended even to the trucks added a touch of elegance. It was not uncommon for a crew of six men to spend up to 60 hours ornamenting a single car.

Inside the cars, the builder's art flourished. Paneled in rare, polished woods such as mahogany, ebony, or rosewood, the cars included inlays, marquetry, and hand carving done by skilled European craftsmen. But as with the elaborate exteriors that had fallen from grace earlier in the century, by the late 1800s the public was tiring of the ornate, darker interiors and demanded more practical, cheerier surroundings. This led to interiors with plainer and lighter color at the turn of the century.

By far the most important advance in car construction was the wholesale use of steel. The transition from wood to steel as the principal material used for car construction was primarily motivated by concern for fire. In 1901 a blaze involving a wooden car in the Paris subway ended in tragedy. The event encouraged engineers to think of using the more fire-retardant steel in the manufacture of cars. The first production model steel cars were built for New York's Interborough subway line and the Long Island Rail Road in 1904 and 1905. The success of these early steel cars and the construction of two massive New York City projects, Grand Central Terminal and Pennsylvania Station, which

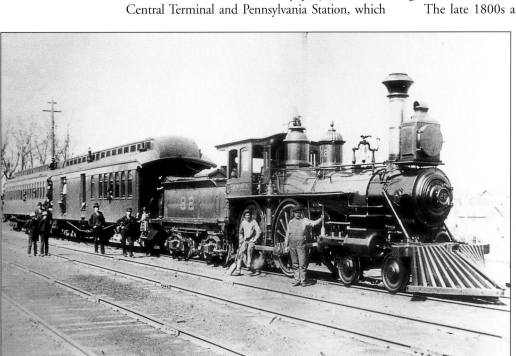

A classic passenger train of the late nineteenth century poses for the photographer at an unknown location on the Chicago & North Western Railway. A high-stepping (i.e., large driving wheels), wood-burning 4-4-0 steam locomotive—the ruling passenger locomotive of the period—has a combination coach-baggage car ("combine") and straight coach in tow, both wooden. Typical of the period, the cars featured "clerestory" roofs which provided added ventilation and light. *Mike McBride collection.*

involved tunnels and underground access, prompted the railroads to think of using steel in the construction of regular passenger cars in addition to subway cars. The Pennsylvania Railroad developed a design for a steel car while out West in 1905 the Southern Pacific constructed a steel coach. Pullman completed the first all-steel sleeping car, the *Jamestown,* in 1907. The idea took hold rapidly. By 1909 almost half the new passenger cars built were constructed of steel. By 1914 nearly 95 percent of passenger cars produced were all steel.

PASSENGER TRAINS OF THE GOLDEN ERA

If ever the sum of the whole was greater than the parts, it was the American passenger train. All trains comprised a set of cars, but the personnel, cuisine, schedule, and the places through which it passed gave a train its personality. Whether it was the faultless service offered on one of the great "Limiteds" (trains that made only a limited number stops) between New York and Chicago or the crew of an all-stops local in Virginia passing out lollipops to their younger passengers, each passenger train took on the character of its market.

The late 1800s and first three decades of the 1900s are considered by many rail historians to be the "golden era" the passenger train. From the turn of the century to the dawn of the great Depression, the American passenger train was undisputed king of the intercity market and essentially the only way to travel fast and comfortably over great distances.

Each train had an agenda. Luxury trains with incomparable appointments, services, and fast schedules galvanized public attention and grabbed headlines. Some became household names. General-service trains formed the backbone of rail passenger transportation in the halcyon years. Like the luxury trains, they provided coaches, sleeping cars, diners, and lounge cars, but at a more basic level of service and speed while serving more communities on varied schedules. Accommodation trains—the all-stops locals—generally moved on even slower schedules, made more (if not all) stops, handled considerable mail and express, and offered minimal amenities to passengers. Together, luxury liners, general-service trains, and accommodation runs formed a cohesive passenger transportation network which spanned the country.

Perhaps the most spectacular of the luxury passenger trains, which blossomed at the turn of the

The *20th Century Limited* launched by the New York Central & Hudson River Railroad and affiliate Lake Shore & Michigan Southern in 1902 was destined for fame. It would soon earn honors as one of the world's most prestigious trains. This postcard from circa 1915 shows the *Century* skimming the shore of Lake Michigan shortly after departure from Chicago behind a hefty new 4-6-2. By this time, the NYC&HR and LS&MS had merged into the New York Central System. *Mike Schafer Collection*

The *Century* was pure elegance. This dining-car scene from 1910 captures a nattily attired crew ready to provide the impeccable service for which the *Century* was known throughout its life. The head chef and steward are at the far end. All-electric lighting was a hallmark of the train. *J. Inbody, Cal's Classics*

Lehigh Valley Railroad's flagship passenger train on LV's New York City–Buffalo route, the *Black Diamond*, illustrates the classic "heavyweight" passenger train of the steam era. A big 4-8-4 Northern-type steam locomotive (see chapter 5) heads up the six-car train which includes an RPO (Railway Post Office)-baggage car, two coaches, dining car, and parlor cars. *Andover Junction Publications Archives*

century, served the New York–Chicago market. Originally inaugurated on June 15, 1887, the Pennsylvania Railroad's *Pennsylvania Limited* operating between New York and Chicago was upgraded in January 1898. This version of the train was typical of the new breed of luxury train. Built by the Pullman Palace Car Company, the wooden cars were painted in cream, red, and green—an eye-catching departure from the norm of that period in which nearly all passenger cars wore solid dark colors like "Pullman green." Each of the train's four sets of equipment (four sets were necessary to "protect" the *Pennsylvania Limited*'s daily schedules between Chicago and New York) included a combination baggage-parlor-smoking-library car (for the gentlemen), a dining car, three sleeping cars, and an attractive compartment-observation

car (where unattached ladies were encouraged to spend their time away from the cigar smoke and frank talk in the library car). The train's cars were decorated with inlaid woods in Oriental or Louis XVI style.

The *Pennsylvania Limited* was joined by the *Pennsylvania Special*, inaugurated on June 15, 1902. Attired in gleaming Tuscan red, the *Special* launched a speed war on the New York–Chicago run between the Pennsylvania and the New York Central & Hudson River railroads. Making the 908-mile run in an amazing 20 hours, the *Special* chopped an unbelievable eight hours off the previous fastest regular time. In June 1905 this schedule was further reduced, to 18 hours (about an hour less than Amtrak's New York–Chicago *Lake Shore Limited* took in 1999, by the way). PRR renamed

the train *Broad Way Limited* in 1912, initially in recognition of the railroad's four-track "broad way" main line. Later the PRR adjusted the name to *Broadway Limited,* acknowledging that the public associated the name more closely with the famous street in Manhattan. The train continued to provide deluxe service until 1967 when it lost its "all-sleeping-car" status when coaches were added. Amtrak operated the *Broadway* from 1971 to 1995.

Rival to the Pennsylvania Railroad in many of the same markets, the New York Central & Hudson River/Lake Shore & Michigan Southern (future New York Central System) introduced what may well have been the greatest American luxury train ever to burnish the rails. Debuting on June 15, 1902, simultaneous with PRR's *Pennsylvania Special*, the *20th Century Limited* operated on a

LEFT: Passenger car furnishings during the passenger train's heyday rivaled that found in well-appointed estates. This is the lounge end of dining room-lounge car *Angel's Camp,* built by Pullman-Standard (the car-building arm of the Pullman Company) in 1928. *Angel's Camp,* along with baggage-dormitory-kitchen car *Donner Lake,* provided swank dining and lounge service on the *Forty-Niner* between Chicago and San Francisco. ABOVE: Railroads wooed passengers by offering luxury amenities, such as free secretarial service, depicted in this scene aboard Baltimore & Ohio's *Capitol Limited* in the 1930s. Note the "Train Secretary" cap at right in the photo. *Both photos, William F. Howes Jr. Collection*

20-hour schedule on NYC&HR's longer (by over 50 miles) New York–Chicago "Water Level Route" main line. It quickly became the darling of business and society earning fame and fortune and an enviable reputation. Attired in classic Pullman green and pulled by one of NYC's Hudson-type steam locomotives, the *Century* of the late 1920s and 1930s was a magnificent operation. Routinely running in multiple sections—as many as seven in one direction on a single day—the *Century* racked up amazing earnings. In 1926, for example, the train grossed $10 million. Faultlessly operated and staffed, the *Century* gave its passengers a level of service, which inspired the title "The Greatest Train in the World." Through two world wars and the Great Depression, the *20th Century Limited*—streamlined in 1938—continued to operate in the grand tradition until it turned into a financial liability and was abruptly discontinued in 1967.

The East Coast–Chicago luxury train market also included Baltimore & Ohio's distinguished *Capitol Limited,* inaugurated in May 1923 between Jersey City (across the Hudson River from Manhattan) and Chicago via Washington, D.C. Though the B&O was geographically the least direct of any New York–Chicago route, the *Capitol* carved out an enviable niche by providing outstanding service to its guests without the snobbery sometimes associated with the *Century.* Aside from a ten-year hiatus (1971-1981), the train survives today, though as a Chicago–Washington run on a modified routing.

Though these luxury trains held the limelight, they were supplemented by a myriad of "lesser" trains—of which some were still quite posh in their own right. In 1932 for example, the PRR operated a dozen passenger trains each way between Chicago and New York aside from the *Broadway.* Some, like the *Western Express,* were all-stops locals while others provided a higher level of amenities and speed, such as the *Manhattan Limited.* Likewise for NYC. Though the *Century* garnered all the press, trains like Central's New York–Chicago *Lake Shore Limited* were really the bread-and-butter operations,

handling coach as well as sleeping-car passengers.

One of the strongest rail passenger markets in America has long been the Florida trade, much of which had its genesis with a train known as the *Florida Special.* Unlike its counterparts, which served primarily business clientele, the *Florida Special* between New York and Miami was a luxury train that catered to tourists. Established in January 1888, the *Special* was introduced to carry an elite group of passengers to Henry Flagler's spectacular new Hotel Ponce de Leon at St. Augustine, Florida.

Partner to John D. Rockefeller in the colossal enterprise Standard Oil, Flagler had retired in late middle age with an enormous fortune and a desire to build an empire. He found an opportunity in pristine Florida, building a series of world-class hotels and a railroad between Jacksonville and Key West and opening the state to commerce and tourism. The *Florida Special* was in the vanguard of that effort. The first electrically lighted train in America, the *Special* helped established one of the most successful rail travel operations in American history—the Florida trains. The Atlantic Coast Line Railroad in partnership with the Pennsylvania, Richmond Fredericksburg & Potomac, and Florida East Coast railroads operated a fleet of luxury trains with evocative names like *Gulf Coast Limited* and *Havana Special*. Competitor Seaboard Air Line, also in partnership with the PRR and RF&P, did the same. Seaboard's *Orange Blossom Special*, inaugurated in 1925, was arguably the most luxurious train ever operated to Florida.

The Florida trains were fun trains and the *Florida Special* and running mate the *Miamian* frequently carried recreation cars during the 1920s and 1930s where passengers could dance to the music of a live orchestra. In one memorable season in the mid-1930s the *Florida Special* even offered a small canvas swimming pool for those anxious to start their Florida vacation early! Patronage on the Florida trains continued strong through the 1960s, and even today the Florida trains comprise one of Amtrak's strongest long-distance markets.

Other Deep South trains served more basic markets. The *Crescent Limited,* inaugurated in April 1925, operated between New York and New Orleans via Washington, D.C., Atlanta, Georgia, and Montgomery, Alabama. Attired in a striking and unusual scheme of green and gold and pulled by equally attractive Southern Railway Class PS-4 Pacific-type steam locomotives, the train came complete with ladies maid.

Great trains populated the Midwest as well. Named for the newly constructed Panama Canal, Illinois Central's *Panama Limited* was introduced in 1911 between Chicago and New Orleans. Refurbished as a deluxe all sleeping-car train in November 1916, the *Panama* was a fixture in the Gulf region—so much so that a local Mississippi judge recessed court every day for five minutes so folks

Text continued on page 79

Delaware & Hudson train No. 1, a run between Albany and Rouses Point, New York, illustrates the classic accommodation train of the first half of the twentieth century. The train, shown taking on coal at South Junction in Plattsburgh, New York, on May 30, 1949, departed Albany at 7 a.m. and stopped at all but one of the 28 intermediate stations on the 190-mile run. The consist includes a baggage car for express, Railway Post Office (RPO) car, another baggage car, and an ancient wood coach dating from the turn of the century. Aside from serving the public at local stations bypassed by more important D&H trains such as the New York–Montreal *Laurentian,* this train would have handled some passenger baggage, a fair amount of mail and a variety of express, including everything from parcels to live baby chicks to intra-office railroad company mail. In other words, it would have accommodated just about anybody and anything. *Phillip R. Hastings, M.D., Collection, California State Railroad Museum*

A Passenger Car Primer, Part I

Like its cousin the freight car, the passenger car evolved in the 1800s to serve a number of needs. As the railroads expanded and the length of a trip increased, passengers now had to be fed, given a comfortable place to sleep for the night, and even entertained. Since passenger cars share an overall similar exterior appearance, unlike freight cars, we will focus on their interior arrangements.

Coach: The term "coach" is often applied to any type of passenger car, but technically it applies only to cars equipped with rows of seats for general travel accommodation. Usually coaches feature a center aisle flanked by seats, which may or may not recline. Though intended primarily for daytime travel, coaches are also used in overnight service for those who do not want to pay the extra fare for sleeping accommodations.

The seating capacity of a coach ranges from the low 40s for long-distance service to 80 passengers for daytime medium- to short-distance travel. In earlier days, not all trains carried coaches; some offered first-class service only. Conversely, some trains were comprised exclusively of coach-class seating—no sleeping or parlor cars. The all-coach long-distance train concept blossomed in the 1930s in part because the Depression had lessened the spending power of the average American and more people found themselves unable to afford the cost of sleeping accommodations. Because of their popularity and capacity, coaches carried—and still carry—the majority of rail passengers. They were and are the most cost-effective passenger accommodation that can be operated.

Backbone of the American passenger train—intercity and commuter—was and is the coach. This B&O coach illustrates the typical 2-and-2 seating arrangement (some commuter coaches feature 3–2 seating for added capacity) found in a vast majority of coaches. Restrooms are located at either or one end of the car. Interior appointments vary widely depending on the car's intended service. This post-World War II coach features reclining seats, window blinds, and fluorescent lighting. *Charles Laird Sr.*

A parlor car's carpeted floor and individual, rotating, reclining seats provided a feeling of being in one's living room. These travelers are taking advantage of such parlor-car comfort on Chicago & North Western's *"400"* streamliner between Chicago and Minneapolis/St. Paul. Medium-distance runs such as Chicago–St. Louis, New York–Boston, and Chicago–Detroit were popular for parlor-car travel. Amtrak offers similar service today, marketed as "club" seating. *Mike Schafer Collection*

THE FAMOUS STREAMLINER "400" — CHICAGO AND NORTH WESTERN LINE

ULTRA-MODERN PARLOR CARS ON THE FAMOUS "400"   9A-H1864

Parlor car: Rich cousin to the common coach, the classic parlor car featured two rows of individual rotating, reclining seats, usually in carpeted surroundings. Parlor cars were a distinct minority and never comprised more than 2.5 percent of the nation's passenger-car fleet. Offering each passenger an individual seat and big picture window as well as the ministrations of a courteous attendant, the parlor catered to those who sought the exclusive atmosphere of a private club and who were willing to pay for it.

Parlor cars could be found where the demand for luxury daytime travel was strongest. Not every railroad operated parlors, and the typical distance over which they operated was usually less than 300 miles. Some commuter trains also offered parlor service, notably those of the Long Island Rail Road.

The parlor car first appeared on the American railroad scene in the 1840s. By the 1860s the concept had begun to flourish and several competing railroads offered parlor service between New York and Washington, D.C. By the 1870s the parlor car was a regular feature of the best trains. Railroads as well as the independent companies of Pullman, Wagner, and Woodruff operated over 300 parlor cars nationwide by the 1870s. Eventually the parlor car's duties expanded to sometimes incorporate the role of lounge car—refreshing thirsts as well as egos. The traditional parlor car flourished and continued strong into the twentieth century, being incorporated into new trains being built as late as 1958.

Ersatz parlor cars still operate, though the term "parlor" has become archaic. Today's versions of the parlor

Modern private-room accommodations aboard a double-deck Amtrak Superliner car. This is a deluxe bedroom for two people. *Mike Schafer*

Patrons enjoy the smart appointments of the diner of Wabash Railroad's new *City of Kansas City* streamliner in 1947. Dining cars were almost always money-losing propositions in their own right, but railroads operated them as loss leaders, knowing that quality food service was a consideration when choosing a train for travel. *ACF Collection, St. Louis Mercantile Library*

car are usually referred to on Amtrak as "Club Class" or "Custom Class" cars. Gone is the 1-to-1 swivel seating arrangement, replaced by spacious although fixed 2-1 reclining seats.

Sleeping cars: Coaches were pretty much coaches, but sleeping cars offered an amazing variety of accommodations for one or as many as four travelers together. In early years, the most common (and least expensive) of these accommodations was the "section." During day travel the section comprised two facing couch-like seats. At night the seats were made up into a lower berth while the upper berth folded down from the ceiling, with heavy curtains hung across the section to afford privacy. Clean, crisp bed linens and a warm Pullman blanket

were all part of the experience. After snapping the curtains shut, the passenger was lulled to sleep by the gentle rocking of the car and the occasional haunting whistle of the locomotive.

The most common type of sleeping car ever operated was the 12-section, 1-drawing-room car—a "12-1." Fully enclosed, the drawing room featured beds for three. Nearly half of the Pullman Company's fleet of 8,000 sleepers built between 1910 and 1935 featured this arrangement. In addition to the 12-1, Pullman also operated a variety of other heavyweight cars which included sections and other enclosed room accommodations such as bedrooms, compartments, and drawing rooms.

In the lightweight car era, which began in the mid 1930s, the section was eventually replaced by the "roomette" as Pullman's standard accommodation for one traveler. A marvel of space utilization, the roomette included a toilet, sink, closet, plush chair, luggage rack, and picture window all in a space barely larger than a broom closet—but big on privacy. Pullman also offered a number of other room accommodations—the double bedroom being particularly popular—to cater to every taste and budget. Today Amtrak continues to offer sleeping accommodations on its long-distance trains, and passengers can enjoy private accommodations for one to four people, some complete with enclosed toilet facilities and even showers.

Dining cars: The most memorable part of a trip by rail was and is a visit to the dining car. Decked out in crisp linens and sparkling silver, presided over by a bustling staff of professionals, the diner was the railroad's showcase. Although passengers once judged railroads by their dining-car service, to the railroad the dining car was an expensive liability, albeit a necessary one.

Traditional diners were amazingly compact vehicles. Carrying 1,000 pieces of china and glassware and 700 pieces of silver, the car also had to have enough provisions on board to feed up to 400 people. A staff of up to ten waiters, a chef, and three cooks were presided over by a steward. Within the confines of an impossibly small kitchen, gastronomic miracles were worked every day. Railroad diners were usually a single car, but some railroads employed twin-unit or even triple-unit cars offering lounge space and a crew dormitory as well as a dining room.

The diner was more than just a diversion for the traveler; it was sometimes the reason the customer had chosen to travel on a specific railroad or train. The railroads understood this implicitly, working hard to distinguish themselves with their fare and their service while frequently tolerating exorbitant operating losses on the cars. Even into the 1950s and 1960s it was not uncommon for the railroads to cook many items from scratch right on board the cars. Baltimore & Ohio was famous for its Crab Imperial, Wabash for its homemade pies. Fresh Rocky Mountain Trout was available in the diners of Colorado trains of the Denver & Rio Grande Western. As America opted for drive-in restaurants in the 1950s and '60s, the railroad dining car continued to be a bastion of civility, albeit in shrinking numbers. Even in 1999 on Amtrak it was still possible to enjoy an excellent meal as the beauty of America rolls by the window.

Lounge cars: The lounge car provides a welcome change of pace for both coach and sleeping-car passengers and can be an inviting place to relieve the tedium of the journey. A comfortable chair awaits in this car with the atmosphere of a private club, and in earlier days if the scenery failed to hold the attention there was frequently a library, a barber shop, or even a shower/bath.

The first lounge car was probably the *Esperanza* built in 1887 for the Pennsylvania Railroad. The lounge car could be found on the great luxury trains and each reflected the personality of the train on which it operated. Operating from New York to Key West, Florida, the *Havana Special* of the 1920s contained mid-train lounge cars which even included a soda fountain, a valet, a ladies maid, and separate lounge areas for men and women. In the lounges of the *20th Century Limited*, a businessman's train, stock quotations were available. Native Americans narrated the scenery across the southwest on Santa Fe's *Super Chief* and today on Amtrak's *Southwest Chief*.

Most lounge cars feature a bar where patrons can slake their thirst. Because space was at a premium and the railroads sought to maximize operating profits, it was less common for a train to carry a full lounge car since none of the lounge seats were considered "revenue" seats, so lounge cars often included sleeping accommodations or baggage storage

Lounge cars are the train's social center (or family room on contemporary trains), a place to settle back with a drink and a newspaper. This is the handsome interior of a Great Northern lounge-observation car. *Mike Schafer*

space. Many dining cars offered a parceled-off lounge area. In the lightweight car era, sleeper-lounges of various floor plans entered service on many trains. Unique lounge cars—many built to a specific theme—often served as signature cars for the trains they graced. Patrons aboard Union Pacific's *City of Denver* could relax in pseudo rustic Western saloon surroundings in the "Frontier Shack" lounge complete with rough-hewn wood décor, a rifle on the wall, and lanterns for lighting. Northern Pacific

customers riding the streamlined version of the *North Coast Limited* could find repose in the Lewis & Clark "Traveler's Rest" lounge. Today, Amtrak's *Coast Starlight* is best known for its "Pacific Parlour Car," a luxury double-deck, glass-roofed lounge which features comfortable lounge chairs, hors d'ouevres, and a daily wine-tasting session for first-class passengers.

Head-end cars: "Head-end" cars don't carry passengers at all; rather, they tote mail, express, and baggage. Traditionally, these cars are positioned between the locomotive(s) and the passenger-carrying cars, hence their group terminology, but it is not unusual for them to also be found at the rear of a train. The most interesting head-end car was the Railway Post Office (RPO), aboard which postal employees sorted mail while the train was en route. Bags of mail were loaded and off-loaded at intermediate stations—sometimes without the train even stopping. During the heyday of the passenger railroading, mail was carried on over 9,000 trains.

The marriage between the railroad and the Post Office officially dated to July 1838 when Congress designated all railroads as postal routes. Mail was carried on a number of routes and there were sporadic attempts to sort it along the way. But it wasn't until 1865 in an effort to relieve the logjam of mail associated with the Civil War that the

post office formally adopted the British concept of sorting the mail en route.

The RPO changed little in format during its 150-year life. The interior contained sorting desks, numerous "pigeonholes" for sorted letters, and racks to hold large canvas mail sacks. Inside, up to 14 mail clerks worked at a frenetic pace to ensure mail was sorted for upcoming stations. Sorted mail was placed into sacks and offloaded during station stops or tossed off the moving train if it was not scheduled to stop at a town. Likewise, mail was loaded at station stops or hung up and caught by a mechanical arm on the RPO while the train roared through some obscure outpost. The cars even featured an individual letter slot into which customers could deposit mail—just as if they were visiting a stationary Post Office.

RPOs were labor-intensive and costly which eventually doomed the concept. The Post Office first turned to trucks in the 1920s and 1930s, began using long-distance trucking in 1951, and then turned to the airlines. As passenger revenues shrank with declining ridership, postal revenues comprised a significantly higher portion of a train's earnings, so whenever

the Post Office decided to remove an RPO in favor of truck or air transport, it often meant the end of the train on which it ran. Widespread abandonment of the remaining RPOs occurred soon after the introduction of the ZIP code in 1963, with the last RPO route in the country, between New York and Washington, terminated on July 1, 1977.

Baggage cars, the most common of head-end cars, are basically rolling storerooms for passenger baggage and sometimes express. Large side doors are their hallmark, but there is little more inside than lights and ample floor space.

Express boxcars look much like freight boxcars, but are equipped with high-speed trucks, special coupling systems, and train lines (electrical cables, and in earlier days steam-heat lines), all necessary for passenger cars. Otherwise, they are indeed similar to boxcars. They carry express—time-sensitive cargo shipped as a premium service—and mail. Much express is now also being hauled behind Amtrak trains in "RoadRailer" trailers, truck trailers equipped with flanged-wheel bogies for use either on rail or road.

Bags of mail are being hoisted on and off the RPO car at the forward end of Illinois Central's *Hawkeye*, a Chicago–Sioux City run pausing at Rockford, Illinois, in 1968. Behind the RPO is the train's only sleeping car and the coaches. *Mike Schafer*

Text continued from page 75
could watch the *Panama* pass. Discontinued for two years during the Depression, the heavyweight *Panama* would eventually become one of the finest streamlined trains ever operated.

The West had its share of great trains, too. The *North Coast Limited* of the Northern Pacific, the *Oriental Limited* of the Great Northern, and Milwaukee Road's *Olympian* competed between the Midwest and the Pacific Northwest. Boasting an all-Pullman consist including a baggage-club car, ladies maid, and an on-board representative who narrated about points of interest, the famous *Overland Limited* was a joint venture between Chicago & North Western, Union Pacific, and Southern Pacific connecting Chicago and California's Bay Area. Santa Fe's heavyweight *Chief* was the heir to the superb legacy of service established by the *de Luxe* and the *California Limited*. The Chicago–Los Angeles *Chief* was launched in November 1926. It quickly established a name for itself and spawned a tribe of other *Chiefs*, the most famous being the *Super Chief*. Introduced as a luxury heavyweight train in 1936, it was quickly replaced by a lightweight, streamlined version and became one of the most famous trains in the world. Many more luxury trains ran nationwide symbolizing the affluence and diversity of America's railroads (and the traveling public) in that optimistic, self-centered time before the Depression and World War II changed the country forever.

In 1921 Congress passed the Federal Highway Act establishing a goal of linking every county seat in the country with improved roads. Coupled with Henry Ford's affordable, mass-produced autos, the change had a dramatic affect. In the ten years between 1920 and 1930, automobile registration skyrocketed from 8 million to 23 million. Predictably, rail passenger ridership began to decline; by 1930 it had dropped 41 percent. Coupled with the impacts of the Depression which began in 1929, the trend prompted the railroads to make significant changes in their passenger service—with a specific focus on the least productive routes, largely the local services whose relatively high costs and low ridership made them a target for elimination.

In some cases the railroads replaced local, conventional steam-hauled trains with less expensive rail motorcars ("doodlebugs") or even buses. But in many other instances the railroads simply stopped providing local service knowing that the slack would be absorbed by the growing network of improved roads that paralleled rail lines throughout the country.

LEFT: As the country's first diesel-powered streamliner, Burlington's *Zephyr* 9900 (left train in photo) was in essence a state-of-the-art motorcar train, the likes of which had been plying branchlines for years. However, the pizazz of streamlining ushered in by 9900 and Union Pacific's M10000 streamliner proved a larger success than railroads might have expected. The result: streamliners proliferated throughout America. In this 1954 scene, 20-year-old *Zephyr* 9900, then having been renamed *Pioneer Zephyr*, stands beside its newest sister, the *Kansas City Zephyr*. Burlington Route, courtesy Ed DeRouin

BELOW: Rock Island's *Rocket* streamliners—one of the original 1937 *Rockets* graces this postcard—served Midwesterners until the end of 1978. *Mike Schafer collection*

THE PEORIA-CHICAGO STREAMLINED ROCKET

THE STREAMLINED ERA

America's railroads watched in horror as intercity ridership dropped over 50 percent between 1929 and 1934, especially in local and intermediate-distance markets. This desperate situation encouraged the railroads to think outside the box and seek new solutions to a growing challenge—how to attract passengers to rail travel. The concept of streamlining had been around since the mid 1800s, but the idea had been treated as an engineering curiosity rather than a sound business effort. That changed in the 1930s as necessity became the mother of invention.

With the assistance of talented industrial designers like Paul Cret, Raymond Loewy, Otto Kuhler, and Henry Dreyfuss, the railroads created new trains with a futuristic look inside and out. The streamliner was something totally new and exciting in an era desperate for change. With attractive designs, bright colors or shiny metal exteriors, sleek new motive power, and fast speeds it symbolized progress and forward motion. The streamliners effectively wed form and function and their Art Deco exteriors and interiors attracted as much attention as their record-breaking speeds. Pulled by colorful diesels or sleekly shrouded steam locomotives, the streamliner did what it was designed to do: entice riders back to the rails.

Acknowledged as the first of the modern streamliners, the Union Pacific M-10000 and Burlington Route's *Zephyr* 9900—the latter being the first successful application of diesel-electric power to mainline service—were introduced in February 1934 and April 1934 respectively. Others quickly followed. The *Zephyr* spawned an entire fleet of similarly named trains including the highly popular *Twin Zephyr*s (between Chicago and the Twin Cities) and the *Denver Zephyr* (Chicago–Denver). Similarly, the UP introduced the *City of Portland* in 1935, the first streamliner with sleeping cars and the progenitor of a whole *City* fleet which included such luminaries as the *City of Los Angeles*, *City of San Francisco*, and *City of Denver*. Steam hauled Milwaukee Road's new *Hiawatha* streamliner introduced in 1935 to link Chicago and Minneapolis/St. Paul. Santa Fe introduced the streamlined *Super Chief* in May 1937. Southern Pacific inaugurated what it called "The Most Beautiful Train in the World," the streamlined *Daylight*, in 1937. The red, orange, and black speedster showed passengers the wonders of the Pacific Coast on its journey between Los Angeles and San Francisco and quickly became one of the most popular trains in history. In 1938 the NYC and the PRR began streamlining their passenger-train fleet, including the *20th Century Limited* and the *Broadway Limited*. Many other railroads followed suit on their own alignments before World War II.

In marketing the new trains, the railroads effectively capitalized on the speed advantage. In May 1934, *Zephyr* 9900, now on permanent display at Chicago's famous Museum of Science and Industry, set a world record with a nonstop run on the 1,015 miles separating Denver and Chicago at an average speed of over 77 mph. The *Super Chief* slashed six hours off the previous best time between Chicago and L.A. The Milwaukee's *Hiawatha*s were scheduled at speeds of over 100 mph on some segments of their run and could cover the 85-mile Chicago–Milwaukee portion of their runs in 75 minutes.

World War II interrupted the introduction of more streamliners, but after the war, prompted by the need to replace equipment and fight off the competition of the auto and the airliner, railroads

Text continued on page 84

GONE are the "good old days" when mother put up the lunch and father wore a duster to protect his Sunday suit on the accommodation train. Gone, too, are the smoke and cinders, and the bone-shaking jolts when pulling into and leaving the station.

*   *   *   *

HERE, now, are the grand new days when smart, semi-local trains such as the Chicago and Eastern Illinois *Whippoorwill* are headed by General Motors Diesel locomotives—with diners and coaches such as once were found only on sleek, streamlined, long-distance trains.

Modern and attractive diner of the Chicago and Eastern Illinois semi-local Whippoorwill, which makes a round trip daily between Chicago and Evansville, Ind., making 12 stops en route with an over-all time of only five hours and thirty minutes.

"Better Trains Follow General Motors Locomotives"

GM GENERAL MOTORS LOCOMOTIVES

Yes, a great many better trains now follow General Motors locomotives in semi-local service as well as in long-distance service—working toward the not too distant day when *all* railroad travel will be "first class." A good thing to remember when you plan a trip *anywhere*.

ELECTRO-MOTIVE
DIVISION OF GENERAL MOTORS • LA GRANGE, ILL.
Home of the Diesel Locomotive

Postwar editions of *Life, Saturday Evening Post, Look,* and other magazines frequently featured ads that extolled how the railroad industry was keeping up with the times by introducing new diesel-powered streamliners, dozens of which hit the rails between 1946 and the mid-1950s. This ad placed in the August 13, 1949, issue of *The Saturday Evening Post* by locomotive manufacturer Electro-Motive told readers that "Better Trains Follow General Motors Locomotives." The ad tied in with the introduction of Chicago & Eastern Illinois' new Chicago–Evansville, Indiana, streamliner, the *Whippoorwill,* pulled by an Electro-Motive E7 locomotive. *Mike Schafer Collection*

Not all postwar passenger trains were slick, diesel-powered streamliners. Steam would reign on regularly scheduled passenger trains in the U.S. until 1960, and the use of heavyweight, steam-era passenger cars could be found into the Amtrak era. The above scene of a Pennsylvania Railroad K-4s Pacific locomotive leading an all-standard train through Jersey City, New Jersey, could serve to illustrate a semi-local passenger train of the 1930s, but it was photographed in June 1956. Although streamliners captured nearly all the attention, they were outnumbered by conventional trains like this until the 1960s. *John Dziobko*

Passenger Car Primer, Part II: Two View

ABOVE: A sleeper-lounge observation car concludes Santa Fe's all-Pullman *Super Chief* rolling through California's Cajon Pass in the 1950s. Near the center of the train is the new Pleasure Dome lounge. *Robert Hale, M. D. McCarter Collection*

LEFT: For a time, a monument marked the location along the Rio Grande main line in Glenwood Canyon, Colorado, where Cyrus Osborn first conceived the idea for a domed passenger car. The monument is shown in 1971 (with Rio Grande's *Rio Grande Zephyr* in the background) and has since been moved to the Colorado Railroad Museum in Boulder. *Mike Schafer*

A major attraction of rail travel has always been the view, and two car types in particular have enhanced that aspect of "training": observation cars and dome cars.

Often confused with dome cars, observation cars were specially designed for end-of-train operation such that patrons could enjoy a 180-degree view of the receding scenery. The first observation car is thought to be a car named *Aladdin* placed in service on the *Golden Gate Special* of the Union Pacific and Central Pacific railroads in 1888.

The hallmark feature of early observation cars were their brass-railed open-end platforms. Although thrilling, the exposed platform, on which patrons sat in folding chairs, was sometimes dusty and always uninhabitable in foul weather. As the streamlined era dawned in the 1930s, the observation car received a sleek, enclosed rounded rear end and the open platform became a thing of the past. Observation cars could be of any type. Most were lounge cars, but some served as parlors, coaches, diners, sleepers, or combinations thereof.

Dome cars feature glass-enclosed upper-level seating areas, a concept that dates from the 1890s but languished in relative obscurity until a General Motors executive named Cyrus Osborn resurrected the idea in the mid 1940s. Riding in the cab of a diesel through Colorado's Glenwood Canyon, Osborn remarked that the magnificent view he was seeing should be available to the traveling public. Osborn's comments caught the attention of CB&Q's progressive president, Ralph Budd, who ordered Burlington's Aurora (Illinois) Shops to reconstruct a stainless-steel coach into an experimental dome car. The result—a car named *Silver Dome*—was so well received by the public that Burlington placed orders for 40 more cars from the Budd Company.

Burlington introduced dome cars on its *Twin Zephyr* trains in 1947, and soon a revolution was under way as numerous railroads followed suit with their own "Domeliners."

Dome cars revolutionized the image of the American passenger train as they became the centerpiece feature of the trains on which they ran. The dome component was applied to nearly all car types, and soon there were dome coaches, dome parlor cars, dome sleepers, dome lounges, and dome diners. The observation-car format and the dome were also combined to form dome-observation cars.

Domes offered an incomparable travel experience. Seated in a glass-enclosed penthouse, passengers had an unobstructed view of scenery. By the late 1950s, 234 dome cars were in operation nationwide. They continued to serve into the 1980s after which most were retired.

Continued from page 81

introduced many more streamliners. Design innovations reached their pinnacle with the introduction of the dome car and perhaps the greatest streamliner ever built, the *California Zephyr*. Inaugurated in March 1949 and scheduled for sightseeing, the *CZ* operated between Chicago and San Francisco showing its passengers the wonders of the Rocky Mountains and California's Feather River Canyon from the windows of five dome cars.

By 1950, over 350 streamliners roamed American rails and the innovations continued, some successful, others less so. Burlington introduced the "Slumbercoach," a popular, budget sleeping car in 1956. That same year, Santa Fe re-equipped its Chicago–Los Angeles all-coach streamliner *El Capitan* with two-story "Hi-Level" cars that improved the passengers' view and improved car utility—and which would inspire Amtrak's current generation of Superliners. New ultra-lightweight designs introduced by Pullman-Standard (*Train X*) and General Motors (the *Aerotrain*) in an attempt to cut costs were much less successful due to design problems and substandard accommodations or ride quality.

THE LONG DECLINE

The passenger train faced the most serious threat of its life after World War II. Losing money since 1929, the rail passenger industry had shown a profit only during that war when tire and gas rationing and war demands had guaranteed high ridership. But afterward, and despite an investment in streamlined equipment which cost the industry $1.3 billion, the railroad's passenger operations again began to lose money—lots of it: at least $500,000 annually. A principal culprit was the automobile which greatly benefited from the development of the Interstate Highway System begun in 1956 and the continued expansion and improvement of the local road network—all tax subsidized. The airliner too was rising to prominence, and in many markets by the 1950s it was possible choose from over 20 flights a day that would reach the same destination as the train in a fraction of time for the same cost. With the arrival of the jet airplane in 1958, the airliner became even more competitive. The railroads' percentage of the total commercial passenger traffic carried dropped from 98 percent in 1916 to just 27 percent in 1960.

The railroad industry was often its own worst enemy. Archaic labor agreements (like the 100-mile day which guaranteed an engine crew a full day's wage for every 100 miles operated, even if it

Representing the alarming decline in passenger-train service (not to mention the railroad industry itself) in the late 1960s is this view of dilapidated Penn Central Detroit–Chicago train No. 355 hobbling into Chicagoland on a summer afternoon in 1969. This was formerly New York Central's *Michigan*, once a top-notch, multi-car streamliner complete with dining and parlor service and an observation car. On this sweltering day, though, the now-nameless train had but three coaches sandwiched by an express boxcar and baggage car. No one would have guessed then, however, that this train would still be operating at the close of the twentieth century—with new rolling stock and locomotives, a cafe car, club service, and a new name (Amtrak's *Lake Cities*), no less. *Mike Schafer*

took only two hours to cover that distance) resulted in labor costs alone eating up 80 percent of passenger revenues. Between 1948 and 1956, expenses rose almost three times as fast as fares. The passenger deficit often severely cut into the railroads' earnings on freight service.

The combination of declining ridership and rising costs spurred the railroads to make severe cuts. The frequency of rail passenger service declined significantly. Between 1951 and 1956 over 1,200 passenger trains were eliminated, and by 1965 over half the national rail network no longer had rail passenger service. Much of the private railroad's passenger equipment and facilities were nearing retirement age or in need of significant and expensive overhaul. No business in its right mind would invest its own money to upgrade something which lost that much money. An American way of life

was in danger of vanishing. By 1970, underscored by the bankruptcy of the Penn Central Railroad which threatened to severe all passenger service between cities such as Boston, New York, and Philadelphia and the Midwest, it became obvious that if passenger trains were to survive, some form of federal support would be required.

COMMUTERS IN PERIL

The urban commuter train was a victim of declining ridership and rising costs, too. Originally established by the private railroads as a profit-making sector, commuter-rail services existed primarily to link the largest of cities to their suburbs. In fact the establishment of commuter rail often preceded and facilitated growth of the suburbs along the lines it served. Chicago, Philadelphia, New York, and Boston all had and still have extensive commuter rail services, some dating to the turn of the century or earlier.

But as the 1950s and 1960s unfolded, suburban Americans abandoned the railroad in favor of the car, and commuter-rail systems became expensive white elephants. The services provided by the railroads were, for the most part Spartan, and a trip in a commuter train during the 1950s and 1960s meant riding in the same cars your grandparents had probably used—right down to the open windows. The railroads deferred capital investment in this costly service, and ancient, non-air-conditioned cars with rattan seats were the norm. Long suffering passengers greeted each other each morning, suffered through late trains, the lack of air conditioning or heat, and at best tolerated the ride.

While passenger commuter ridership did drop between the 1920s and 1960, suburban commuters still accounted for nearly a fifth of the rail passenger-miles operated nationally. And those miles were largely operated in the morning and evening peak periods while midday usage dwindled, forcing the industry to invest in an operation which was used for perhaps only four hours per day, five days per week.

Whether it be intercity or commuter runs, as the 1960s drew to a close, the passenger train was in peril. Few could foresee the interesting—if relatively modest—turnaround that awaited.

A NEW ERA

In October 1970 President Nixon signed legislation creating the National Railroad Passenger Corporation popularly referred to as Amtrak. On May 1, 1971, Amtrak began operation of a national, 21,000-mile intercity passenger system—less than half the passenger mileage operated the day prior by the nation's private railroads. Using 1,200 cars and 300 locomotives provided by the member railroads and operating over the railroads' trackage, the company provided service to 43 states.

Almost immediately the new carrier encountered trouble. The dilapidated condition of locomotives and rolling stock and the sheer variety of the equipment used made providing consistent, on-time service an impossible task. Amtrak's first publicity campaign had stated "We're making the trains worth traveling again." By the mid 1970s the company's efforts had begun to reflect that. Purchasing its first new passenger cars and locomotives, Amtrak lowered the average age of its equipment and improved its reliability. Perhaps the most important step the company took was the 1976

At Madison, New Jersey, in 1981, former Delaware, Lackawanna & Western electric M.U. (multiple unit) commuter cars built in the 1920s still reign on the New Jersey Transit, successor to the commuter operations of the erstwhile Lackawanna, Erie, Pennsylvania, New York & Long Branch, Reading, and Jersey Central railroads. Eventually, NJT replaced these and other elderly cars with all-new rolling stock, thanks in part to local taxes devoted to public transit. *Mike Schafer*

acquisition of 456 miles of track comprising the Northeast Corridor between Boston and Washington, thus laying the groundwork for future high-speed rail linking many of America's largest cities.

The national carrier focused on maintaining intercity services and enhancing fast corridors with mixed success. Building on the success of the high speed *Metroliner*s introduced by Penn Central in 1969, Amtrak developed faster *Metroliner* service in the Northeast corridor and enhanced service in other corridors. But in the late 1970s several long-distance trains were eliminated due to Congressional-mandated budget cuts.

Long-distance trains got a boost in 1979 and 1980 with the arrival of new Superliner cars. Additional Superliner cars were delivered, but long-distance service consistently struggled to find its

place. Amtrak's long-distance routes cover many thousands of route-miles nationwide but carry roughly half the amount of passengers hauled in the 456-mile Northeast Corridor.

Envisioning the future of Amtrak is difficult. Essentially a creature of politics and funded at the whim of Congress, Amtrak operation is not guided by a cohesive, consistent national policy or funding. Regardless, there have been strategic business improvements, such as Amtrak's restructuring into business units in the 1990s. The Amtrak West unit controls the services provided between the Pacific Northwest and Southern California, including corridor services between Seattle and Portland, Sacramento and Oakland, and Los Angeles and San Diego. The Northeast Corridor business unit operates trains in the vitally important Northeast

Corridor. The Chicago-based Intercity business unit operates everything else—primarily long-distance trains but also corridor services radiating from Chicago to Detroit, Milwaukee, St. Louis, Kansas City, and Carbondale, Illinois.

This restructuring has permitted the company to control costs more effectively. It has also resulted in significant innovation in service design, and some of those efforts are likely to serve as examples for future Amtrak services.

The passenger train can be competitive with the auto and the airplane in medium- and short-distance markets especially if it can achieve speeds that will significantly reduce travel times. True high-speed service is already under way in the Northeast Corridor and will be enhanced by the arrival of new state-of-the-art equipment as this book goes to

and mail and an expected trend will be for more long-distance trains to do so in the future—just as they did in the past before Amtrak. In a few instances, such as on Amtrak's *Coast Starlight* between Los Angeles and Seattle, enhanced luxury services provide the amenities usually encountered only on ocean cruises and attract affluent passengers as well as coach passengers.

Another concept, borrowed from a pre-Amtrak effort which ultimately failed, is the *Auto Train*. Amtrak currently operates daily *Auto Train* service between northern Virginia and central Florida to serve the Northeast-to-Florida market. The train offers on-board amenities to passengers whose cars ride behind them in special auto carriers attached to the rear of the train.

It remains to be seen whether these efforts will be successful in the long run, but more service innovation has

ABOVE: Amtrak's eastbound *Southwest Chief* at La Plata, Missouri, in May 1994 typifies the American long-distance train of the closing decade of the twentieth century: futuristic new diesels (these are General Electric models), a multitude of head-end express cars, and a string of double-deck Superliner coaches (including two 1960s-era former Santa Fe Hi-Level cars), diner, Sightseer Lounge, and sleepers. Although the *Chief* is a Los Angeles–Chicago train, much of its patronage comes from more modest online cities like La Plata that often are without any other form of public transportation. *Dan Munson*

LEFT: Union Pacific's famed *City of Los Angeles* is winding through Cajon Pass in Southern California for the very last time on May 2, 1971. The train made its final departure from Chicago on April 30, 1971, on the eve of Amtrak startup. The following day, Amtrak began operating a skeletal network of passenger trains inherited from Amtrak member railroads. Alas, the *City of Los Angeles* was not among them. *Jim Heuer*

press. At the other side of the country, Washington State has introduced Spanish-designed Talgo trains that employ tilt technology to allow faster operation through curves. With arrivals and departures in the hearts of downtown and with excellent intermodal connections available with some of the finest transit systems in North America, corridor services will likely gain riders directly at the expense of the auto and air carriers.

In other areas as well, cooperative arrangements between the state governments and Amtrak has resulted in expanded services, and the capital and operating partnerships these endeavors represent are models for future relationships elsewhere. In Washington State, the cooperative effort with Amtrak has caused ridership to virtually double on the Seattle–Portland "Cascadia Corridor."

If the long-distance train is to survive, it will need to support its own operating costs. This means potentially higher fares for premium accommodations, higher ridership, and new sources of revenue. Several intercity trains are carrying express

taken place in the last five years than in all the previous years of Amtrak's existence and that in itself is a good start.

COMMUTER RAIL REBORN

As traffic congestion increased dramatically beginning in the late 1960s, regional planners began to look at commuter and intercity rail with renewed interest as a way of controlling the growing traffic problems. At the same time, the rising cost of the service coupled with the losses incurred had caused the railroads to take even less interest in providing commuter service, so government stepped in to preserve and improve the condition of commuter operations. In 1965 the Pennsylvania Railroad sold the Long Island Rail Road—the nation's largest commuter line—to the State of New York for $65 million. At the time, with nearly 1,200 passenger cars and 754 miles of track, the LIRR was carrying 170,000 riders a day. (By contrast, today's entire national intercity Amtrak system carries roughly 58,000 passengers per day.)

The Bilevel Concept

Few advancements in technology have enhanced the bottom line of rail passenger service—commuter as well as long-distance—more than the bilevel concept. Though hardly new—visionaries rendered proposals for bilevel railcars as early as 1900—not until the 1950s did the format really gain widespread acceptance.

Though dome cars introduced multi-level car design in 1945, the true two-story passenger-car design dates from 1950 when Chicago, Burlington & Quincy introduced stainless-steel bilevel commuter cars (which were still in service as this book first went to press in 1999) on its busy commuter route out of Chicago. Neighbor Chicago & North Western soon followed suit, replacing its ancient fleet of single-level, steam-era commuter coaches with gleaming new air-conditioned bilevels.

Why bilevel? Bilevel design offered tremendous cost savings. Basically, twice as many passengers could fit comfortably into a bilevel car, and yet the cost of building that car was far less than it would have been to build two single-level cars to carry the same number of people.

The bilevel concept spread to intercity passenger trains in 1954 when Santa Fe introduced its first "Hi-Level" coaches. In 1956 Santa Fe converted its Chicago–Los Angeles *El Capitan* coach streamliner to Hi-Level status. Now, Santa Fe could accommodate 500 passengers in a 9-car train rather than a 14-

The interior of a Chicago & North Western bilevel commuter car illustrating the "gallery" format of upper-level seating. *C&NW*

car train—which meant lower capital investment, lower maintenance costs, and lower operating costs (fewer locomotives and less fuel was required to move a 9-car train versus a 14-car train).

Basically there are two types of bilevel design. Most bilevel commuter cars (and a small group of intercity cars built in 1958 for C&NW) employ the "gallery" format in which the upper levels are balconies hung on both sides of an open-interior car. In other words, passengers seated in the upper level can see down into the main level and

vice versa. Most bilevel intercity cars are true double-deckers, with two completely separate levels. Steps connect the two levels, of course, in both arrangements.

Bilevel commuter cars caught on quickly in the 1960s, but only Santa Fe and C&NW embraced the bilevel design for intercity trains initially. Not until Amtrak—inspired by the success of Santa Fe's Hi-Level trains—introduced its Superliner cars in the late 1970s did the bilevel concept again flourish in intercity car design. Now, most Amtrak long-distance trains are of bilevel design.

Likewise, commuter-rail operators in other areas began to seek support through local government transportation agencies. New York's Metropolitan Transportation Authority and the Connecticut Department of Transportation supported capital and operating costs for service between New York and New Haven.

The 35,000 daily passengers using Philadelphia's numerous commuter-rail lines received a lift when the Southeastern Pennsylvania Transportation Authority stepped in to provide operating and capital support, buying new equipment and linking the city's two major downtown commuter rail stations, Suburban Station and Reading Terminal, with a new tunnel. Regional public support for vitally important commuter rail services in the Chicago area has maintained commuter service on the former Burlington, Milwaukee Road, Chicago & North Western, Illinois Central, Wabash, Rock Island, and South Shore railroads. Commuter rail services in the Boston area are publicly supported and provided under a contract with Amtrak.

Driven by concerns about being unable to build enough roads to support commuters' single-occupant use of vehicles, regions which for years lacked significant rail-transit routes are now creating (or recreating) them with public funds. Los Angeles is served by new commuter rail lines as well as by new subway and trolley (light-rail) service. Miami, Florida, likewise has new service. Seattle is to be linked to its northern and southern suburbs by a new commuter rail service by the year 2000.

Once an unwanted stepchild, commuter rail is now seen as one of the most cost-effective options of mitigating the impacts of traffic congestion. It is even being discussed as a catalyst for downtown redevelopment in the suburban communities which it serves. The concept has come full circle.

RENEWED INTEREST AND HOPE

In addition to government-subsidized passenger trains, several private operations have been created where nothing similar ever existed before. They include the *American Orient Express*, a luxurious private land-cruise train whose interiors imitate the inlaid woods and fine designs of Europe's Wagons-Lits Company's trains which once graced Europe, Asia, and the subcontinent. Those with less time or money may spend an evening on one of the many "dinner trains" which operate in various parts of the country. Offering passengers a chance to dine while enjoying the passing scenery, dinner trains replicate the experience of dining by rail in the

New commuter-rail operations have blossomed in territories either long devoid of them or never having had them at all. On October 19, 1998, the *Altamont Commuter Express* service began operations on Union Pacific trackage between Stockton and San Jose, California, via Livermore and Altamont Pass. The diesel-powered tri-level ACE trains, one of which is shown at Altamont on October 20, 1998, provide a saner alternative to commuter-choked interstates connecting the San Joaquin Valley with Silicon Valley. *Phil Gosney*

One of Amtrak's Bakersfield–Oakland *San Joaquin* trains trundles through the streets of Jack London Square in Oakland in October 1998. Amtrak and state government partnerships in California and Washington have resulted in something that has been missing from the Amtrak system since its inception–individuality. Unique equipment, paint schemes, and interesting new on-board services such as regional menu selections have met with enthusiastic passenger response. The *San Joaquin* and other California corridor trains feature new bilevel "California Cars" whose design inside and out has been influenced by Caltrans, the state public agency which works with Amtrak. *Phil Gosney*

golden days of the railroad—even if passengers do end up where they started at the end of the evening. A couple private railroads still make a go of offering regularly scheduled passenger service. The New York, Susquehanna & Western, for example, offers regularly scheduled passenger service at Syracuse, New York. And numerous tourist railroads offer excursions and regular service to those who come to relive the romance of the rails.

The passenger train has survived financial crisis, government intervention, the automobile, and the airplane. In places where rail is truly competitive with the car and plane, there's a better than even chance our children will grow up with commuter and high-speed trains that will rival the best the world has to offer. Everywhere else, the average American continues to reinvent reasons to take the train, whether for a business endeavor, Sunday excursion, or a relaxed vacation, extending a love affair with the rails that has existed since the 1800s.

The year 1998 was one of Amtrak's best ever in terms of ridership and revenues, however the carrier continues to rely on some federal funding. Amtrak has succeeded in purchasing new passenger rolling stock and motive power while revitalizing or building a great number of passenger stations, but despite the fact that most industrialized nations subsidize intercity rail passenger operations, America's ambiguity about doing so has left Amtrak without a clear sense of direction or reliable future funding. While corridors such Boston–Washington receive ample support because of their obvious importance, other significant intercity corridors such as Philadelphia–Harrisburg and St. Louis–Kansas City are dependent on the whims of individual state subsidy while yet others—Cleveland–Columbus–Cincinnati to name one—have not been fortunate at all, primarily due to states' unwillingness or inability to assist. Air carriers can and do fill these gaps, but short runs are less cost-effective for airlines and many have abandoned these markets. The problem is also critical in rural America where the abandonment of city pairs by for-profit bus companies has sometimes left rail as the only public transportation option. Yet, Amtrak's future as an intercity carrier is, at this writing, far from secure.

Regardless of the daunting challenges, true high-speed rail is finally on America's horizon, and with the significant new interest in urban and suburban rail passenger service, there remains some hope and optimism for some aspects of the American passenger train.

5 *The Railroad* Locomotive

When the Industrial Revolution produced the steam locomotive in England in the late 1820s, most of the United States was still a wilderness, and to this day the North American railway system reflects that untamed heritage. This is not mere rhetoric. The shape, size, and style of America's locomotives can be traced right back to those pioneering railways in England. Today's giant turbocharged diesel-electrics haul two-mile-long container trains over track that was determined by Roman chariot wheels (the British and American "standard gauge" of 4 feet, 8¹/₂ inches is the width of the grooves of Roman chariot roads in Medieval England). But from this Genesis, the American and British railways and locomotives developed very differently from each other.

The "locomotive" had its beginning at the Rainhill Trials in England in October 1829, when the then-abuilding Liverpool & Manchester Railway sponsored a competition to come up with a machine that could pull its trains. The Trials proved that steam was a viable power source, and the competition was won by the *Rocket*, a four-wheel locomotive built by Robert Stephenson & Company of Newcastle. It had direct-drive cylinders and a horizontal boiler with a very tall smokestack to provide draft for its wood-stoked fire. Many other less successful locomotives of this period had vertical cylinders connected to the driving wheels through complex walking beams (a configuration derived from stationary steam engines of the time which were used to operate water pumps with vertical shafts).

That same year, another Stephenson locomotive, the vertical-cylinder/walking-beam *Stourbridge Lion*, had made test runs on the Delaware & Hudson Canal Company's 16-mile horse-powered, coal-hauling railroad between Carbondale and

Honesdale, Pennsylvania. Though it proved too heavy and rigid for the track, the *Lion* did earn the honor of being the first locomotive to pull cars for a commercial railway in North America.

In this era there were many famous "first" locomotives. Peter Cooper's diminutive *Tom Thumb* hauled a trainload of Baltimore & Ohio Railroad directors 13 miles in 57 minutes in 1830 but was immortalized in history when it lost a race to a horse (Chapter 1). The *Best Friend of Charleston*, built by the West Point Foundry in New York City for the South Carolina Canal & Railroad Company that same year, served successfully until its fireman, irritated by the sound it was making, tied down the boiler's safety valve and shortly thereafter became the first American victim of a locomotive boiler explosion.

While these locomotives and their brethren were true historic landmarks, the most significant of the group was the *John Bull*. In 1830 the Camden & Amboy Railroad was completing an overland link between New York and Philadelphia, and its manager ordered a locomotive from the Stephenson Company in England. In August 1831 a sailing ship docked in Philadelphia and unloaded two great crates of machinery. There to receive them was Isaac Dripps, a 21-year-old mechanic. Dripps was hampered by the fact that the crates had arrived without plans or drawings,

and he had never seen a locomotive and had no idea what it should look like nor how it should work! But he had it together and operating by September 15, 1831.

The *John Bull* was the first locomotive in North America to have all the proper elements arranged in the right proportions. It had a wood-fueled firebox, a horizontal fire-tube boiler, a smokebox and stack for draft, and two cylinders connected directly to the driving wheels. The Camden & Amboy made some modifications that made it distinctively American, including an oil-burning headlight and a "cowcatcher." This long wooden plow-like projection, which would protect the locomotive from wayward livestock it might encounter, rode on an unpowered set of wheels that helped to guide the locomotive around curves. The brake system was like that of a horse-drawn wagon, consisting of a large lever on the tender that forced wooden brakeshoes against the wheel treads.

The *John Bull* was officially C&A No. 1 and didn't actually get its nickname (which reflected its British heritage) until after it was in service. It was an unqualified success, and over the next six years no less than 15 more wood-burners were built to its design, making the *John Bull* the first locomotive to be duplicated in kind—all locomotives built up to this point had been one-time experiments that were never duplicated. In September 1833, the C&A began regularly scheduled service with trains up to seven cars long and speeds up to 30 mph with its fleet of *Bull*-class locomotives. C&A No. 1 was used in revenue service until retired in 1866 and stored.

In 1871 the Pennsylvania Railroad took over the C&A, and in 1884 the *John Bull* became the first engineering specimen in the new Smithsonian Institution in Washington, D.C. In 1980, it was overhauled and fired up for its 150th birthday,

FACING PAGE: Two Santa Fe locomotives, both of them products of the Electro-Motive Division of General Motors, illustrate one of the most well-recognized diesel locomotive designs ever—that of a locomotive cab set high above a rounded nose, a format that was an industry standard from 1937 to 1964 for freight and passenger diesels. *Jim Boyd* ABOVE: Standing at its birthplace, the Reading Company shops at Reading, Pennsylvania, in 1985, restored Reading 4-8-4 No. 2102 is a fine example of modern steam power. Big Northern-type locomotives such as this were at home on heavy coal trains as well as fast passenger runs. *Jim Boyd*

Stephenson's *Rocket* of 1829 featured a horizontal boiler, direct-drive cylinders, and an extra tall smokestack for creating a strong draft for the fire. The real *Rocket* has long since vanished into antiquity; the above is a replica from a British museum in York, England. *Jim Boyd*

becoming the second-oldest operable self-propelled vehicle in the world (the oldest being a steam-powered road vehicle in France). The *John Bull* performed like a "real" locomotive, with a strident exhaust and snappy response. B&O's *Tom Thumb*, by comparison, seemed like a frail mixture of handcar and sewing machine!

"Strident exhaust?" you might ask. "What's that got to do with it?" A steam locomotive is a wonderfully simple machine in which a fire heats water to produce steam. But it takes a draft to make a good fire, and in a locomotive the steam is exhausted from the cylinders into the "smokebox" at the front of the boiler. As it rushes out the smokestack, it creates a partial vacuum within the boiler which causes air to be drawn in from beneath the firebox, intensifying the fire as it is pulled through the boiler flues to the smokebox. The harder and faster the locomotive works, exhausting more and more steam through the smokebox, the more draft is forced through the fire, creating more complete and efficient combustion of the fuel.

THE AMERICAN STYLE

Built in England, the *John Bull* was characteristic of the type of design and construction that would shape the British railway system. Although both America and England would adopt the same standard gauge for track, the railways of the New World took on a much different character from those of the home kingdom.

In England the railways were being built into an already densely populated countryside, and fairly restrictive side and overhead clearances were established for station platforms and overhead bridges. The civilized British immediately adopted the idea of high-level passenger boarding platforms—so that passengers would not have to climb steps to board a train—but they were designed for cars and locomotives the size of the *John Bull.* As trains grew in size over the years, they still had to fit into these 1830s clearances for the station platforms, which severely limited the ability to design large locomotives.

In America, on the other hand, station platforms were minimal affairs with wood planking or gravel at rail-top height, and the passenger cars were constructed with steps for ground-level loading. This kept the clearances above the rails much less restricted, and American equipment grew much larger as a result.

In England the rights-of-way were fenced, and all grade crossings were guarded by watchmen and gates, while in North America the rails simply stretched unprotected into the wilderness. The British never felt the need for headlights because their tracks were well protected, while the Americans wanted headlights to see unexpected obstructions at night and long, pointed cowcatchers to protect the equipment from wayward livestock or wild animals. Loud whistles and bells also became standard on American locomotives to warn the countryside of a train's approach. (The British attitude to this day is reflected by a railway inspector who, when asked what would happen if something should stray onto the track, replied simply, "It's got no bloody business being there.")

Up to this point, most locomotives simply sat upon four or more driving wheels. In 1837 a four-wheel swiveling pilot truck was developed to help support the weight of increasingly large boilers. The resulting "4-4-0" locomotive (four pilot wheels, four driving wheels, no trailing wheels—yet), embraced by the Baldwin Locomotive Works of Philadelphia in 1845, quickly became the most popular design in the States. This "American Standard" placed a narrow firebox between the driving wheels and extended the boiler forward to rest on a cylinder saddle above the center of the four-wheel non-powered pilot truck. The arrangement permitted a long open space between the first driving wheel and the cylinders in which to hang the valve gear between the frames (the valve gear controls the admission of steam into the cylinders and is used to reverse locomotive direction). The 4-4-0 was easy to maintain and rugged, and its perfect three-point suspension (center of the pilot truck and one spring saddle on each side of the firebox between the drivers) provided an amazingly stable ride on the often crudely graded American track.

Although the details would vary, the general size and proportions of the 4-4-0 remained remarkably unchanged for the next 40 years. They were the first true "dual service" locomotives, equally at home on passenger or freight trains. Driving-wheel diameter ranged from 50 to 70 inches, giving many of them mile-a-minute capability on good track—but good track was often hard to find. It is worth noting that even by the 1850s the speed of a train was usually more limited by the condition of the track than the design of the locomotive.

The 4-4-0 got America through the Civil War. When Union raiders under the command of James J. Andrews stole a Confederate train at Big Shanty, Georgia, on April 12, 1862, resulting in the fabled "Great Locomotive Chase," both the stolen *General* and pursuing *Texas* were 4-4-0s. And when they

The original *Best Friend of Charleston* locomotive was blown into history by an irate fireman (and he along with the locomotive). This replica operating at the Baltimore & Ohio Railroad Museum in Baltimore, Maryland, in 1977 shows the *Best Friend*'s vertical boiler, a holdover from early stationary steam-engine technology. Clearances, ride stability, and other considerations quickly altered boiler positioning on future locomotives. (Can you imagine a 4-8-8-4 Big Boy locomotive with a vertical boiler? Union Pacific would have had the tallest tunnels in the world.) *Jim Boyd*

A truly functional locomotive, Camden & Amboy No. 1, the original 1831 *John Bull*, had a cab, headlight, spark-arrestor stack, and eight-wheel tender at the time of its retirement from regular service in 1866. Fortunately, the *Bull*'s new owner, the Pennsylvania Railroad, saw fit to store the locomotive and later donated it to the Smithsonian Institution. *Jim Boyd collection*

drove the golden spike to complete the transcontinental railroad at Promontory, Utah, on May 10, 1869, both the wood-burning Central Pacific *Jupiter* and coal-burning Union Pacific No. 119 that met "head-to-head" were 4-4-0s. In 1876 the Baldwin Locomotive Works catalogued a line of "Centennial" 4-4-0s (commemorating America's 100th birthday), and the brightly painted and brass-bound 4-4-0 became an icon of America's "Wild West."

MOGULS AND MORE

The 4-4-0 was not the only wheel arrangement in common use in America, but until the 1880s it was by far the most popular. Similar in size and weight to the 4-4-0 was the 2-6-0 "Mogul" type, which can trace its origins back to the 1850s but which became a truly practical locomotive with the development of the "radial" (able to swivel) two-wheel pilot truck in 1866. The 2-6-0 placed more of its weight on the driving wheels, and it usually had smaller drivers than a 4-4-0 of similar weight. This produced a somewhat slower but considerably more powerful locomotive, and the distinction between a freight locomotive and passenger locomotive began to develop, with the four-wheel pilot truck becoming typical of a passenger or dual-service machine and a two-wheel truck characteristic of a freight locomotive.

By the 1880s the 2-6-0 had added another set of drivers and grown into the 2-8-0, and the 4-4-0 had been similarly enlarged into the 4-6-0. Wood fuel was also giving way to much more efficient coal. Heavy, thick fuel oil could also be used in steam locomotive fireboxes and became popular in the Western states where coal had to be brought in.

As America neared the end of the nineteenth century, wrought iron and copper in locomotives were replaced by steel as the Industrial Revolution provided the manufacturing skills and economic strength to change the railways from crude

pathways into vital arteries binding the nation together. The trackwork was getting better, and the railroad was well established as the fastest and most efficient means of overland travel. Not only could locomotives make the magic 60-mph "mile-a-minute" mark, but by 1897 they hit the "century mark" of 100 mph (with a 4-4-0, no less), just in time for the new century.

It was more than just bigger locomotives that permitted American railroads to develop into the massive transportation network of the century. While all sorts of advances had been made in trackwork and signaling, it was Eli Janney's

Western & Atlantic's *General* of Civil War fame was a classic wood-burning 4-4-0 of the period with diamond smokestack, high drivers for speed, ornate brass trim, and colorful livery. The restored locomotive is shown at (of all places) Green Bay, Wisconsin, during a 1963 barnstorm tour. *Robert Bullerman*

knuckle coupler and George Westinghouse's air brake of 1873 (Chapter 1) that made possible the trains that we know today.

The air brake also affected the appearance of American steam locomotives. The system required one or two steam-driven reciprocating air pumps along with a system of storage tanks and cooling coils. The era of spit-and-polish elegance was rapidly giving way to utilitarian black paint over a rolling exercise in plumbing! While tight British clearances continued to restrict the size of their locomotives and cars, and their vacuum brake system severely limited train length, the Westinghouse air brake permitted American trains to grow not only in size but much greater in length.

THE QUEST FOR SPEED

In the 1890s America was impressed with speed, and the big railroads competed intensely with one another for the lucrative passenger business, like the giant New York Central System and Pennsylvania railroads, with their rival multiple-track main lines between New York and Chicago. On May 10, 1893, New York Central & Hudson River locomotive 999, an 86-inch-drivered 4-4-0, rolled the *Empire State Express* to the speed of 112.5 mph en route to the Columbian Exposition world's fair in Chicago. That was the fastest man had ever traveled and lived to tell about it.

While the 999 had made speed news en route to the Columbian Exposition, an even more significant locomotive was already on display there: Baldwin's new passenger 2-4-2, which introduced the idea of the "trailing truck" to permit a large firebox to be placed behind the drivers, rather than between them. The bigger firebox allowed for a much larger boiler with more potential horsepower, and over the next five years it resulted in the development of the 4-4-2, 4-6-2, and 2-8-2 locomotives that would become the workhorses of American railroads for the next 50 years.

In 1896 Baldwin built the first 4-4-2 for the Atlantic City Railroad, and the Pennsylvania Railroad followed in 1898 with its own 4-4-2 "Atlantic" type. Three years later the Pennsy introduced its big Class E-2 4-4-2s (see following section for an explanation of steam-locomotive classes) for fast passenger service. With tall 80-inch drivers, these engines were designed for speed and power, and by 1914 more than 500 had been built.

In 1902 the PRR's Juniata Shop in Altoona, Pennsylvania, turned out Class E-2 7002, which on June 12, 1905, turned in the fastest speed run ever claimed for a steam locomotive: 127.1 mph across Ohio on the *Pennsylvania Special*. Although the proof of this record is so unscientific that the "official" world steam speed record is recognized as the carefully-documented 126-mph performance of London & North Eastern's streamlined 4-6-2 *Mallard* in England in 1938, that didn't stop the mighty Pennsylvania Railroad from publicizing the 7002's record as authentic.

The size of the driving wheel is a significant factor in determining the speed and power of a locomotive. In general terms, the larger the driver diameter, the faster the locomotive. But this "taller drivers for higher speed" had its limits, because above 80 inches, the drivers tended to be too large and prone to spinning wildly, losing traction and delivering little or no pulling power. By contrast, smaller driving wheels, 50 to 64 inches, could deliver tremendous power to the rails but were capable of lower potential speeds because they needed to rotate faster to make the same track speeds. Thus steam locomotives were designed for specific power and speed ranges. A high-drivered passenger engine would not work well on a slow, heavy freight train, and a powerful freight engine could not make the speed necessary for passenger service.

THE LOCOMOTIVE COMES OF AGE

While high drivers and world speed records captured the nation's imagination and made newspaper headlines around the turn of the century, it was quite likely that the pulpwood from which that newsprint was made and the final rolls of paper that were fed into the presses for the daily edition were carried from the forest to the mill to the printing plant behind a 2-8-0 freight engine. With its design dating back to the 1860s, by 1900 the 2-8-0 "Consolidation" had became America's

Wheel Arrangements and Class Distinction

By the turn of the century (1901, not 2001) there were enough different types of locomotives that some sort of standard classifying system was needed, and in 1901 the American Railway Master Mechanics Association adopted the system devised by New York Central's Frederick M. Whyte, which identified locomotives by their wheel configurations, with numbers separated by hyphens representing the pilot truck, driving wheels, and trailing truck—4-4-0, 2-8-2, and so forth. These wheel-arrangement designations made no specific reference to the size or power of a locomotive but merely identified the general configuration of the machine. The various wheel arrangements were also given names. The names were generally universal, though rival railroads often used different names for the same wheel arrangement for "political" reasons.

Wheel arrangements and names were not sufficient to identify specific locomotive designs, and many railroads also used "class" designations comprised of letters and numbers (the PRR 8063, for instance, was built as an "E-2" and reclassified "E-2s" when equipped with a superheater in 1918). These classes applied only within a given railroad and were not standard from one railroad to another.

Some common steam-locomotive wheel arrangements, names, and intended service

Switching		**American Standard**		**Freight service**		**Passenger service**	
0-4-0	Four-coupled	4-6-0	Ten-Wheeler	2-8-0	Consolidation	2-4-2	Columbia
0-6-0	Six-coupled	4-8-2	Mountain	2-8-2	Mikado ("Mike"),	4-4-2	Atlantic
0-8-0	Eight-coupled		("Mohawk" on NYC		MacArthur	4-6-2	Pacific
			lines)	2-8-4	Berkshire	4-6-4	Hudson ("Baltic"
General-purpose		4-8-4	Northern ("Nia-	2-10-0	Decapod		on Milwaukee Road)
(freight and pas-			gara" on NYC,	2-10-2	Santa Fe	4-4-4-4	T1 ("T1" is a class
senger)			"Pocono" on DL&W,	2-10-4	Texas		designation for the PRR,
2-6-0	Mogul (freight		"Greenbrier" on C&O,	4-10-2	Overland		which had these loco-
	more than passenger)		GS series on SP,	2-6-6-6	Allegheny		motives in quantity;
2-6-2	Prairie (freight		"Dixie" on L&N)	2-8-8-4	Yellowstone		they were non-articulat-
	more than passenger)			4-6-6-4	Challenger		ed, rigid-frame engines)
4-4-0	American or			4-8-8-4	Big Boy		

Chicago, Milwaukee & St. Paul 851, a 4-6-2 ("Pacific" type) fresh out of the American Locomotive Company shops in 1912, illustrates how the addition of a trailing truck permitted a larger firebox, which sits behind the last set of driving wheels and above the trailing wheelset. The trailing wheels helped support the weight of the firebox. Pacifics became very common on passenger runs during the twentieth century span of the steam era. *Milwaukee Road Historical Association*

When the Pennsy wanted to outdo rival New York Central's display of its world-record speedster 999 at the Chicago Railroad Fair in 1948, it went to get its own even faster 7002—only to discover that it had been scrapped without ceremony in 1934! Pennsy found, however, identical Class E-2 sister 8063, which like the 7002 had been built at PRR's Juniata Shops, Altoona, Pennsylvania, in 1902 and set aside for preservation in 1940. When the "World Record 7002" went on display for the Chicago Railroad Fair's second year of 1949, there was no mention that it was actually the 8063. Fortunately, the Pennsylvania Railroad was one of the few American companies to have the foresight to preserve significant examples of its steam fleet, and the ersatz 7002 was included in the collection that was donated to the Railroad Museum of Pennsylvania in 1979. Due to its appropriate size and excellent condition, in 1983 the "7002" was pulled out of the museum and overhauled by the adjacent Strasburg Rail Road for regular service hauling tourists. It is shown during a special outing on the Strasburg in 1985. *Jim Boyd*

most popular freight engine with nearly all of its weight on its low and powerful driving wheels and a pilot truck to guide it smoothly at speed. And it was a simple matter to increase the size even more by adding an additional set of driving wheels to create an even more powerful 2-10-0.

But the future of locomotive development had been introduced in 1893 with the Baldwin 2-4-2. The concept of the trailing truck to support a large firebox completely behind the driving wheels would be the key to the modern steam locomotive. And while it was the 4-4-2 Atlantic of 1896 that would grab the headlines with world speed records, an even more significant machine was created the following year by Baldwin for an order of locomotives to be exported to Japan. Baldwin moved the firebox of a 2-8-0 to the rear of the drivers and added its two-wheel trailing truck to create the first 2-8-2, dubbed the "Mikado" in honor of the Emperor of Japan. This would become the most popular steam locomotive type of all time, in use in virtually every corner of the world. And the Mikado became America's freight workhorse right up to the very end of steam.

The difference between freight locomotives and passenger locomotives was primarily in their driving wheel size and numbers, so it was not uncommon for freight and passenger locomotives to share the same boiler design. The classic example is the 2-8-2 Mikado and 4-6-2 Pacific. You could take the standard boiler and put a two-wheel pilot truck and four sets of low freight drivers ahead of the trailer truck to create a powerful 2-8-2, or replace those with a four-wheel pilot truck and three sets of higher drivers to create a similar-sized 4-6-2.

With the success of the 2-8-2 and 4-6-2, it didn't take long for the locomotive builders to add an additional driver set to each to produce the first true main line giants, the 2-10-2 and the 4-8-2. With these machines, the steam locomotive had truly come of age in the first decade of the twentieth century.

COMPOUNDS AND MALLETS

But the engines with trailing trucks and big fireboxes were not the only developments between the 1880s and World War I. In an effort to gain more efficiency from the steam produced in the boiler, the concept of "compound" cylinders was introduced in the 1880s, where the exhaust steam from one cylinder was then routed to another larger cylinder and used a second time. The superheater, a few years later, accomplished the same task with

Though hauling a passenger excursion in this early 1960s scene in northern Illinois, Chicago, Burlington & Quincy 4960 represents one of the most common steam locomotive wheel arrangements for freight service in the twentieth century, the 2-8-2 Mikado type. Rebuilt and with a somewhat modified look, 4960 can be observed today, active, hauling passengers on Arizona's Grand Canyon Railway. *Jim Boyd*

much simpler machinery, and compounding immediately became obsolete technology.

However, compounding did find one area where it was extremely effective. By the late 1880s it had become obvious that boilers could be made bigger and longer, but there was a severe problem in getting more than five sets of driving wheels to negotiate curves. In 1888 a Swiss designer named Anatole Mallet produced a locomotive with a hinge in its frame and two independent sets of driving wheels and cylinders. The boiler and firebox rode on the frame affixed to the rear set of drivers, while the front set could swivel from side to side to negotiate curves.

In 1903 the American Locomotive Company built the first "Mallet" in North America for the Baltimore & Ohio. An 0-6-6-0, *Old Maud* was a compound, with small high pressure cylinders on the rigidly affixed rear "engine." These cylinders exhausted their steam through a flexible pipe to the much larger cylinders on the movable front engine, which then exhausted through another jointed pipe into the smokebox and out the stack. The small high pressure cylinders in the rear and large low pressure cylinders up front would produce nearly identical power, and the Mallet

(commonly pronounced MAL-ley) proved to be a very workable arrangement for drastically increasing the size and power of a steam locomotive.

It wasn't long before a trailing truck and big firebox were added, and the Mallet quickly grew into monster 2-6-6-2s, 2-8-8-2s and even 2-10-10-2s. As boilers increased in size and capacity, compounding was abandoned, and high-pressure cylinders were applied to both engine sets. These locomotives were known as "simple articulateds" and would eventually grow to become the world's largest steam locomotives. The term "articulated" refers to the hinge in the frame, and the Mallets were technically "compound articulateds."

THE STANDARD ERA

By 1914 America had developed the technology to build what we recognize as "modern" steam locomotives. There were three big commercial locomotive builders: Baldwin, American Locomotive Company (Alco) and Lima, plus numerous railroad shops which were constructing complete locomotives. Each railroad had its own operating conditions and management philosophies about locomotive design, and as a result, steam locomotives were nearly all custom designed for each

individual railroad. Although an expert could discern detail differences among the builders, it was far easier to recognize the design quirks of the different railroads. In general, steam locomotive design varied greatly from one railroad to another.

In April 1917 America was dragged into the Great World War in Europe, and by the following winter its railroads were being severely stressed by the sudden burden of wartime traffic. In the name of the war emergency, the United States Railroad Administration (USRA) was established on December 28, 1917, to take over the operation of America's railroads. As part of its authorizing legislation, the USRA had a mandate to create a series of standard locomotive designs that could be used everywhere in the country. This idea of standardization was greeted with hostility by the industry, as each railroad considered its needs to be unique. The Pennsy and New York Central operating the same locomotives? Unthinkable!

Undaunted by the outcry, the USRA assembled a blue-ribbon team of designers from the locomotive manufacturers. By the end of April 1918—within four months of its creation—the committee submitted twelve standard designs that were the state of the art for their time. They were 0-6-0 and 0-8-0 switchers, compound 2-6-6-2 and 2-8-8-2 Mallets and light and heavy versions of the 2-8-2, 2-10-2, 4-6-2 and 4-8-2. They were all superheated and equipped with as many standard design elements as possible. And, indeed, the arch-rival Pennsy and New York Central both ended up with USRA light Mikados (84 NYC and five PRR).

Before the railroads were returned to private ownership following the war in 1920, a total of 1856 "government" engines had been built—but the locomotives were so well designed that 3,251 more were built on orders from the railroads themselves after the war. The idea of standardization had obviously won some converts.

But the railroads and builders continued to develop their own designs for newer and more powerful locomotives.

SUPER POWER

By the late 1920s American steam locomotives were typically big, simple, robust, and rugged. They were built for ease of maintenance and raw endurance, compared to the more efficient and finely tuned but temperamental locomotives found elsewhere in the world. At this time there were three major commercial builders in the United States, and although each could crank out identical

American Locomotive Company—Alco, as it was popularly, and later officially, known—was the result of the consolidation of Schenectady Locomotive Works with seven smaller companies at the turn of the century. By 1928, all Alco production was concentrated at Schenectady and its Canadian subsidiary, the Montreal Locomotive Works. This postcard view shows Alco's headquarters building in Schenectady early in the twentieth century. *Mike Schafer collection*

ABOVE: Baltimore & Ohio 4-6-2 No. 5202 marching out of Cincinnati Union Terminal with a passenger train bound for Louisville, Kentucky, in the late 1950s illustrates a USRA Pacific. Though the USRA was dissolved shortly after World War I, its design specifications would live on to the end of the steam era. *Alvin Schultze*

RIGHT: Steam switchers such as the 0-6-0 and 0-8-0 lacked pilot and trailing wheels, and their absence enhanced the locomotives' ability to negotiate convoluted yard and industrial trackage at low speeds. It also put all of a locomotive's weight on the small drivers, which gave it better pulling power. N&W 226, which employs USRA designs, was less than a year old is at Petersburg, Virginia, in 1952. *A. A. Thieme, Charles T. Felstead collection*

Shay-type locomotives such as Cass Scenic Railroad No. 7 at Cass, West Virginia, in 1969 were designed to lug at slow speeds over very light rail, roughly laid track, and steep grades—just the type of conditions you'd find on logging railroads (where track was hastily built and shifted around to reach new logging areas) and at mining companies. Rather than traditional drive wheels, steam operated in three vertical cylinders connected to a universal-jointed crankshaft which was geared to the locomotive's wheels. The result was an engine that sounded as if it were moving at 80 mph, though in reality crawling at the speed of a fast-walking person. Geared locomotives also reduced the likelihood of a runaway on steep grades. *Jim Boyd*

USRA standard locomotives or uninspired workaday power, each also developed its own distinct style of product.

The oldest and largest was the Baldwin Locomotive Works, founded by Matthias Baldwin in 1831. By 1928 its huge Eddystone Works on the south side of Philadelphia had 108 acres under roof! Baldwin's products could be best described as basic and rugged, and the company was one of the first to standardize components and production techniques. It built everything from switchers to huge mainline articulateds.

In Upstate New York, Albany was the home of the American Locomotive Company (better known as Alco), which had been created in 1901. While Baldwin built workaday locomotives, Alco constructed the aristocrats in the form of sleek passenger engines and ultimately the world's largest articulateds. Alcos tended to be clean of line and sharp in detail.

In 1880 Ephraim Shay had taken his idea for a geared logging locomotive to the Lima Machine Works in northwest Ohio, and the overnight success of his invention propelled Lima into the locomotive business. By the 1920s, this smallest of the "Big Three" locomotive manufacturers was also building conventional engines in addition to the Shays and had gained a reputation for unparalleled craftsmanship and well-engineered designs. Under the leadership of Will Woodard, Lima was about to exploit the basic physics of steam and combustion through design concepts that would carry the steam locomotive into the new realm it termed "super power." Harking back to 1893 and the development of the trailing truck and the firebox behind the drivers, Woodard calculated that enlarging the firebox without enlarging the overall boiler would produce a locomotive of greater thermal efficiency and much higher potential horsepower, giving it the ability to combine power with speed. In 1925 Woodard built the first locomotive

Boston & Albany 2-8-4 No. 1409 is a duplicate of the Lima A-1 demonstrator which was the first true "Super Power" steam locomotive, designed to deliver power at speed. The 1409 was photographed in Boston on September 12, 1947. The B&A was one of the more prominent subsidiaries of the New York Central System. *Charles T. Felstead collection*

Nickel Plate 2-8-4 No. 765 was one of a number of Berkshires built by Lima and Alco for several railroads that were under the control of the Van Sweringren brothers of Cleveland. Nickel Plate's 700s are probably the best-remembered of the "Van Sweringren Berkshires," but Chesapeake & Ohio, the Pere Marquette, the Virginian, and the Richmond, Fredericksburg & Potomac also had them. Four such Berks—NKP 759 and 765, C&O 2716, and PM 1223—have seen active excursion and special-duty service in recent years following retirement and restoration. Here, the 765 hustles a freight train through the Illinois farmlands during a week of trips over host railroad Toledo, Peoria & Western in 1980. *Jim Boyd; Lima postcard from Mike Schafer collection*

Southern Pacific 4449 illustrates the modern Northern-type (4-8-4) steam locomotive as well as streamlined steam, popularized by the streamliner passenger train movement which began in 1934; SP X2472 in the background is a Pacific. They are shown, restored and fully operable, in 1992. Originally appearing on the Northern Pacific (hence their name), Northerns were popular on a number of railroads for heavy-duty, high-speed freight and passenger service. Selected SP Northerns were decked out in streamlined metalwork for assignment to the road's famous *Daylight* streamliners, inaugurated in 1937. In most situations involving streamlined steam, the streamlined elements were merely cosmetic sheathing or shrouding and not integral to the locomotive's construction. *Jim Boyd*

with a huge firebox riding on a four-wheel trailing truck, the "A-1" 2-8-4 demonstrator. Highly successful tests on the Boston & Albany in the Berkshire Mountains of Massachusetts gained this wheel arrangement its "Berkshire" name. The B&A placed an order for the new 2-8-4s.

That same year, Lima stretched the A-1 by one set of drivers to produce the first 2-10-4 for the Texas & Pacific (hence, "Texas" type). Every locomotive with a four-wheel trailing truck that followed in the history of steam can trace its design origins to the Lima A-1 demonstrator of 1925.

Within a few years the Berkshire would grow from relatively slow 63-inch-drivered machines into true high-speed locomotives with 69-inch drivers. Seeking a powerful mainline locomotive for its hotly competitive fast freight service between

Chicago and Buffalo, the Nickel Plate Road hit on the perfect balance between speed and power, and the resulting "Berks" became one of the most successful steam locomotive designs of all time, perfectly matched to the railroad's operating needs. They could easily make 70-mile-per-hour speeds with 100-car freight trains and were reliable and easy to maintain. Near-duplicates of the 80 Nickel Plate Berkshires were built over the years for the Chesapeake & Ohio; Pere Marquette; Wheeling & Lake Erie; Richmond, Fredericksburg & Potomac, and the Virginian—a total of 257 Berkshires of the same basic design, differing only in details.

NORTHERNS AND HUDSONS

When Will Woodard created the four-wheel trailing truck in 1925, it didn't take long for the

idea to sweep the industry. In the following year, 1926, Alco enlarged a passenger 4-8-2 into the first 4-8-4 for the Northern Pacific, and the "Northern" type was born. One year after that, Alco enlarged the 4-6-2 into a 4-6-4 for the New York Central, creating an instant classic, the "Hudson." Never before had the first example of a wheel arrangement been such an unqualified success. Even though its design was refined over the years as 275 were built, the NYC Hudsons' 79-inch drivers and basic dimensions remained essentially unchanged.

The addition of the larger firebox and four-wheel trailer truck to a 4-6-2 or 4-8-2 would produce a locomotive with roughly one third more power for a machine of comparable size. And the Northerns and Hudsons quickly developed into

New York Central 4-6-4 5335 has the *Cleveland Special* under control at Dayton, Ohio, in 1951. The mighty New York Central will always be synonymous with the Hudson-type locomotive. Working with Alco, NYC's Paul Kiefer designed the Hudson format, and Alco delivered the first Hudsons (NYC's main lines into metropolitan New York followed the Hudson River) in 1927. They and later Hudsons would become a signature of steam-era NYC passenger trains. Even toy-train manufacturers American Flyer and Lionel churned out models of the NYC Hudson. *R. D. Action Sr.*

locomotives even larger than their genesis 4-8-2s and 4-6-2s, with more generous proportions and larger driving wheels. This was particularly true of the 4-8-4s, which were produced with drivers from 69 to 80 inches, compared with 63 to 73 inches for 4-8-2s. The 4-8-4 could thus deliver both power and speed and became the first wheel arrangement since the 4-4-0 to become a true "dual service" design, suitable for both fast passenger and heavy freight service.

Throughout the 1930s and 1940s, the Hudson became America's premier fast passenger locomotive, and the 4-8-4 became the railroads' favorite dual-service machine. The Santa Fe owned both the largest 4-6-4 (with 84-inch drivers) and the biggest 4-8-4s (with 80-inch drivers), and both were Baldwin designs. The "Big 800" 4-8-4s built

by Alco for the Union Pacific during the 1940s were designed for sustained operation at 100 miles per hour but saw service on both passenger and freight trains. The Southern Pacific's magnificent streamlined Daylight 4-8-4s were comparable to the UP and Santa Fe passenger engines, while the New York Central squeezed equal passenger performance into a more compact package with its 4-8-4 "Niagaras." In the Midwest, the big 4-8-4s for the CB&Q, Milwaukee Road, C&NW and others tended to be more dual-service machines with drivers in the 74-inch range for more power than sheer speed.

THE LAST OF THE GIANTS

While Berkshires and 4-8-4s and 2-10-4s and Hudsons pushed the conventional two-cylinder

designs to their logical extremes, it was the realm of the articulated where America's true giants came into being. The USRA 2-6-6-2 and 2-8-8-2 Mallets had become the workhorses of the coal fields by 1924 when Alco built the first simple articulated 2-8-8-2 for the C&O with high-pressure steam going to all four cylinders. In 1928 Alco carried this concept one logical step further by enlarging the firebox and adding a four-wheel trailer truck to create the 2-8-8-4 "Yellowstone" for the Northern Pacific. With 63-inch drivers, this was a true mainline locomotive, easily capable of 60-mph speeds. In the years that followed, the 2-8-8-4 gained a fine reputation as a massive freight locomotive, hauling iron ore on the Duluth, Missabe & Iron Range and coal and merchandise on the Baltimore & Ohio. The Southern Pacific even "turned around"

As the world's largest steam locomotives, Union Pacific's "Big Boys" were legendary and heralded American railroading at its classic best. These multi-footed monsters were built by Alco early in the 1940s, just in time to help out with the war effort. Here the last of the clan, the 4024, creates its own little storm as it works eastward through Hermosa Tunnel on Sherman Hill in Wyoming in August 1957. Eight Big Boys have been preserved. *Jim Shaughnessy*

the 2-8-8-4 and ran it with the cab and firebox to the front and the smokebox trailing to keep the crew ahead of the smoke from the oil-fed fire when running through tunnels.

In 1926 the Union Pacific was looking for the ultimate fast and powerful road freight locomotive to replace its ponderous 2-8-8-0 Mallets. In conjunction with Alco, the UP developed an incredible three-cylinder 4-12-2 riding on 67-inch drivers. The third cylinder sat in the saddle beneath the smokebox and drove an internal crank on the second driving axle. But while the fleet of 90 long-legged monsters performed very well on the straight and flat prairie main lines, the UP still needed a more flexible machine for the curves and grades of its mountain routes.

In 1936 the UP worked with Alco to put the 4-12-2 onto an articulated frame, and the result was

the first 4-6-6-4. Riding on 69-inch drivers, the new "Challenger" differed from earlier articulateds in that it permitted almost no vertical movement in the hinged lead engine unit—the boiler was supported on a horizontal sliding joint, which gave the locomotive an amazingly stable ride. These 4-6-6-4s could run at well over 70 mph and immediately proved themselves to be excellent dual-service machines.

The 40 UP Challengers ushered in an era of high-speed, high-horsepower articulateds all across the country from the home-built 2-6-6-4s of the Norfolk & Western to the massive Lima 2-6-6-6s for the C&O and Virginian. Challengers saw service from coast to coast from the Northern Pacific to the Western Maryland and Delaware & Hudson.

In 1940 the UP's motive-power chief, Otto Jabelmann, began working with Alco on a locomotive

even larger than the Challenger. Using eight sets of 68-inch drivers riding on roller bearings and a massive boiler carrying 300 p.s.i of pressure, they created the 4-8-8-4, the largest steam locomotive ever to be built. War was already raging in Europe when the nearly completed UP 4000 was on the erecting floor at Schenectady in September 1941, and an Alco mechanic chalked a "V" for victory on the smokebox front, along with the words "Big Boy!" The name stuck, and between then and 1944, 25 of these world's largest steam locomotives went to work on the Union Pacific. Capable of speeds up to 80 mph, they did most of their work between 30 and 50 mph, where they developed their greatest horsepower—over 6000 drawbar horsepower at 35 mph.

Ironically, the Big Boy was not regarded as Jabelmann's best locomotive, for in 1942 he

Text continued on page 110

ABOVE: Only with a broadside view of an articulated can one fully appreciate its size. Norfolk & Western in cooperation with the Roanoke Transportation Museum restored A-class 2-6-6-4 No. 1218 to service during the 1980s, operating it on systemwide steam excursions. The homebuilt (at N&W's Roanoke Shops) simple articulated is putting on quite a show crossing the Suwaunee River in Florida in 1987. *Jim Boyd*

LEFT: The steam locomotive had developed from its earliest days with crew riding in a cab at the rear, because the fireman fed fuel by hand, and the firebox had to be coupled up to the "tender" which carried the wood or coal. The cab-forward concept would work only with an oil fire, because only liquid fuel could be piped to the other end of the locomotive. The 95 Baldwin-built SP "Cab-Forward" 4-8-8-2s were among America's most distinctive and successful articulateds, being used in both freight and passenger service. *Jim Boyd*

The Electric Locomotive in America

An all-time favorite among historians of U.S. electric railways was Pennsylvania Railroad's GG1 locomotive, one of which is shown storming along with a New York & Long Branch train near Perth Amboy, New Jersey, in June 1956. Developed by the PRR with style refinements by noted industrial stylist Raymond Loewy, the GG1 was the ultimate electric locomotive for high-speed passenger service or heavy-duty freight assignments. The GG1's reign continued after the demise of the PRR, serving on Penn Central, Conrail, and Amtrak until the 1980s. *John Dziobko*

The steam locomotive came into being in 1829, but the seeds of its destruction had been sewn eight years earlier in the physics laboratory of an Englishman, Michael Faraday, who had discovered mysterious electromagnetic forces, and by 1835 Thomas Davenport had demonstrated at Rensselaer Institute in New York how to harness those forces in an electric motor. In 1847 the motor was applied to a small battery-powered locomotive,

and by 1860 generators had replaced fragile batteries as a source of electricity. In the spring of 1880, Thomas Edison built a 1,400-foot loop of track in Menlo Park, New Jersey, and operated on it a small electric locomotive that hauled two passenger cars at speeds up to 40 mph.

In 1885 Frank J. Sprague developed a simple means of mounting a "traction motor" on a railway axle that made possible electric locomo-

tives and self-powered streetcars. A year later Sprague replaced horsecars on the Richmond (Virginia) street railway system with electric streetcars, and within a decade, electric streetcars had become commonplace in America. In 1894 General Electric riveted together a 35-ton electric locomotive that went to work for a Connecticut cotton mill for the next 70 years!

Soon the streetcar grew into railroad-sized "multiple-unit" passenger cars, where each car carried its own control circuits and traction motors which could be operated by the motorman from one controller at the front of the train through a series of wire "jumper cables" between the cars. These "m.u. cars" (see page 85), which could draw power from overhead wire or from third-rail installations, were very effective and economical for commuter service in and out of big cities, since they could be made up into trains of any length and did not need to be physically turned around after arriving at a stub-end terminal station—the engineer simply took control from the compartment at the other end of the train.

Electrification was spreading rapidly at the turn of the century in metropolitan areas where m.u. cars could handle heavy commuter traffic and where tunnels posed a smoke problem

for steam locomotives. Indeed, without electrification, it would not have been possible to build Grand Central Terminal and Pennsylvania Station in the middle of Manhattan due to smoke-abatement ordinances. Only electrification permitted the long tunnels necessary to reach these stations.

By the mid 1920s, heavy electric locomotives were hauling freight and passenger trains over hundreds of miles of America's busiest or most rugged main lines, from the high speed passenger-hauling New Haven Railroad to the Norfolk & Western in the Appalachian coal fields. Out West, the Great Northern ran wires through Cascade Tunnel, and Milwaukee Road electrified 647 miles of its mountainous main line to Tacoma. These electrifications used massive riveted box-cab locomotives riding on steam-locomotive-sized driving wheels,

ABOVE: Charles City Western 300 is a typical "steeple-cab" electric locomotive, ideal for local and switching service on interurbans and other electric railways. It is shown at Charles City, Iowa, in 1963. *Jim Boyd*

LEFT: Early electric locomotives often incorporated a no-frills "box-cab" design, reflecting the relative simplicity of electric locomotives in general. This three-unit set of Virginian box-cabs (known as "squareheads" or "flatnoses" by VGN crews) had hoisted many a coal train over Appalachian grades by the time this photo was taken at Roanoke, Virginia, in August 1956—the 640-ton locomotive set dated from the mid 1920s. Neighbor Norfolk & Western—which also had electric operations—and VGN merged in 1959 and the former Virginian electrification was terminated in 1962. *John Dziobko*

Most electrified rail operations in the U.S. were concentrated in the East, but Milwaukee Road had several hundred miles of electrified track on its Pacific Extension. The segment of main line over the Rocky Mountains in Montana and Idaho was electrified as was the section over the Cascade Mountains in Washington State. Milwaukee employed box-cab-type electrics and center-cab "Bi-Polars" for most of the duration of electric operation, which lasted from 1915 to 1974, but in 1950 the Milwaukee took delivery of a dozen General Electric streamlined electric locomotives, nicknamed "Little Joes" (because they had originally been built for the Soviet Union, which reneged on the order) to supplement or replace older power. Here, one of the Little Joes is shown in 1969 assisting an eastbound Tacoma (Washington)–Chicago freight up the heavy grade out of Avery, Idaho, to St. Paul Pass. The diesels behind the Joe worked all the way through from Tacoma to Chicago. *Mike Schafer*

and jumper cables permitted the electrics to be joined in multiple-unit sets to match or surpass the power of even the largest steam locomotives.

In 1929, the Pennsylvania Railroad announced the most ambitious electrification project in American history: the complete electrification of its four-track main line between New York City and Washington, D.C. To supplement box-cabs and m.u. cars, in 1934 the Pennsylvania unveiled its magnificent streamlined GG1 dual-service electric locomotive.

For all of electrification's benefits—low pollution, low noise, smooth and fast acceleration, and longer equipment lifespans—it has its drawbacks. Overhead wire systems are expensive to build and tricky to maintain, while third-rail systems, which are largely exposed at ground level, work best where the right-of-way can be fenced

off from trespassers. Mainly, it was the infrastructure expense that limited the scope of electrification to only those areas where traffic density, tunnels, or rugged operating conditions made it economically viable. Other cost considerations have already turned the power off on Conrail's former-PRR electrified freight operations. Milwaukee Road's last electric operations occurred in 1974, and Chicago South Shore & South Bend's freight operations were dieselized a few years later. Nearly all the conventional railroad electric operations (versus subway and trolley) that remain are those of commuter carriers serving New York City, Chicago, Philadelphia, Baltimore, and Washington.

Unless there is another widespread fossil fuel shortage, new electrification in the U.S. will probably be limited to

rail-transit systems rather than convention railroads, with one major exception. As this book goes to press, Amtrak is putting the finishing touches on its 160-mile electrification extension from New Haven, Connecticut, to Boston. Once in place, Amtrak will inaugurate new locomotive-powered, high-speed trains between Boston,

New York, and Washington. It is the first major electrification project in America in decades.

Although they could not be used everywhere, the sheer speed and silent but awesome power of electric locomotives easily demonstrated their inherent superiority over steam—and sometimes diesels.

Continued from page 104

applied the Big Boy's design elements to the 4-6-6-4 and began construction of 65 new "Super Challengers" that turned out to be the railroad's most useful and versatile locomotives, capable of passenger-train speed and freight-train power. While the 25 Big Boys were restricted to freight duty on the rugged Wyoming main line, the 105 old and new Challengers roamed nearly the entire UP system, handling freight and passenger assignments with equal ease.

DOODLEBUGS OF DESTINY

The electric streetcar of the 1890s was a wondrous means of economical transportation (see sidebar beginning on page 106), but it was limited in where it could go by the necessary overhead trolley wire from which it got its power. It wasn't long before the car-builders began to wonder if it was possible to put the generator and some form of internal combustion engine aboard the car and thus free it from the need for overhead wire. Around 1906 General Electric mated a gasoline engine to a generator and an elementary control system and fed two traction motors beneath a railroad-sized passenger car. Thus was born the "gas-electric" motorcar, which was essentially a streetcar that carried its own electrical power supply. As an economical alternative to short steam-locomotive-powered passenger trains on lightly traveled branch lines, these noisy and rambling motorcars soon found their way to remote locations all across the country, where they acquired the endearing nickname "doodlebugs."

General Electric and various trolley-car builders teamed up on various motorcar projects until 1917, when GE , busy with mainline electrifications, abandoned the market. In 1924, however, a fledgling enterprise in Cleveland, Ohio, the Electro-Motive Company, resurrected the idea. Using GE traction motors and generators, gasoline engines from Winton Engine Company, and heavy

steel carbodies from the St. Louis Car Company, over the next decade EMC turned out over 400 rugged and reliable doodlebugs.

In 1913 GE had placed two 175-horsepower V-8 gasoline engines and electrical generators inside a "box-cab" carbody riding on two doodlebug powered wheel assemblies (trucks) carrying two motors each to create the first true gas-electric *locomotive*. It was sold to the Dan Patch Electric Line in Minnesota. This was America's first internal-combustion locomotive. In 1927 the Chicago, Rock Island & Pacific did essentially the same thing by taking the power plants and power trucks from two EMC motor cars and putting them together in one stubby box-cab carbody to create a four-motor, 550-horsepower locomotive. EMC soon followed with seven 800-horsepower units built new for the Rock Island, which proved quite successful in both freight and passenger service.

Thus, by 1929, both GE and Electro-Motive had produced reliable and economic internal-combustion locomotives by extrapolating doodlebug technology at a time when the steam builders were just beginning to exploit the concepts of Super

Railcars and locomotives powered by internal-combustion power dated to almost the beginning of the twentieth century, but most employed gasoline or distillate (crude gasoline) engines which had limitations. Gas-electric motorcars ("doodlebugs") such as this Burlington car still in active service (as a branchline freight locomotive rather than hauling passengers, however) in western Illinois 1965 were the precursor to diesel-electric power. *Jim Boyd*

Power—but few suspected just how deadly these snorting little motorcars would be to the magnificent steam locomotives that were already running and yet to be built.

VEST-POCKET STREAMLINERS

While rambling doodlebugs and strange little box-cab locomotives were welcome money-savers at the onset of the Great Depression, they inspired the accountants more than the traveling public. What was needed in the depths of the Depression was something exciting and futuristic to lure customers back to the rails. The result was the "streamliner," which took its first form in early 1934 in the Union Pacific's M-10000, a bright yellow-and-brown, 204-foot, 85-ton aluminum train of three permanently coupled cars with a 600-horsepower souped-up doodlebug power plant. Electro-Motive supplied that power plant, and it had something even better in mind.

Back in 1925, GE, Alco, and Ingersoll-Rand had teamed up to produce a 300-horsepower box-cab switcher using an IR diesel engine. Using compression to ignite spray-injected fuel, a diesel engine would substantially outperform even the best gasoline or spark-ignition "distillate" (lightly refined) oil engines of the time. Jersey Central 1000 thus went into the history books as America's first successful diesel-electric locomotive.

Even as it was powering the M-10000 with a distillate engine, Electro-Motive knew that it needed a diesel, but developing a lightweight, powerful, and reliable diesel engine was an expensive task far beyond the scope of little EMC or even its engine supplier, Winton. In 1930, however, they had both become a part of an outfit which had the resources to do just that: General Motors Corporation. With GM's bankroll, Winton was developing the model 201A two-stroke-cycle diesel engine that would be well suited for railroad work.

LEFT: The nation's first two true streamlined trains, Union Pacific's M-10000 and Burlington's *Zephyr* 9900, introduced in 1934 did more than launch the streamlining movement. The *Zephyr*, which carried a diesel power plant (the M-10000 had a distillate engine), helped prove the worth of diesel-electric power in mainline application. Subsequent new streamlined trains, such as UP's *City of Los Angeles* shown in this 1930s-era postcard, employed diesel-electric power plants. This early version of the *City of Los Angeles* looked much like its M-10000 ancestor, but its diesel-electric power-car set were able to haul a much longer train; the M-10000 was but three cars long. *Mike Schafer Collection*

BELOW: Many early streamliners had power cars (versus true, independent locomotives) that were integral to the train set they powered. However, in 1935 Santa Fe took delivery of these two box-cab diesel-electric locomotives built by Electro-Motive. They were true independent locomotives that could be assigned to any mainline passenger train, be it a streamliner or a standard heavyweight train. In the case of "Mike & Ike," as these two units became known, they went to work on the new *Super Chief* between Chicago and Los Angeles. *Santa Fe*

UNION PACIFIC STREAMLINER "CITY OF LOS ANGELES"

The 201A made its debut in a shiny stainless-steel articulated streamliner just slightly smaller than the UP's M-10000. *Zephyr* 9900 (see Chapter 3), built by the Budd Company of Pennsylvania for the Chicago, Burlington & Quincy, made instant headlines by hitting 100 mph on its first run and then on May 26, 1934, dashing non-stop from Chicago to Denver, covering 1,015.4 miles in 13 hours, four minutes and 58 seconds. The traveling public was dazzled—and the diesel-electric locomotive was here to stay!

Within the next few years EMC put the 201A into a line of switching locomotives, and more than a dozen more streamliners were built, each refining the design and growing in size. But these early lightweight streamliners were limited to a fixed number of cars and did not have the operational flexibility of a modern steam locomotive and a "heavyweight" train of conventional coaches, sleeping cars, diners and mail cars—configured with each trip to match the traffic demand. Electro-Motive's design engineer Dick Dilworth knew that the diesel-electric would remain a novelty until it could match the performance of a 4-6-4.

He calculated that a CB&Q 4-6-4 was putting out about 3,600 horsepower, and he needed to match that figure with his little diesel engine. The 12-cylinder Winton 201A could put out only 900 horsepower, but four of them together equalled 3600 horsepower. So Dilworth mounted two 12-cylinder 201As inside what was essentially a boxcar riding on two four-wheel power trucks to produce one 1800-hp locomotive. And two of those boxcabs coupled together and operated as one by electrical jumper cables produced a 3600-horsepower machine that could equal the CB&Q 4-6-4.

The Santa Fe bought near-duplicates of Dilworth testbeds in September 1935 to power its new Chicago–Los Angeles heavyweight deluxe train, the *Super Chief.* The box-cabs were ugly and utilitarian, but they proved that they could keep the fancy new train on schedule.

By 1937 EMC was nearing completion on a huge new locomotive factory at LaGrange, Illinois, just west of Chicago, and one of its first products was a superbly streamlined version of the bulky box-cabs. To provide protection for the crew, the operating cab was moved up and back behind a smoothly sculpted nose, and the four-wheel freight trucks were replaced by smooth-riding six-wheel passenger trucks, with a non-powered center axle between the outer motor-driven axles. Baltimore & Ohio No. 51 became EMC's first "E-unit," its model designation "EA" referring to its eighteen-hundred horsepower and "A" or, cab unit, configuration. Along with the E-unit also came the concept of the cabless booster "B" unit; the A and B combined would produce the 3600-horsepower set to match the performance of a 4-6-4—and cabling three E-units together in A-B-A or A-B-B

In 1937, Electro-Motive Corporation introduced the E-series passenger diesel, destined to become the most successful passenger diesel in America, with production continuing to 1964. E-units contained two engines—900 hp each on early models—which doubled reliability (but also maintenance). The "E" in the designation indicated Eighteen hundred horsepower, although later models had as much as 2,400 hp. This artist's rendering shows an E6 model for the Southern Railway that would be delivered in 1941. *EMD*

Although *Zephyr* 9900 and early passenger diesels helped sell the diesel-electric to railroads, they still weren't convinced the diesel could outperform the tried-and-proven steam locomotive in heavy freight service. That changed with the introduction of Electro-Motive's FT-series freight locomotive in 1939. Here, four Santa Fe FT units hoist a heavy train through California's Tehachapi Mountains in the 1950s. *Robert Hale, M. D. McCarter Collection*

formation would produce a diesel-electric that could outperform even the biggest 4-8-4!

The numerous E-units built in 1937 and 1938 were powered by 900-h.p. Winton 201As, but in 1939 EMC introduced its own new 567-series diesel engine*, built from scratch at La Grange. The 567 (567 cubic inches of displacement per cylinder) was simple and rugged and had plenty of

---

*The terms "engine" and "locomotive" are often used interchangeably, but in diesel technology they are two different things. Diesel-electrics are locomotives that contain one or more engines or "power plants." An engine's power generator produces electricity for the traction motors, which rotate the locomotive's wheels. An E-series passenger diesel, for example, contains two engines, and some later, rebuilt models even contained three engines—two for motive power and one to power a separate generator for train-heating and lighting.

room to grow, with the V-12 version initially rated at 1000 horsepower. Utilizing a pair of the new 567 V-12s in each unit, in March of 1939 EMC created the first "standard" passenger road diesel locomotive, the 2000-hp E3, and the steam locomotive was doomed. It just didn't know it yet.

DIESELS FOR FREIGHT

While E-units and shiny passenger trains caught the attention of both the public and the railroads, EMC knew that the real challenge for the diesel-electric would be heavy freight service. Dick Dilworth went back to his horsepower calculations and concluded that he would need about 5000 horsepower. His tool was the new 1350-hp 16-cylinder version of the 567 engine, but it was

too large to mount two in one carbody like an E-unit. So Dilworth created a permanently-coupled cab-and-booster set that packed 2700 hp. Two of these sets coupled back to back in an A-B-B-A configuration produced a 5400-hp locomotive utilizing four diesel engines and 16 traction motors to equal or surpass the performance of almost any steam locomotive. Dilworth's machine was dubbed the FT, "F" for freight and "T" for twenty-four hundred horsepower. In 1939 EMC built an A-B-B-A FT demonstrator set numbered 103 and sent it on a year-long coast-to-coast tour that proved the capability of a diesel to outperform steam locomotives at almost any task. The Santa Fe bought the first production FT's in October 1940, and a new era in railroading was about to begin.

113

Early on, Alco read the handwriting on the wall and entered into diesel production, having dabbled in diesel technology as early as 1924. Like many locomotive companies, Alco's first offerings were switchers—an arena where internal-combustion power first began to prove itself in the railroad world. This Frankfort & Cincinnati locomotive is one of Alco's popular S-series switchers, which began production in 1940 and lasted until 1960. The F&C was a Kentucky-based shortline. For many shortlines throughout America, switchers were the mainstay motive power. *Jim Boyd*

While EMC was turning out streamliners and switchers, the steam builders were still working on developing bigger and better steam locomotives—but they were not oblivious to the threat of the diesel-electric. Baldwin and Westinghouse Electric had been teaming up on electric locomotives for years, and in the late 1930s they continued this relationship into diesel switcher production. Meanwhile, Alco was following a similar path, teamed up with General Electric for electrical equipment and in 1929 buying the McIntosh & Seymour Engine Company to develop its own line of diesel engines. By 1940 Alco was producing a very successful line of standardized diesel switchers and had introduced a line of twin-engine passenger units to

compete with EMC's E-units. The Alco "DL109" passenger units featured a sharply angled nose and carbody styled by industrial designer Otto Kuhler. Only Lima remained totally dedicated to steam.

Electro-Motive and Winton were merged into the parent corporation on January 1, 1941, to become the new Electro-Motive Division of General Motors, headquartered in La Grange. The EMD FT freight unit was the wake-up call to Alco and Baldwin, but an international incident at Pearl Harbor, Hawaii, on December 7, 1941, froze diesel locomotive development while the nation mobilized again for war.

While the railroads remained free of government takeover during World War II, the War

Production Board put severe restrictions on strategic materials and limited production to existing designs of switching and freight units and banned the construction of passenger units. Thus EMD gained a tremendous competitive advantage in the diesel market by being able to produce and gain valuable experience with FT road units throughout the war, while Alco was restricted to switch engines—although it was able to continue producing the DL-series locomotives by claiming they were dual-purpose, freight and passenger. Both Alco and EMD diesel *engines* (not locomotives), however, were delivered in great numbers to the U.S. Navy, where they were used to power submarines and small combat vessels. And the EMD FT diesels are credited with keeping the mighty Santa Fe Railway moving during the war, where they replaced steam in the bad-water territory of the desert Southwest.

With the Japanese surrender at the dawn of the nuclear age in 1945, the war on the steam locomotive swung into full force, as EMD went back into passenger production with its new 2000-hp E7 and upgraded the freight FT into the 1500-hp F3. Alco got immediately into the freight diesel fray with its FA1 cab unit and stunned the railroad world with its impressive 2000-hp PA passenger diesel, using a single 16-cylinder engine instead of EMD's twin 12-cylinder power plants.

Fresh from a solid success in powering submarines, in August 1944 Fairbanks-Morse of Beloit, Wisconsin, put its unique opposed-piston two-stroke cycle diesel engine (most others used a four-stroke) into a 1000-h.p. switching locomotive and jumped into the railroad market with a vengeance. In 1945 even Baldwin was working on a competitor to the EMD F3 and Alco F3. Lima finally got the message in 1947 and began building diesel switchers while aggressively advertising bigger and better steam locomotives.

THE ROAD-SWITCHER

In the late 1940s there were essentially two ways to build diesel-electric locomotives: on a switcher "platform" or in a truss-sided "cab unit" carbody like the E and FT. The cab unit had excellent forward visibility and crew protection, but its high cab and full-width hoods made rearward visibility difficult for the engineer. What was needed was a big switcher that was powerful and fast enough for road service.

Interestingly, Alco had created just such a locomotive in 1940. The Alco RS1 put a 1000-hp

Part of the assembly line for Alco-G.E. diesel-electric switchers at the Schenectady Works of the American Locomotive Company

Alco-G.E. Diesel-Electric Locomotives

A Complete Line, Built for Stock in Standard Sizes

THE Alco-G.E. line of diesel-electric locomotives is the product of the combined resources of American Locomotive and General Electric.

American Locomotive has been building steam power for a century. G.E. has been building electric locomotives for fifty years. The first Alco-G.E. diesel-electric was built in 1925.

In offering railroads the extra quality and performance of this diesel-electric line, Alco and G.E. also offer the distinct advantage of an impartial advisory service to help railroads select the right type of power for each particular job.

Recognizing the advantages inherent in each type of power—steam, electric, and diesel-electric—it is our policy to work together on all problems of motive-power application and recommend the type of power economically best suited to any particular set of traffic and geographical conditions.

The purchaser of Alco-G.E. diesel-electric locomotives, therefore, is assured of the economies and profits which result from the proper application of motive power.

AMERICAN LOCOMOTIVE AND GENERAL ELECTRIC

Introduced prior to World War II, the DL-series diesel-electrics were Alco and General Electric's answer to Electro-Motive's E-series passenger diesels and were touted in this handsome brochure produced by Alco-GE. However, the DLs—which like E-units were twin-engined—were marketed as dual-purpose locomotives for either freight or passenger service. This allowed Alco to produce DLs through the war while other manufacturers were required by the War Production Board to suspend the production of passenger-only diesels. *Mike Schafer collection*

ABOVE: Alco's postwar PA-series passenger diesel, a single-engine 2,000-hp locomotive (the locomotive set to the left of the Electro-Motive F-units in this scene at Santa Fe's passenger locomotive facility in Chicago in 1956), were highly acclaimed for their good looks. However, good looks aren't everything. The locomotive's sometimes troublesome power plant dogged Alco, and only less than 300 PAs and booster PBs were sold—though a few could be found operating on U.S. passenger trains into the late 1970s. *John Dziobko*

RIGHT: Nearly all the major locomotive builders—Alco, GE, Baldwin, and Fairbanks-Morse—that built diesels attempted to offer competing models to Electro-Motive's wildly successful F-series. Baldwin's attempt was its DR-series (for Diesel Road locomotive), illustrated here by a cab-booster set of Jersey Central "Babyface" DRs (so-nicknamed account of the squat nose and large cab windows) at Aldene, New Jersey in 1954. *John Dziobko*

Alco pioneered the road-switcher concept with the 1940 introduction of its RS1 locomotive, which offered versatility by being able to function as a switcher, a road-freight unit, or even as a passenger locomotive. In this 1967 scene at Chicago's Dearborn Station, a Chicago & Western Indiana RS1 serves as the station switcher, shunting Monon Railroad's *Thoroughbred* passenger train into the depot for boarding. C&WI RS1 263 is coupled to another unit of note—Monon No. 37, an Electro-Motive BL2 which will lead this evening's *Thoroughbred* to Louisville. The BL-series was Electro-Motive's early and short-lived attempt at road-switcher design. In the background sit two Electro-Motive E8s which later in the evening will take Erie Lackawanna's *Phoebe Snow* passenger train on its overnight journey to Hoboken, New Jersey. *Mike Schafer*

6-cylinder engine atop a lengthened switcher frame beneath a narrow hood with side walkways. The rear-end cab was moved forward on the frame, and a short rear hood was added to accommodate a steam boiler for passenger service (steam was used to heat passenger trains), if it was needed. The whole package was placed on standard four-wheel road freight trucks. This "road-switcher" concept was so successful that the entire pre-1941 production of RS1s was "drafted" by the U.S. Army for use overseas, but civilian production

resumed in 1943. The RS1 was a bit shy on horsepower, but its road-switcher configuration was just the versatile package the railroads were looking for.

Baldwin was quick to jump on the road-switcher bandwagon and by 1946 was producing a true road unit at 1500 hp. That same year Alco produced its 1500-hp RS2, and in 1947 Fairbanks-Morse upped the ante to 2000 hp with its H20-44 heavy duty road-switcher. EMD's first major marketing blunder was to answer the road-switcher challenge in 1948 with its BL2 "Branch Line"

unit, which retained the side trusswork and looked like an F3 with a slightly narrowed hood. But the truss carbody made the innards of the engine room more difficult to access for maintenance. One of the big advantages of the narrow road-switcher hood is that the outboard walkways and side doors make diesel engine maintenance very easy.

But EMD would have the last laugh. In October 1949 Dick Dilworth produced his own 1500-hp "General Purpose" GP7 road-switcher, which immediately picked up the nickname

"Geep"—pronounced "Jeep" and an apparent take-off of the well-known Army vehicle of that name. With the GP7, the popular EMD 567 engine could be marketed in a package that would do almost any job a railroad could come up with, from high-speed passenger trains to road freights and midnight yard switching jobs. The Geep would become the most popular diesel locomotive of all time.

Throughout the 1950s, EMD, Alco, Baldwin and FM cab units and road-switchers overwhelmed even the mightiest of steam locomotives. By September 1949 the commercial builders had turned out their last steam locomotives. The last new steam locomotive for a Class 1 U.S. railroad was an 0-8-0 built in December 1953 by the Norfolk & Western's home shop in Roanoke, Virginia.

THE SECOND GENERATION

Steam was still hauling coal on the Norfolk & Western and Illinois Central when diesels entered their "second generation' in the late 1950s. At that time, the basic four-motor freight diesel was still at the 1500-to-1800-hp level, and it was becoming obvious that greater horsepower per unit could reduce the number of overall units needed. Heavier units riding on pairs of six-wheel ("C") trucks with three motors each were pushing into the 2400-hp range. The road-switcher had all but doomed the cab unit for anything but passenger service, and the earliest road diesels were nearing the end of their projected 12–15-year economic service life.

But the banner for change was taken up by an unexpected player: General Electric. Alco had been building locomotives with GE electrical gear since the 1930s, but GE was ready to strike out on its

The two principal formats of early diesel carbody design—that of the full-width "cab unit" body versus that of the "road-switcher" design—are aptly illustrated in this view at Rock Island's Silvis (Illinois) Shops in 1966. At left is an Alco FA model (Alco's answer to Electro-Motive's F-series) while at right is an Electro-Motive GP7. Although cab units provide excellent forward visibility and crew protection because of the crew cab being set above and behind a large nose, they were not practical for switching. With the road-switcher, crews could see fore and aft while brakemen could easily ride the steps during switching operations, as shown here. *Mike Schafer*

Though a latecomer in diesel offerings, Fairbanks-Morse may have been ahead of its time when it introduced, early in the 1950s, its hulking "Train Master" road-switcher, several of which are lined up here at San Francisco in 1971 ready to take Southern Pacific commuters back home. The 2,400-hp locomotives were powerful forces in freight railroading, and they also worked well hauling passenger trains account of their ability to accelerate fast. For railroads of the period, 2,400-hp locomotives may have been too much. That plus F-M's unusual opposed-piston power plant—a somewhat for-eign concept to railroad mechanical departments (but not the U.S. Navy and other marine-based endeavors, which had long embraced F-M engines)—limited the Train Master's popularity. *Jim Boyd*

As an independent, General Electric was another latecomer to the manufacture of road diesels—but destined for great success in the field. It all started with an experimental U-series locomotive introduced in 1956, but things really took off with the 1959 introduction of the U25B. Powered by a Cooper-Bessemer FDL-16 four-stroke-cycle diesel engine (GE had acquired the Cooper-Bessemer company), the U25B—a trio of "U-boats" are shown here on the Erie Lackawanna at Griffith, Indiana, in 1965—cranked out 2,500 hp. GE continued to produce newer, improved models of its Universal series, and by the 1980s had become a serious contender to Electro-Motive. *Mike Schafer*

own, and it did it in an impressive way by designing a new freight locomotive from the ground up at 2500 hp. GE's "Universal" road-switcher, the U25B, significantly modernized air filtering, cooling, and electrical systems, in addition to upping the horsepower threshold. When it hit the road in 1959, it was marketed as a "unit reduction" locomotive, with two U25Bs replacing three conventional 1500-hp units, either cabs or road-switchers, that could be traded in as part of the purchase deal. EMD and Alco both scrambled to compete. EMD boosted the output of its 16-cylinder 567 from 1800 to 2400 hp by adding a turbocharger. Meanwhile, Alco introduced its Century-series locomotive line.

And the road-switcher took on a new look at about the same time. The earliest road-switchers had operated with the cab behind the diesel engine, with the "long hood" forward, because

crews liked the sense of protection that the hood ahead of them provided. The GP7, however, was promoted with its high short hood as the front for better visibility. In 1959 the Santa Fe ordered its new EMD SD24s and Alco DL600s with cutdown short hoods so the engineer could see completely across the front of the locomotive. Thus was born the "low-nose" or "chopped-nose" roadswitcher that would become the industry standard for the next three decades.

The GE U25B was a stunning success that soon bumped its former partner Alco out of the market. Baldwin and Lima never made it to the second generation, and Fairbanks-Morse gave up the locomotive business in 1963. By the mid-1960s, EMD and GE were slugging it out toe-to-toe at the 3000-hp range. Making the first major change in internal dimensions since 1939, EMD enlarged the bore of its 567 engine to create the new 645

engine with additional growing room.

The horsepower race was on in 1965, and both EMD and GE were now using more efficient a.c. alternators in place of the d.c. main generators and rectifying the output through solid-state diodes to d.c. for the traction motors. The alternators had much greater capacity, and EMD upped the ante again by stretching its new 16-cylinder 645 to 20 cylinders to produce the 3600-hp SD45 20-cylinder (a record for cylinder count), six-motor unit. In spite of some early mechanical bugs, the SD45 was a great success with larger railroads.

But while the big SD45 made the headlines, EMD's 3000-hp six-motor SD40 and four-motor GP40 and their GE counterparts would become the workhorses of the next decade. They were solid and reliable, and the railroads loved 'em. What the customers wanted was locomotives that ran well on minimal maintenance, day-in and day-out.

A contemporary of GE's U25B was Electro-Motive's GP30, which packed in 2,250 hp. This was the first diesel in Electro-Motive's catalog to offer a low nose as standard. Though some railroads, notably Norfolk & Western, still preferred high-nose road-switchers, most went with the low-nose option, which offered crews better visibility. Chicago & Eastern Illinois GP30 No. 240 is on a "caboose hop" at Chicago in 1966. *Jim Boyd*

Not to be outdone by Electro-Motive and GE, Alco offered its own line of heavy-duty road-switchers. While Electro-Motive offered its GP- and SD- series and GE its Universal series, Alco's equivalents were in its "Century" line of locomotives. A whole string of Centurys lead this New York, Susquehanna & Western freight at Binghamton, New York, in 1985. Despite the presence of burly Alcos on this train, Alco had gone out of business in 1969, though its patents and designs were carried forth by its Canadian counterpart, Montreal Locomotive Works. *Jim Boyd*

One of Electro-Motive's demonstrator SD45 diesels is shown testing on the Chicago Great Western at Sycamore, Illinois, in March 1966. The SD45 was a landmark locomotive for Electro-Motive, the first (and only) diesel-electric locomotive to employ a 20-cylinder power plant. Introduced in 1965, the SD45 churned out a record (for single-engine locomotives of the period) 3,600 hp. *Jim Boyd*

Two Clinchfield SD45s sandwich an SD40 on a north-bound freight flying high over Copper Creek Viaduct in Virginia. Their higher-than-average maintenance requirements limited the popularity of the SD45, although many were still in use at the close of the twentieth century, notably on the new Burlington Northern & Santa Fe Railroad as well as on regional railroad Wisconsin Central. The SD40, however, can still be widely found throughout America. *Jim Boyd*

Gas 'n go! Stay on the road. Don't spend time in the shop. Old units made fine trade-ins on shiny new chopped-nose units. The Second Generation was taking over.

LAST OF THE GIANTS REVISITED

In 1949 the Union Pacific was operating the world's largest steam locomotives, its 25 4-8-8-4 Big Boys. It had always bothered management that four 1500-hp diesels were required to replace one Big Boy, and they wanted to reduce that ratio by creating bigger and more economical diesels.

General Electric offered an intriguing alternative in 1949 with a 4500-hp gas-turbine-electric locomotive which essentially harnessed a jet engine to a generator and spread the power over four trucks beneath a huge cab-unit carbody. The UP bought two dozen "Big Blows" before GE offered an even bigger two-unit 8500-hp turbine in 1958—and these monsters were soon uprated to 10,000 hp each! The 30 upgraded turbines were the most powerful locomotives to ever operate in the world.

But the turbines, while incredibly powerful, were also incredibly fuel-hungry, and the economics of second-generation diesels caught up with them. In 1963 both GE and Alco took the frames and trucks from the 4500-hp turbines and rebuilt

RIGHT: A footnote—though a large one— to the diesel era was Union Pacific's experimentation with gas-turbine-electric technology, the result of which was a series of the most powerful locomotives ever to operate. These monsters incorporated what was essentially a jet engine (which is what they indeed sounded like) to drive traction motors. They used crude Bunker C fuel oil, carried in a separate tender. One 10,000-hp set is shown, in tandem with one of UP's mammoth 5,500-hp Alco Century 855 diesels, at Omaha in 1965. There's more than 15,000 hp at the head of this train! *Jim Boyd*

BELOW: One of UP's DD40AX dwarfs its SD40-2 companion moving tonnage through California's Feather River Canyon in 1984. The Centennial's amazing length (for a single-unit locomotive) and 6,600 hp earned it the honor of being the world's largest diesel locomotive. *Jim Boyd*

Why the Diesel Prevailed

It has long been a popular topic for discussion that dieselization was a fraud perpetrated by the industrial giant General Motors threatening to takes its business "elsewhere" that convinced railroads to scrap brand new steam locomotives in favor of diesels. The federal government even investigated the charge and found it to be completely groundless—GM's Electro-Motive Division had always been a fair market competitor. It simply had the best locomotives.

How could the upstart diesel upset the 125-year reign of steam? The answer is found in three places: (1) the basic physics of the traction motor; (2) the jumper cable; and (3) manpower.

A diesel-electric of almost any size is immediately superior to even a much larger steam locomotive because of the performance characteristics of the electric traction motor. A steam locomotive standing still is all potential energy, but it cannot develop horsepower or traction until it actually begins to move—and since it begins at zero, that first movement is the most difficult. For this reason, a steam locomotive would often need to back up and "take slack" in the couplers to be able to lunge forward to get its train moving.

The diesel's output, electricity, can be immediately applied to the wheels through the traction motors, which exert tremendous pulling power at starting speeds. As the locomotive begins to move, its speed potential is then limited by the maximum output of the diesel engine, and when that is reached, the locomotive will pull no harder and go no faster. A steam locomotive, on the other

One of Electro-Motive's earlier offerings of third-generation diesels was the SD70MAC, featuring ac traction and the new full-width "safety cab" nose. Not surprisingly, Electro-Motive MAC-series locomotives have acquired the nickname "Big Macs." Sharing the Conrail SD70MAC's limelight in this 1993 photo is a Morristown & Erie Alco Century 424 built in 1964 for the Toledo, Peoria & Western. With Alco, Baldwin, and Fairbanks-Morse all gone from the locomotive-manufacturing arena, Electro-Motive and GE continue to battle it out as the two primary competing suppliers of new diesel locomotives. *Jim Boyd*

hand, starts with theoretically zero power and increases in output as the machinery speed increases, up to the steaming capacity of the boiler. As a result, a steam locomotive could get up to track speed with almost any train it could get started, while a diesel could start almost any train but would usually be limited in potential speed.

This is why a 1000-hp diesel switcher can move slowly with a mile-long train that would require a 4-8-4 or three 1500-hp road diesels to get up to track speed. And while the 4-8-4 would have to take slack and struggle at maximum effort to get the train moving, the little diesel switcher or three-unit road set would start with a very low throttle and ease the big train into motion before

gradually applying power. Since most railroad work is actually performed at low speed, the diesel-electric had an inherent advantage due to elementary physics.

Since the horsepower of the diesel engine limits the locomotive's potential speed, the way to go faster is to add more diesel engines to the power set. This is where the jumper cable strangled the life out of the steam locomotive. Since diesel locomotives are self-regulating machines that are controlled by electricity, it was a simple matter to equip them with jumper-cable control wires between units to add more and more units to build the power block needed for any job. While steam could be doubleheaded, each locomotive required an engineer and fireman to

operate it. A single engineer could run a six-unit diesel, while two steam locomotives needed two engineers and two firemen.

And therein was the manpower element. Steam was very labor-intensive, requiring a two-man crew on each locomotive and a vast support staff all along the railroad to provide coal and water and lubricant every 40 miles or so. A diesel just needed liquid fuel, sand for traction, and a minimum of in-service maintenance. Steam required huge backshops and heavy machinery to keep them running, while diesels could usually survive with a good mechanic and a toolbox. And the diesel, being an "automatic" machine like an automobile, could be left running or worked 24 hours of every day, while a steam locomotive required firebox cleaning about every eight hours and a visit to the roundhouse after every road trip or workday in the yard. The diesel could work harder and for a much longer time and required much less manpower to keep it running.

An excellent example of the diesel's economic superiority was the Illinois Central. It would take two or three Electro-Motive GP7s to replace a single 4-8-2 or 2-10-2 steam locomotive in fast or heavy freight service. In 1950 the IC was operating 1,166 steam locomotives and 89 passenger and switching diesels. When the last steam locomotive dropped its fire in early 1960, the IC was operating its entire railroad with only 600 diesels. It's called "utilization," and that is why steam was vanquished and the diesel prevailed.

them with two 16-cylinder diesels on each platform, producing 5000-hp (GE) and 5500-hp (Alco) locomotives. EMD responded with a new four-motor ("D") power truck and two turbocharged 2500-hp 567s to produce its 5000-h.p. DD35. By 1969 these diesel giants had bumped the fuel-hungry turbines off the rails.

That same year, EMD applied its new 645 turbocharged V-16, rated at 3300 hp, to the DD35 format to produce the largest single-unit diesel-electric locomotive ever built. The 6600-hp monster DDA40X was introduced on the 100th anniversary of the May 10, 1869, completion of the transcontinental railroad, and the diesel Big Boys were officially dubbed "Centennials." By 1971 the UP had acquired a fleet of 47 of these world's largest diesel-electric locomotives. While diesels with more horsepower may be built in the future, it is doubtful that any single units will be built exceeding the nearly 100-foot length of the DDA40X.

HIGH TECH

The railroads were very happy in the early 1970s, with the UP running the world's largest locomotives and everybody else moving trains with 3000-hp road-switchers that were reliable gas-'n-go workhorses. Then came the Arab oil embargo and the "energy crisis." Fuel supplies dwindled and prices skyrocketed in 1973 as American motorists sat in gas lines to fill their tanks. The national speed limit was reduced to 55 mph, and the railroads were caught with fuel-hungry locomotives.

The price of simplicity and reliability is reduced fuel efficiency. Suddenly the railroads valued fuel efficiency more than simplicity. But the cost of fuel efficiency is a complexity. Air compressors and cooling fans that ran all the time with a direct drive from the diesel-engine crankshaft added "parasite drag" that ate up horsepower and increased fuel consumption. Putting in clutch and control systems to turn

them on only when needed saved fuel but added to internal complexity and maintenance cost.

But again, locomotive builders had a new tool at the perfect time—the computer. Using computers, locomotives could be engineered to squeeze every bit of energy from the fuel consumed. Further, on-board computers could turn on and off auxiliary components for maximum efficiency and take over the control systems to apply power to the rails in the most effective manner. "High tech" complexity was making fuel efficiency a more economically viable goal.

State-of-the-art diesel-electric technology is brightly stated by this pair of General Electric model AC4400CW locomotives, at Lee, Illinois, bound for Chicago with a Burlington Northern & Santa Fe freight out of St. Paul. Alternating-current traction motors and computer-operated control systems brought diesel-electric locomotive technology to a new magnitude during the 1990s. *Mike Schafer*

The final development stage for the American locomotive in the twentieth century was the use of alternating-current for traction motors. Although ac motors had been used for 100 years, they have always been difficult to control over a wide output range of speed and power, while dc motors are extremely simple to control, though less efficient. Solid-state technology and computers came to the rescue in the 1990s with electronic "choppers" that create an artificial wave in the ac current to supply the motors with precisely the frequency and power needed for any throttle position, load and track

speed. The first ac motors were applying so much power to the rails that they were actually twisting the steel axles.

The "third generation" of American diesel locomotives hit the rails in the mid 1990s in the form of computer-controlled ac traction locomotives. Horsepower was again the name of the game, and the 3000-hp plateau jumped quickly to the 4300-hp level, as both GE and Electro-Motive worked frantically on new, more powerful diesel engines of completely new design to pick the race up to the 6000-hp level that the ac motors were already capable of handling—a single-engine, six-motor locomotive capable of delivering the power of a four-unit set of 1948-era F3s—or a steam Big Boy.

And the newest locomotives even look dramatically different. With the elimination of the caboose in the 1980s, all crew members would ride the locomotive (even though the steam-era six-man crew was now usually down to a radio-equipped two men). To provide the conductor with an "office" for his paperwork, the cab was enlarged, and a new "safety" short hood with massive internal collision posts spread the full width of the nose. Many locomotives even carry computers in the cab for the conductor to use to keep in touch with the railroad's car-tracking and work-assignment computer systems. Bright "ditch lights" at the front corners of the locomotive frames combine with the high-mounted headlight to give the modern diesel a "flying pyramid" of light for added safety and visibility.

But with all this high-tech equipment, the pioneer spirit of the American locomotive has not been lost. It is not by accident that the most popular type of air horn, the K5LA, was designed by music-trained technical engineers to duplicate the sound of a five-chime steam-locomotive whistle. So a bit of the steam era lives on.

6 The Railroad Station

There was a time, two generations or so ago, when virtually every adult American could identify a railroad station which had played a significant part in their life. In fact, for well over a century, beginning in the 1830s, the nation's appetite for mobility, information, and the fruits of commerce had drawn people to the town depot—the community's "gateway to the world;" one's entree to new experiences. It was here that you once stood on the platform and talked to the engineer of the *Limited,* shipped a trunk by Railway Express, and departed for camp, college, or war; received mail-order packages; wired money to a son or daughter; departed aboard a Pullman on a business trip or vacation. For recent generations, contact with railroad depots has perhaps meant brief, weekday encounters while commuting between home and work, or an occasional intercity trip on Amtrak, or encouraging preservation of the endangered hometown depot. More likely, however, it has involved nothing more than just passing a site where a depot once stood and speculating on how things used to be.

With the rapid expansion of railroads in the second half of the nineteenth century and their extraordinary impact on the growth and economic well-being of communities throughout the country, the town depot became the focal point for many aspects of daily life. Here worked—and sometimes resided—the railroad's agent, its representative in the community, and, often, an essential player in the monitoring and control of train movements between stations along the line. With the railroad's arrival in town, new opportunities opened up for contacts with other communities and the nation's expanding frontier by encouraging personal travel, facilitating commerce, and providing the means for more rapid and reliable communication.

The railroad depot was the center of this activity. Here you could purchase a ticket and board a train to conduct business in a distant city or visit places heretofore unseen. Your personal belongings would be accommodated in the baggage car by having the agent issue a metal or paper "check" identifying the items as your property for redeeming at your destination. Arrangements could be made for the shipping or receiving of goods aboard the railroad's freight trains. The United States mail arrived and departed at the depot. By the 1840s, express companies were contracting with railroads to offer expedited service aboard passenger and express trains for small, valuable, or time-sensitive shipments. Most of this traffic was handled across the platform of the railroad depot. As telegraph lines were strung along the railroad network in the middle of the nineteenth century, the depot became the town's communications center. Agents honed their skills as telegraph operators to receive and send messages governing the movement of trains. Utilizing lines of companies such as Western Union, these agent/operators also handled messages for the public. The telegraph key, wire, and sounder brought news from afar, and it was quickly disseminated to all who gathered at the depot.

In time, as towns grew, activities in and about the railroad depot also expanded and became more diverse. Restaurant and hotel facilities were added. Passenger terminals in some major cities provided barber shops, showers, changing rooms, and retail stores to serve the traveler. The railroad's agents could help you plan a complex itinerary, rent a hotel room, and even buy travel insurance.

By the turn of the century, the railroad depot had become part of the social fabric of most communities, as well as a center of commercial activity. Here was the place where much of the town's business was transacted, its residents and visitors passed, its social commentators gathered. For more than a hundred years, in thousands of towns large and small, train time was an event that commanded attention—even if for no better reason than to see who was arriving today on the *Limited, Flyer,* or *Special.*

ORIGINS: STATIONS AND DEPOTS

Coincident with the operation of the first American railroads in the 1830s, stations were established at specific points along the route for the management and control of train movements between terminals. The location of these stations was initially dictated by the distance a locomotive could travel before refueling or servicing (or horses replaced on horse-drawn trains), and where crews would be changed. As operations became more complex with several trains running on the line at the same time, means had to be found to keep them separated to avoid collisions. Stations, spaced at distances to facilitate efficient train movement, served as a frame of reference by which a dispatcher could give a train crew authority and instructions to proceed down the track to another location (station) to meet a train or receive further orders. Following introduction of the telegraph,

FACING PAGE: Nearly every American community, large and miniscule, at one time had a railroad station as its connection to the outside world. In 1997, Muleshoe, Texas, still had its Santa Fe depot. *Tom Kline* ABOVE: One of America's most stunning large-city depots is Cincinnati Union Terminal, shown on a summer night in 1997. Opened in 1933 when the U.S. was in the grip of the Great Depression, CUT foretold an impending era of streamlined passenger trains, the first of which wouldn't be introduced for another year. One can still catch a passenger train at CUT, but only about once a day. *Mike Schafer*

ABOVE: This view of the Duluth, Shore Shore & Atlantic depot at L'anse, Michigan, in 1915 beholds a classic station scene during railroading's heyday. Passengers watch the arriving steam train as a horse-drawn carriage awaits parcels and perhaps mail that will be transferred once the train halts. Cans of cream on the platform will be forwarded to a downline dairy. At many locations, depot agents lived on the premises, usually in an upper-story apartment in the depot itself, as was the case here. *Mike Schafer collection*

RIGHT: The telegraph was instrumental in early railroad operations, and the telegraph key and sounder were fixtures at nearly all depots (the tobacco tin was also a fixture; agents always kept an empty one at hand to place over the sounder to amplify the Morse code signals). Working with station operators through the telegraph network, dispatchers governed train movements via train orders. Train orders were dictated to operators via Morse while the operator copied them out in longhand on "flimsies"—special train-order tissues. Once complete, the train orders were given to train crews when their train reached the station. *Mike McBride collection, Andover Junction Publications photo*

"operators" at the various stations could relay orders from a central dispatcher to passing train crews, as well as report on each train's progress.

Stations were normally identified in a railroad's timetable by name. If manned, there would usually be a building (depot) for shelter as well as facilities for operating and maintaining the railroad. Other stations might be nothing more than a defined point along the rail line with an identifying sign. In outlying areas, station buildings often included housing for the railroad's employees in the area and their families.

In time, towns developed around many of these stations. In such cases, as well as when stations were initially located in populated areas, they often became a convenient place for the railroad to conduct business with the public, load its passenger trains, and handle mail, express, and freight traffic. Here, railroad agent/operators not only monitored the movement of trains, they also served as the company's contact with the community and the users of its services.

Depots were structures designed to house the unique functions of railroad stations. Each reflected the character of its station's activities, the community it served, and its owner. Some depots were merely a rudimentary shelter and platform at an unmanned "flagstop" where passengers would use a flag or lantern to signal approaching trains of their desire to board. Others housed the multiple functions of the typical station in a structure that might be as simple as a wood frame Cape Cod "saltbox" or as complex as a gingerbread-ladened "Victorian." Depots at urban terminals were often truly monumental edifices in style and scale.

EARLY DEPOTS

Colonial stagecoach stations and early turnpike toll houses might be seen as the antecedents of the railway depot. Indeed, like stagecoach lines, some railroads originally used nearby hotels, taverns, and other public buildings for handling passengers and freight. However, the unique functions of the railroad station in the control of train movements, as well as the sheltering of passengers and goods and the sale of transportation, soon prompted the design of structures tailored to these varied activities.

The station agent or "operator" was as much a depot fixture as the telegraph key. Aside from relaying train orders to crews, agents sold tickets to passengers and handled the paperwork on local freight business that passed through the station. The duties of this agent for MARC (Maryland Rail Commuter) at Harpers Ferry, West Virginia, in 1990 were pretty much limited to the sale of train tickets—train dispatching having evolved to direct radio contact between dispatcher and train crew, and local freight business having become a thing of the past. *Steve Smedley*

Initially, most railroad depots were strictly functional in design and of wood, stone, or brick construction. The building was situated adjacent to the track, with an entryway, or carriage court, fronting a public thoroughfare for ease of access. A waiting room offered protection from the weather until the train's arrival. Some designs supplemented the main waiting room with a smaller one for women and, in the segregated South, a separate "colored" waiting area. The railroad's agent oversaw train operations and transacted business from an office facing the track and with a window opening to the waiting room. To enhance his ability to observe train movements and platform activities, the agent's office was usually equipped with a polygonal bay window extending out onto the platform. In depots which also handled freight, a store room was provided, generally on the opposite side of the agent's office from the waiting room. Both the passenger waiting room and the freight room exited to a platform running parallel to and abutting the track. While the portion of the platform for loading passengers, mail, and express was at track level, freight was generally handled in and out of rail cars across an elevated platform, often adjacent to a side track. A canopy or shed constructed over the platform area provided limited protection from the elements. Frequently, a second floor was built to house the agent and his family.

Rapid expansion of the railroad system in the U.S. right after the Civil War prompted standardization of station designs at all but the most important cities en route. These were generally the work of the railroads' own civil engineers. Meanwhile, in Europe, railroads were often turning to leading architects for the design of stations reflecting aesthetic tastes of the times. Some U.S. roads employed these European designs for their major station complexes.

THE GOLDEN ERA

As a national network of rail routes took form, grew, and consolidated during the last half of the nineteenth century, the railroad depot took on even more importance. The expansion of telegraph lines along railroad rights-of-way coupled to the growth of rail-related express companies also increased the role of the depot in community affairs. Cities continued to thrive, and additional

129

towns formed around stations of the railroad. In fact, some communities were started by a railroad to support its expansion, and they often continued to subsist almost entirely on that road's activities in the area. These were commonly known as "railroad towns" and were typically the headquarters of an operating territory, or division, of the railroad or the home to an equipment maintenance shop or freight yard.

The railroad depot was often viewed as being a gateway, a place where outsiders would form their first impressions of a locale. Thus, its size and appearance were factors by which the entire community's success might be judged. Not surprisingly, railroads found themselves under pressure to enhance their depots in stature and architectural embellishments. At first resistant, most roads eventually relented as their own sense of self-worth, competitiveness, and even "civic pride," began to influence depot design. It was not uncommon for the depot to be the largest and, architecturally, the most interesting structure in the area. Being a focal point in the community, the depot frequently sported a tall, imposing clock tower.

Many American architects of the mid-to-late 1800s drew upon European railway practice and adopted styles reflecting popular tastes of the times, such as Italianate, for the design of mid-size and large depots. An early example that is still extant is the head house of Baltimore & Ohio Railroad's Camden Station (1865) in Baltimore.

Victorian styles were frequently employed at the turn of the century for station structures of all

Some stations were not much more that remote outposts that existed primarily for purposes of train dispatching. At the time of this photo in November 1957, there was no more passenger service to Irwin, Illinois, on Illinois Central's Kankakee–Bloomington line. However, the railroad maintained a depot there since Irwin was near a junction point with a limestone quarry spur, and trains often stopped here to work the branch or meet other trains—situations in which the dispatcher and an operator had to communicate. *Howard Patrick*

The Colorado & Southern depot at Broomfield, Colorado, northwest of Denver was a picturesque structure with dormers, wainscoting, green trim, and a one-time necessary appliance for nearly all depots, a train-order signal. There was no passenger service on the C&S (a Burlington Route subsidiary) at the time of this photo, but Broomfield was still an "active" meeting point for trains and still had enough local freight business to warrant an operator/agent. In operator mode, the agent notified trains (by lowering the train-order signal to the horizontal "stop" position) that he had orders from the dispatcher for them. As an agent, he or she dealt directly with the public regarding freight shipments or, if there was passenger service, train tickets. *Mike Schafer*

ABOVE: The windowed tower that tops the depot at White River Junction, Vermont, reflects an era when architecture dwelt on details—right down to the locomotive weather vane. Alas, since this 1974 view was recorded, that functional piece of decoration has been stolen—the victim of weather-vane collectors. White River Junction served the Central Vermont and Boston & Maine; today, Amtrak passenger trains still call at the Junction. *Mike Schafer*

LEFT: Depots often reflected a town's pride and not necessarily its size. The former Chicago & Alton depot at Dwight, Illinois, is a handsome, ponderous stone structure that dominates the downtown of this burgh of 4,000 inhabitants. *Steve Smedley*

sizes. The Keokuk, Iowa, Union Station (1891) and St. Louis Union Station (1894) are typical of this design.

Some railroads retained nationally recognized architects to design their more important stations, such as in major cities and along suburban commuter lines, at state capitals and county seats, and for centers of railroad activity. In fact, the reputations of several architects of the period were built upon the work they did for railroads. Henry Hobson Richardson became widely known for his Romanesque depot designs for the Boston & Albany and other New England lines. Daniel H. Burnham's "City Beautiful" concept of Roman- or Beaux Arts-style buildings set in landscaped parks received popular acclaim with his Washington Union Station. Frank Furness produced numerous designs for stations on the Reading Lines, Pennsylvania, and Baltimore & Ohio, as did Frank Milburn for the Southern Railway. Other notable architects were actually on the staffs of railroad engineering departments. Among E. Francis Baldwin's many

Union Depot, Milwaukee, Wis.

ABOVE: Milwaukee Road's Everett Street Station in the railroad's namesake city was a classic Victorian structure of imposing proportions, in particular its looming tower. Soo Line also used the station for a time, hence the postcard's notation that this was a "union" depot. Part of the tower was removed after World War II, and in 1965 the depot was razed, replaced by a modern depot two blocks away. *Mike Schafer collection*

LEFT: Many larger city terminals were stub-end facilities whereby the station tracks, located under the train shed, ended at the "headhouse" of the depot, as illustrated by this view at Milwaukee Road's Minneapolis depot early in the 1960s. Soo Line and Rock Island were tenants at this depot, which was undergoing restoration as this book was being prepared. *Jim Boyd*

E. Francis Baldwin of Baltimore & Ohio's engineering department designed a number of memorable depot structures for the railroad in the later half of the nineteenth century. The depot at Oakland, Maryland, shown in 1979, incorporated the Queen Anne style that was all the rage in the 1880s. *Mike Schafer*

Resembling a stately university building more than a railroad station, the Chesapeake & Ohio depot/railroad office at Huntington, West Virginia, incorporated "Federal" styling that was a hallmark of a number of C&O structures. A statue of railroad magnate Collis P. Huntington, father of the C&O, guards the depot in this 1969 view. *Mike Schafer*

buildings for the B&O are several depots which exist today. Arguably, the finest of these are at Point of Rocks (Gothic Revival, 1875) and Oakland (Queen Anne, 1883), Maryland, the former of which still sees regular passenger-train service.

Some styles, building materials, and even colors came to be associated with certain railroads or parts of the country. Wood-frame depots were popular throughout the rural South on roads such as the Atlantic Coast Line. Mission-style structures of stucco, terra cotta, and tile were widely used in the Spanish-influenced West, particularly along the Southern Pacific and Santa Fe. Mediterranean Revival buildings with light-colored stucco walls and covered open-air waiting rooms became popular on Florida's railroads in the 1920s. Where stone and brick were readily available, such as the East and Midwest, they became the depot building materials of choice, especially for urban and suburban stations on roads like New York Central. Of them all, the Eastern railroads probably had the greatest variety of depot designs.

Although various track and platform layouts were tried in the early days of railroading, particularly in Europe, three basic designs quickly emerged as meeting the needs in most situations.

The "head" or "stub-end" station is generally configured with tracks and adjacent platforms running perpendicular to, and ending at, a head-building housing a concourse, waiting rooms, ticket office, and related facilities. This design became popular for large terminals and boasts the advantages of generally requiring less land area than through stations and permitting passengers to reach their trains without having to cross tracks.

In the through- or side-station layout, the principal tracks extend through the facility allowing a train to continue its run without having to reverse direction. The two-sided version has platforms on both sides of the tracks and is frequently used on routes of two tracks or greater. More economical, and far more common, is the single-sided through station with a platform abutting only one side of the track(s). The principal advantages of the through station are the relative ease of train movements and, frequently, a shorter and less congested walk to and from trainside for the passenger.

Along many railroad routes, especially lightly trafficked branch lines, depot design and construction reached its zenith at the end of the nineteenth century. The loss of local short-haul passenger, mail, and express business to electric interurban railways, plus the growing availability of the household telephone as a substitute for the depot's telegraph service, lessened the importance of hundreds of small stations in their communities. The advent of the automobile, and the improvements in streets and highways that soon followed, simply accelerated this trend in the years leading up to and following World War I.

Although the small-town depot may have begun fading as the focal point of community life,

the large terminals in the nation's leading cities were becoming virtual cities unto themselves. Passenger traffic between major cities and from expanding suburbs to urban centers was still increasing. This, plus the relative prosperity of the railroads at the turn of the century, spurred the planning of ever larger and grander depots in these areas. Also, the railroad consolidations of the late 1800s had produced some inflated management egos anxious to flaunt the power and success of their companies. At the same time, urban congestion and increasing conflict with street traffic at

Kansas City Union Station opened in 1914 to a 21-gun salute and a crowd of some 100,000 people—an indication of how important railroad stations once were to Americans. Designed by Jarvis Hunt of Chicago, the Beaux Arts Classical structure over the years served Santa Fe, Burlington, Rock Island, Missouri Pacific, Kansas City Southern, Frisco, Wabash, Union Pacific, Chicago & Alton (later, Gulf, Mobile & Ohio), Chicago Great Western, Katy, and Milwaukee Road—undoubtedly a true union station! Amtrak continued to use the station after 1971 until deterioration rendered it closed. As this book first went to press, there was a movement under way to heavily restore the noble depot for new uses as well as possibly its intended use, as a train station. *Joe Welsh Collection*

grade crossings were leading to demands for railroad line relocations and the consolidation of operations at a "union station" serving all railroads in the area. Here was a golden opportunity for the leading architects and railroad civil engineers of the day to create monumental depots of extraordinary beauty and utility. Many rose to the occasion, only to have the lasting significance of their work undermined by the long decline in intercity rail

passenger traffic which began in the 1920s and was abated only in wartime.

The Chicago World's Columbian Exposition of 1893 had triggered interest in Daniel H. Burnham's vision of the City Beautiful with its vaulted Roman and Beaux Arts structures in a spacious parklike setting. This seemed well suited to the idea of depots as urban monuments and by the second decade of the twentieth century had largely replaced the Victorian designs previously favored for urban depots such as St. Louis Union Station. Kansas City Union Station and Washington Union Station are fine and still-existing examples of railroad depots as monuments.

While no two of these massive edifices were identical, most included these basic components: A main waiting room, with one or more subsidiary waiting rooms, rest rooms and toilets; a ticket office, baggage room, and various services for the traveler; a concourse for assembling passengers at gates preparatory to boarding trains; track gates and platforms under a shed; and the layout of track comprising the entry/exit "throat" of the terminal.

The principle design objectives were to accommodate recurring peak loads; expedite outbound passenger movement from the building's entrance to the ticket office, baggage room, waiting room and/or concourse track gates, in that order; and separate inbound from outbound, and commuter from intercity passenger flows.

Ideally, the main waiting room was situated adjacent to the line of flow of departing long-distance passengers, for they were more likely to use it than arriving passengers or commuters. The room was usually impressive in scale and decor. Until

TRAIN SHED, LA SALLE STREET STATION, CHICAGO

LEFT: To shelter passengers from the elements, major city terminals often incorporated huge train sheds which themselves were sometimes architectural wonders. The train shed at Chicago's La Salle Street Station, opened in 1903, warranted placement on postcards of the era. The shed was later torn down and replaced with individual platform canopies. The head house in the distance housed offices above the cramped waiting room and was itself torn down in the 1980s. Interestingly, La Salle Street Station has appeared in two well-known movies with two famous movie stars, with Cary Grant in Alfred Hitchcock's famous "North by Northwest" and—with actor Robert Redford—"The Sting." *Mike Schafer Collection.*

BELOW: At first glance what appears to be a cathedral is in fact the elegant interior of Amtrak's San Antonio depot, built for the Missouri Pacific. Stained-glass windows and "starlight" ceiling lights enhance the elegance of the structure, photographed in July 1996. *Tom Kline*

ABOVE: Chicago Union Station's interesting iron-and-glass platform canopies protect Metra and Amtrak passengers from Windy City elements. Such canopies became favored over train sheds. *Mike Schafer*

RIGHT: A short distance north of Chicago Union Station stands what some have termed a "giant 1930s-style radio." Such is the new pseudo Art Deco-styled Northwestern [sic] Atrium Center, which replaced the headhouse of North Western Terminal in the 1980s. *Mike Schafer*

terminals built in the twentieth century, there was generally another, smaller waiting room for women and, occasionally, one for immigrants. In the South, separate facilities were provided for blacks. A smoking room, shoeshine stand, and barber shop were typically provided for men, and a retiring room for women, in both cases with adjoining toilets. A wide variety of other services were normally in easy reach of the waiting room, including the telegraph and telephone office, retail stores, restaurant, newsstand, red caps, Travelers Aid, and so forth. Behind the scenes, there were

mail and express facilities, utility rooms, offices and, in some instances, a public hotel and dormitory space for train crews.

A concourse generally separated the ticket office, baggage room, and waiting room from the tracks. This area often housed an information booth, newsstand, and lunch counter. Tracks entered the station through a "throat" of turnouts (switches) and crossovers and fanned out along platforms under a shed. The track and signal layout of the throat was critical to the safety, flexibility and reliability of train operations at the terminal.

The construction of massive train sheds of glass framed in iron arching over a wide expanse of tracks and platforms had its genesis in Europe following the popular acceptance of this design in a 1891 London exhibition hall called the Crystal Palace. Although highly favored by architects striving for impressive, well-lit open space, these sheds were costly to build, virtually impossible to adequately ventilate and clear of engine exhaust, and difficult to clean.

Text continued on page 144

137

A Depot Sampler

Five major U.S. passenger terminals deserve special mention. All still exist and all still at least in part serve rail passengers. One facility—Pennsylvania Station—has undergone draconian decimation while two others— Chicago Union and Cincinnati Union—have see drastic, though thankfully partial, alterations. However, in all cases there has been either a happy ending to the story or an interesting twist that will result in a revival.

PENNSYLVANIA STATION, NEW YORK CITY

It is not surprising that the nation's leading metropolis has had some of its finest railroad terminals, the Pennsylvania Station of 1910 being among them. The demolition of its depot building beginning in 1963 was one of the country's most regrettable architectural losses.

The building of Pennsylvania Station was an integral part of a complex plan by Pennsylvania Railroad president Alexander Cassatt to bring his tracks from New Jersey under the Hudson River into Manhattan and proceed beneath the East River to Long Island City to link up with the Long Island Rail Road, a road controlled by the Pennsylvania. Cassatt also envisioned through service to New England via the New York Connecting Railroad, a line to be jointly owned with the New York, New Haven & Hartford Railroad for the

Likened to Berlin's Brandenburg Gate, the imposing edifice of New York City's Pennsylvania Station—Pennsylvania Railroad's principal Eastern terminal—stretched for hundreds of feet and encompassed a whole city block in midtown Manhattan. PRR advertised the station, shown in the 1930s, as the "gateway to America." *A. F. Sozio, Joe Welsh Collection*

purpose of bridging Hell Gate, a waterway to the east of Manhattan. It was a dream made possible by turn-of-the-century advances in railroad electrification and tunnel construction. For his Manhattan terminal, Cassatt chose a Roman-influenced Beaux Arts structure designed by Charles F. McKim of the prestigious firm of McKim, Mead & White—one truly monumental in style and scale—to sit atop the 21-track layout of America's largest through station.

A colonnade vestibule greeted passengers at the main entrance on

7th Avenue. After a walk along an arcade flanked by upscale stores (the length of which becoming a source of frequent complaint), one descended a grand marble staircase into the General Waiting Room, a space modeled after the the Roman baths at Caracalla. Here, passengers stood—there were no benches—among Corinthian columns and travertine walls extending six stories high to a vaulted and coffered ceiling. Candelabra-topped lampposts and clerestory windows provided lighting.

Bench seating could be found in two subsidiary waiting rooms; one for men, the other for women. The ticket office, baggage and parcel room, restaurants, telephones and telegraph facilities and rest rooms fronted on the waiting rooms. Beyond stood the concourse and train shed enclosed in soaring canopies of steel and glass. Stairways descended to 11 platforms.

Although all tracks were on one level, Long Island Rail Road customers used a concourse, waiting room, and ticketing facility located below the

The roof of the majestic waiting room of the original Pennsylvania Station in Manhattan was over 150 feet high. In its new incarnation, Penn Station is located entirely underground. As the twentieth century drew to a close, a new plan called for Amtrak to move into the nearby vacated United States Post Office, which features architecture and spaciousness similar to the original Pennsylvania Station. The grandeur of the former Pennsylvania Station may indeed return. *A. F. Sozio, Joe Welsh collection*

main concourse. This had the advantage of separating the pedestrian flows of commuter and intercity services. Likewise, since all platforms had access to both levels, arriving intercity passengers could be routed away from travelers boarding trains.

Declining long-distance travel and general financial problems prompted the Pennsylvania to take measures to increase revenue and decrease costs. In the 1950s a modernistic, semicircular ticket counter was installed, a structure, critics claimed was in conflict with the station's classical decor. Retail vendors and advertising displays invaded open spaces. Far more damaging, however, was the sale in the early 1960s of air rights for the construction of a new Madison Square Garden arena and the subsequent demolishing of the depot structure above ground level. Currently, Amtrak's depot facilities at the site can most charitably be described as uninspiring and congested.

GRAND CENTRAL TERMINAL, NEW YORK CITY

Sharing honors with Pennsylvania Station as one of New York's two great depots of this century, Grand Central Terminal, although shorn of its once-heralded long-distance trains, still functions today as a busy commuter station. Opened for service in 1912, this was actually New York Central's second depot of that name at 42nd Street and Park Avenue. Rail traffic growth, steam engine smoke and noise, and grade crossing congestion had rendered the 1871-built and 1899-enlarged Grand Central Depot obsolete. Legislation in 1903 requiring electrification of train operations into Grand Central put additional pressure on the railroad. Furthermore, large tracts of valuable urban real estate were being consumed by railroad yards. Together, these factors led to the decade-long planning and construction of an electrified line below street level and a new Grand Central Terminal. It was a monumental structure of granite and limestone, in the Beaux Arts style, sitting as a head house at the end of two levels of tracks tunneling beneath now-ritzy Park Avenue. The New Haven Railroad, entering the city over Central's tracks from Woodlawn in the Bronx, was a tenant.

The focal point of Grand Central has always been its concourse, a spacious room with a floor of Tennessee marble and walls of Botticino marble and buff-tinted stone rising 125 feet to a vaulted turquoise blue ceiling depicting stars and constellations. Natural light enters through tall, arched windows. In the center stands an octagonal information booth topped by four clock faces. Here, New Yorkers have been "meeting under the clock" for more than 80 years. The separate ticket windows of NYC and New Haven fronted on the concourse.

Off to one side of the concourse, and out of the flow of most pedestrian traffic, was a large waiting room with a 50-foot ceiling from which were suspended bronze chandeliers. On the opposite side of the concourse from the waiting room were track gates leading to the 29 platforms and 42 tracks on the upper level. From these tracks departed trains such as the Central's *20th Century Limited* and

Empire State Express and New Haven's *Yankee Clipper* and *Merchants Limited*.

A second concourse located below the main level and reached by ramps and stairs opened to gates serving the 17 platforms and 25 tracks on the lower level devoted exclusively to suburban commuter services.

Virtually a city within itself, the Grand Central complex included

hotels, restaurants, theaters, and a wide assortment of retail shops. Still among its most famous eateries is the Oyster Bar on the ramp between upper and lower levels. Although it has undergone many changes over the years, including construction of a 59-story office building adjacent to it, Grand Central Terminal retains its status as one of America's greatest

railroad stations. Preservation of the famous depot was championed by the late Jackie (Kennedy) Onassis, who almost single-handedly began a movement thwarting proposals to demolish the depot, replace it with an air-rights skyscraper, and render the concourse to nothing more than a mundane pedestrian way for commuters. In 1998, the Metropolitan Transportation Authority, who leases

the building from Penn Central Corporation, completed a major restoration of the facility.

CHICAGO UNION STATION

A joint venture of the Pennsylvania Railroad, Chicago, Milwaukee, St Paul & Pacific, and the Chicago, Burlington & Quincy, the Beaux Arts-style terminal opened in 1925. Basically a double

stub-end facility, but with limited capability for through operation, the station was approached from the south by the Pennsylvania, Burlington, and tenant Chicago & Alton (later absorbed by Gulf Mobile & Ohio).

Designed by the firm of Graham, Anderson, Probst & White, successor to the late Daniel H. Burnham's firm, the colonnade facade of the head house, and skylit waiting room with its ornate interior columns, sculptural figures, and vaulted ceiling, mirrored the work of Burnham as well as the new Manhattan station of its principal owner, the Pennsylvania. Acknowledging the growing importance of automobile access, U-shaped internal driveways facilitated the loading and unloading of passengers. The head house, which contains a lofty waiting room and eight-story office complex (originally intended to be many stories taller) was separate from, but connected via a passageway under Canal Street to, the concourse building.

Having long been a commuter station as well as handling intercity trains, Union Station has fared relatively well during the decline in long-distance rail patronage. Nevertheless, the beautiful concourse structure was razed in 1969 for an unaesthetic air-rights development, significantly impeding passenger movement to and from the track

THE GRAND CENTRAL TERMINAL SHOWING HOTEL COMMODORE, YALE CLUB, AND BILTMORE HOTEL.

NEW YORK CITY.

Grand Central Terminal as it appeared in the 1920s. The depot remains fully intact, and following major interior and exterior restoration work in the late 1990s, it looks better than ever. The surrounding scene has since changed, however, as new skyscrapers went up on land surrounding GCT, dwarfing the world-famous structure. *Mike Schafer collection.*

Chicago Union Station as it appeared in 1969 shortly before the concourse building (forward building) was razed. The large office/waiting room building in the background remains, but the concourse area is now covered by a non-architecturally significant office building. The view looks northwesterly, with the Chicago River in the foreground. Some of the track area can be seen as well as the tops of most of the south-side platform canopies (see page 137). *Mike Schafer*

platforms. Amtrak, the station's current owner, has tried to make the best of the situation by recently refurbishing the public areas and improving pedestrian flows for its own passengers and Metra's commuters.

ST. LOUIS UNION STATION

Serving as an east-west gateway city second only to Chicago, it is understandable that St. Louis' railroads would build a Union Station worthy of that role. The 1894 castle-like Victorian head house design by Theodore C. Link and 600-foot wide balloon train shed (page 40) by civil engineer George H. Pegram remain to this day

one of the largest and finest examples of the stub-end urban terminal. Unfortunately, instead of being a train station, it now functions as a hotel and shopping mall, although some of the tracks have been retained for railroad displays and the occasional visit of an excursion train.

Viewed from the front of the head house, the dominant exterior feature was a 230-foot clock tower which also stored water for the sprinkler system and housed the terminal's ventilating system. Entry to the second floor of the head house brought you into the Grand Hall with its ornate vaulted ceiling and huge chandelier. Off the

Grand Hall were the women's waiting room, men's smoking room, formal dining rooms, and a wing housing the Terminal Hotel. Below, on the first floor, were the general waiting room, ticket office, lunch room, shops, and a post office. This area opened onto the concourse, a 606-foot long expanse called The Midway. Gates to more than 30 (later 42) tracks stretched along The Midway.

Reaching to a maximum height of 75 feet, an inverted arch balloon shed extended over three-and-a-half miles worth of tracks and an area of nearly ten acres. The original 630-foot long shed was lengthened to 810 feet in

1903. Utilizing a unique double wye-and-crossing track layout at the throat of the station, all trains backed in. This had the advantage of keeping locomotive exhaust outside the shed.

Union Station has undergone numerous changes over the years, but none so debilitating as the erosion of train traffic. Having hit its peacetime peak in 1921 with an average of 269 trains arriving or departing a day, service declined to just four arrivals and four departures daily with Amtrak's takeover of intercity rail passenger operations in May 1971. Remarkably, the station had never seen any significant amount of commuter

St. Louis Union Station stands majestically along Market Street south of the downtown area; this 1986 view looks westward. Since its transformation into a hotel/mall complex, Union Station has become one of the top attractions of downtown St. Louis. The addition of a light-rail line serving the complex as well as other downtown sites has further spurred patronage at Union Station, where crowds gather for shopping or lunch or to view the historical displays that show Union Station when it was one of the nation's leading rail passenger terminals. *Mike Schafer*

service. Finally, Amtrak pulled out in 1978, prompting a renewal of efforts to rehabilitate the facility for an adaptive use. In 1985, the headhouse and former Terminal Hotel reopened as a hotel, utilizing the Grand Hall as its lobby. A shopping mall occupies The Midway and a portion of the train shed, which has been walled in with glass to keep weather out. The former Railway Express building south of the train shed now serves as a theater, and the nearby Railroad YMCA has been beautifully rebuilt as a Drury Inn hotel.

CINCINNATI UNION TERMINAL

Although Cincinnati has always been a major transportation gateway between the North and the South, its railroads took a long time in consolidating their various passenger stations in the city. Finally, in 1927, just as rail passenger traffic was starting its decline, the Pennsylvania, Baltimore & Ohio, Chesapeake & Ohio, Norfolk & Western, Louisville & Nashville, New York Central's Big Four, and Southern's Cincinnati, New Orleans & Texas Pacific agreed to form the Cincinnati Union Terminal Company to build a union station. The resulting complex of station structures, maintenance facilities and yards, occupying nearly 300 acres of land more than a mile from downtown, entered service in 1933. Although designed as a through station, most of the trains using the station originated or terminated in Cincinnati.

Behind a landscaped elevated plaza rose a semispherical dome with an entrance portal of limestone and marble on which hung a 20-foot wide clock with neon red hands. Through a series of circular ramps, including one for buses and taxis, vehicle flow to the entrance or underground parking garage was handled remarkably well. There were even provisions for a transit line and airplane runway.

The moderne, streamline styling of the exterior was carried inside the soaring rotunda with more hints of Art Deco in curved surfaces and the use of aluminum, polished steels, chrome, and exotic woods. Around this spacious semicircular waiting room were arranged the ticket office, restrooms, newsstand, theater, restaurant, and shops. Above these were stunning mosaic murals by Winold Reiss depicting the development of Cincinnati and events in American history. In the center of the room was a round information booth and settees.

An additional 14 Reiss mosaics decorated the train concourse which bridged the tracks. A semicircle of seats occupied the space in front of each gate where a ramp descended to the platform. The platforms were protected with traditional umbrella canopies.

CUT was designed to handle 216 trains a day. Except during World War II, it never came close to its capacity. Lacking any suburban services, the fortunes of the terminal paralleled the downward slide of the long-distance passenger train. Amtrak moved to another location in 1972, following which most of the concourse was removed to accommodate expansion of Southern's intermodal yard. Most of the Reiss mosaics were moved to the regional airport. Following the failure of a mall development in the rotunda, a museum center was established. Various other sections of the building are available for rent for wedding receptions, dinner parties, and even railfan-related gatherings. Amtrak returned in 1991 with the service of just three trains a week in each direction.

LOS ANGELES UNION PASSENGER TERMINAL

Despite recognition decades earlier of the need for a new union station, it was not until 1939 that the doors of Los

Sprawling LAUPT is seen in all its glory in this memorable time exposure from a night in the 1950s. *Robert O. Hale, M. D. McCarter collection*

Angeles Union Passenger Terminal opened. A joint venture of the Santa Fe, Southern Pacific, and Union Pacific railroads, the roads' architects adopted a design combining Southern California's Spanish heritage with then-popular Art Deco styles. In a nod to Californians' growing attachment to the automobile, the design provided for easy vehicle access and plenty of parking.

The head house, located on the west side of the stub-end tracks, was constructed of steel clad in concrete.

Entry from the street was through a 50-foot arch decorated with colorful mosaic tiles and patterned glass. The foyer, flanked by a ticketing concourse and open-air arcade, led to a spacious waiting room of carved woods and ceiling beams, massive leather settees, marble, travertine, and mosaics. The room was lit by large chandeliers and tall windows, and its side doors opened to landscaped patios. The complex of Fred Harvey restaurants, stores, and barber shop

was decorated by the firm's highly regarded interior designer, Mary Colter. Beyond the waiting room, at the track end of the building, was a concourse with gates leading to the arrival and departure lobby and a tunnel under the tracks with ramps rising to the platforms above.

Interestingly, LAUPT appeared as the centerpieced of a movie, "Union Station," filmed shortly after the station opened. In the movie, the depot portrayed a major Chicago terminal. Since then, LAUPT has

made numerous cameo appearances in TV shows and movies.

From the beginning, LAUPT catered almost exclusively to the intercity traveler. Following the surge during World War II, passenger traffic through the terminal declined steadily. Within the last few years, however, there has been a new injection of Amtrak, subway, trolley, and Metrolink commuter business, accompanied by extensive refurbishing of the station.

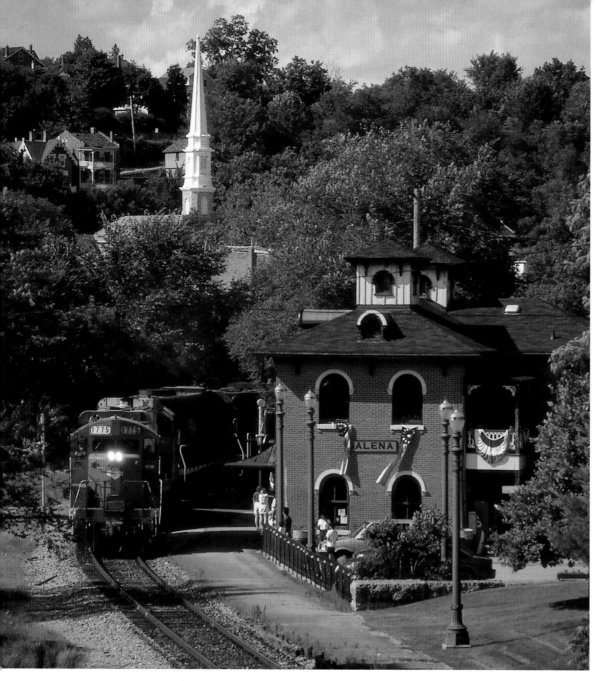

Restoration has become a battle cry in America, where "old" was once "out." With citizens across the country becoming more historically aware, numerous railroad depots have been spared the wrecker's ball, even if they no longer function in their original intended use. Shown in 1996, the Illinois Central depot in Galena, Illinois, now serves as that city's Chamber of Commerce and tourist center, although excursion trains occasionally still disgorge passengers here. *Mike Schafer*

Continued from page 137

By the second decade of the twentieth century, railroad civil engineers were exercising greater control over the track and platform areas, while the architects retained their influence with the head house waiting rooms, offices, and concourse as well as any landscaping. Soon, the towering balloon sheds of the Victorian era were giving way to more practical designs. Among these was the low-standing Bush shed, first introduced in 1906 at the Hoboken, New Jersey, terminal of the Delaware, Lackawanna & Western. Named for its designer, Lincoln Bush, one of Lackawanna's civil engineers, it incorporated skylights framed in steel extending over both the platforms and tracks, but with a slotted opening over each track center to vent locomotive stack exhaust. The design was adapted for use

in numerous cities. However, it was to be the "butterfly" or "umbrella" style canopy, supported by platform-mounted poles, that became the favored method of protecting passengers and cargo from the elements when loading or unloading trains.

DECLINE

Rail passenger traffic peaked in 1921 and commenced a downward slide interrupted only in wartime. Not surprisingly, depot construction also slowed, with new facilities generally being built to replace damaged or economically obsolete structures, or in response to line relocation or grade separation projects and consolidations into union stations. Buffalo Central Terminal (1930), Cincinnati Union Terminal (1933), Philadelphia's 30th Street Station (1933), Los Angeles Union Passenger Terminal (1939), Toledo Central Union Terminal (1950), and New Orleans Union Terminal (1954) were among the principal depots built in the face of erosion in railroad patronage.

Although the dramatic decline in long-distance rail passenger service obsoleted some of these and many other downtown terminals before their time, a few are enjoying a revival as a result of new or expanded rail transit or commuter services. At Los Angeles Union Passenger Terminal, for example, this has produced train and passenger volumes that rival its best years of the past.

In other than local suburban commuter districts and Amtrak's urban corridors, community depots have been hard hit by the loss of passenger traffic. However, this has not been the only factor rendering most of them obsolete. The loss of Railway Express Agency business and most mail traffic to highway and air transport in the late 1960s cut deeply into the activities of the typical small-town depot. Meanwhile, there had been a revolution in railroad freight transportation as the less-than-carload (LCL) shipments, historically handled at local depots, were now moving more efficiently in intermodal truck-on-flatcar piggyback service from centralized terminals—or directly over the highway. As telephone, two-way radio, and other electronic communications tools were perfected, the railroad's and public's reliance on the telegraph ended. Dispatchers could now communicate directly with train crews without the need for operator intervention at stations along the line.

Whereas for more than a hundred years the depot agent had been the railroad's regular contact with freight customers as salesman, troubleshooter, and preparer of shipping documents, advances in computer and communications technology have permitted centralization of these functions, with substantial savings in labor costs.

By the 1970s, the historic roles of the local railroad depot had largely disappeared except in the few instances where Amtrak or commuter trains still stopped. Consequently, railroads have demolished thousands of vacant depots, converted some for alternative railroad purposes, and sold others for such varied uses as private homes, restaurants, barber shops, libraries, museums, and commercial or civic offices. Still others stand today only through the efforts of community leaders and historic preservationists wanting to save significant examples of this piece of the nation's industrial and cultural heritage.

PRESERVATION

At the beginning of this century there were approximately 80,000 railroad depots dotting the American landscape. At the close of the twentieth century there were somewhat over 10,000. The best hope for most of these is the growing interest, emanating mainly from the local level, in saving some of these architectural gems and momentos of an institution once deemed essential to the commercial and social well-being of many communities. Some observers trace this interest to the public outcry following the 1963 demolition of the magnificent depot structure of New York's Pennsylvania Station and various threats to its midtown neighbor, Grand Central Terminal. Certainly, the National Historic Preservation Act of 1966 and subsequent legislation, including the Intermodal Surface Transportation Efficiency Act (ISTEA) of 1991, have encouraged and assisted these efforts by providing a means for protecting and financing the rehabilitation of these structures. Today, there are numerous examples of superb restoration projects, including many stations along Amtrak's Northeast Corridor as well as in cities and small towns across the country. Hopefully, these will inspire similar undertakings in the future.

Washington Union Station provides a stunning example of how "adaptive reuse" can restore life and vigor to depots, even if they are still serving passengers. Once basically a huge empty area designed for milling crowds waiting for train gates to open, Union Station's concourse section is shown in 1988 shortly after the depot's revamping. Where in 1952 a runaway Pennsylvania Railroad passenger train crashed through the end of track and through the concourse floor into the basement, people now happily sample a wide variety of eateries and shops and purchase Amtrak and commuter-rail tickets. *Mike Schafer*

7 *The Railroad* Work Force

The Baltimore & Ohio Railroad distributed this admonition to the cooks and waiters aboard its dining cars:

"No matter how well a meal may be prepared and served, if the coffee is not well brewed it can very readily spoil the meal. When the brew has been held for two hours, around 25 percent of the flavor has disappeared. And at the end of three hours, the loss ranges from 30 percent to 50 percent. SEE THAT OUR GUESTS ARE SERVED THE FINEST CUP OF COFFEE POSSIBLE."

Complying with this instruction did not always guarantee customer satisfaction, however. At least one B&O dining-car crew found it had to bend the rule a bit to satisfy passengers aboard the road's streamliner, the *Cincinnatian*. The train's early morning departure from Baltimore en route to Washington, before continuing on to Cincinnati, made it popular with commuters heading for the nation's capital. Many congregated in the diner for breakfast and a cup of coffee. A recurring complaint was that the coffee was too weak. Nothing the crew did seemed to mollify the commuters until they began brewing the morning "eye-opener" pot upon the eastbound train's arrival in Baltimore the previous evening. The complaints of weak coffee stopped.

Although railroading is normally a highly disciplined business—even quasi-military in character—with codified rules and instructions born of more than a century and a half of experience, most railroaders succeed at what they do, in large measure, by their own wits.

At its peak, in the second decade of the twentieth century, the railroad industry employed over 1.7 million people, or about 4.5 percent of the nation's entire work force. The drama attending the building of America's railroads in the nine-

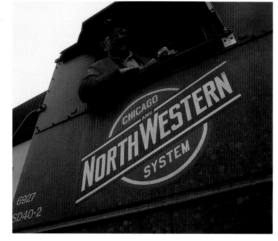

teenth century, and their pivotal roles in opening the frontier and in the defense of the nation, endowed the industry with a mystique of power and romance that had propelled railroaders into the national folklore of heroes and villains. Although women have long worked in the industry, especially during wartime, railroading has more typically been viewed as a man's world of hard labor, fast running, and high living. Yet for every Casey Jones (not a fictional being, by the way) at the throttle making up time with Illinois Central's "Cannonball," or Joseph "Steve" Broady doing 90 mph down White Oak Mountain with Southern's "Old 97," or moguls Vanderbilt, Gould, and Harriman scheming against each other and rival railroads, there have been thousands of unheralded men and woman handling the essential tasks of keeping the railroads running.

For many it has been hard and dirty work, often performed far from home at irregular hours and while exposed to extreme weather conditions and the hazards associated with heavy, moving equipment. More than a few have been severely or fatally injured on the job. But whether they toiled aboard trains, on the track, in repair shops, at depots and lonely signal towers along the route, or in administrative offices, there has always been a bond tying railroaders together as a family. As they

say, "It gets in your blood." For more than a century and a half, sons and daughters have been following in the footsteps of their railroading parents. Notorious as gossips, braggarts, and complainers, railroaders remain fiercely loyal to their "home" road, division, terminal, or shop when outsiders, especially other railroaders, dare to criticize.

More than 85 percent of all railroad workers belong to a labor union. Early to unionize—locomotive engineers were first, starting in 1863—railroad labor-management relations have often been contentious. Historically, each major job category, or "craft," was represented by a different union. By 1940, there were 21 railroad craft organizations. In recent years, several of these unions have merged. Through years of collective bargaining, railroaders have become among the best-paid workers in the nation. Union-negotiated work rules have enhanced on-the-job safety, as well as promoted job security. Unfortunately, the latter rules have sometimes impeded the industry's ability to compete with other modes of transport by imposing restrictions on the use of new technologies and operating practices.

Railroaders generally work in close-knit teams, or crews, of two to a dozen or more individuals, often with little on-scene supervision. However, even when working alone, communication between employees is essential for personal safety as well as the safe and efficient operation of trains. To understand the role of each major railroad craft, and its relationship to the rest of the team, it's helpful to review the typical railroad organization. A headquarters staff sets general policy and procedures for the railroad and centralizes the coordination of departmental field activities. It is in the field—out along the tracks, at stations and terminals, and in equipment maintenance shops—that most of the activity of the railroad takes place. On

FACING PAGE: A locomotive engineer on the Chicago & North Western. *Steve Smedley*

LEFT: Gulf, Mobile & Ohio's South Joliet, Illinois, yard, 1972. It takes people to run railroads. From the company president down to track laborers, every person plays an important role in railroading. *Doug Steurer*

147

large railroads, many of these field functions are organized by geographic territory, generally called a division, with each division typically made up of several hundred miles of track, two or more train crew terminals, and numerous stations, all under the management of a superintendent. Many railroaders relate their "seniority," or length of service, to the date they hired out on a specific division, terminal, or shop.

Railroad functions are broadly categorized as Operations, Traffic, or Administration. Operations includes activities of the Transportation, Mechanical and Engineering departments. Transportation has responsibility for safe and efficient station and train operations, including management of the car and locomotive fleet. The largest group of employees in the Transportation Department are train crews comprised of engineers, firemen, conductors and trainmen. Other Transportation jobs include dispatchers, station agents and operators, yardmasters and clerks.

The Mechanical Department inspects, repairs and sometimes even designs and constructs the railroad's rolling equipment, principally cars and locomotives. This has been the work of the car and locomotive inspector and other shop crafts such as carman, machinist, blacksmith, boilermaker, pipefitter and, increasingly as diesel-electric locomotives replaced steam engines, the electrician.

Until late in the twentieth century, railroading was a particularly labor-intensive endeavor with many tasks at hand. During the servicing of Katy Railroad's *Texas Special* at San Antonio in 1947, a man tosses ice to another worker to ice the diner's refrigeration system. *Phillip R. Hastings*

Three Illinois Central "hostlers"—people who move locomotives about an engine terminal for servicing—pose beside one of their steeds at IC's Paducah, Kentucky, facilities in 1957. *Howard Patrick*

The design, construction, inspection, and maintenance of fixed facilities such as track, bridges, signals and buildings falls to the Engineering Department. Trackmen, machine operators, signal maintainers, and carpenters are typical job categories in this department.

Packaging the railroad's services to meet the transportation needs of potential customers is the role of the Traffic sector with its specialists in marketing, pricing, and sales. Here, along with the local station agent, have been the principal contacts between the railroad and those who decide on which carrier to use for the movement of freight or passengers.

The Administrative organizations of the railroad include such diverse departments as Finance and Accounting, Law, Human Resources, and Public Relations. Most of these activities are performed at headquarters.

Since topping 1.7 million in 1916, railroad employment has tumbled to barely a quarter of a million today, even as the industry moves record amounts of freight. Reductions in train crew size were made possible by the shift from steam locomotives to diesels after World War II (eliminating many of the fireman's duties), electronic communications between crew members, and the reduction in local switching work. The

diesel locomotive also greatly reduced the manpower required for locomotive servicing and repair. Modern communications technology, including the railroad industry's widespread use of the computer, has simplified many tasks, such as accounting, and vastly reduced the labor required for others, including train dispatching and locomotive and rolling-stock fleet management.

Fortunately, the human and property carnage that characterized early railroading has been largely relegated to the history books and the nation's folklore. Through the combined forces of technology, union perseverance, government

A Illinois Central crewman tends to a hotbox that has halted the progress of a St. Louis–Chicago freight at Gibson City, Illinois, on an August day in 1960. *Howard Patrick*

THE LOCOMOTIVE ENGINEER AND FIREMAN

The aristocrat of railroading; honored in folklore as virile, fearless, and heroic, the locomotive engineer put in motion and kept under control the "iron horse," for almost a century the fastest machine on earth. He and his locomotive were the most visible and respected embodiments of railroading for the public and fellow railroaders, alike. In the lingo peculiar to railroading, his locomotive was a "hog" and he was the "hoghead" or "hogger."

Assisted by a fireman, the engineer marshaled the resources necessary to get a train across the railroad safely, efficiently, and on time. In the days of steam locomotives, they were judged by their immediate supervisor, the road foreman of engines, by their ability to stay on schedule with the least use of coal and water, and to keep stack exhaust clean. This meant maintaining the prescribed level of water in the boiler, mix of fuel and

regulatory intervention, management enlightenment, and changes in a workplace culture that once glorified risk-taking, railroading has finally become one of America's safest industries. Adoption of the automatic coupler and air brake in the latter half of the 19th century played a major role in increasing the life-expectancy of trainmen. Telegraph, telephone and radio communications and electronic signaling have enhanced the safety of train movements.

BELOW: At one time every American boy dreamed of sitting in the right-hand side of a locomotive cab in the position of engineer, in control of thousands of tons of locomotive heading up a thundering freight or fast passenger train. Union Pacific engineer Steve Lee is fulfilling that dream while working a steam-excursion train powered by UP Challenger locomotive No. 3985 in 1990.

RIGHT: In the steam era, the fireman played an instrumental, if back-breaking, role in locomotive operation. This fireman is doing his best to build an evenly hot fire in the firebox of a Shay locomotive on the Cass Scenic Railroad in 1989. *Both photos, Jim Boyd*

oxygen in the firebox, lubrication on moving parts, and steam and brake-line pressure. For as much as railroading was a science, its best practitioners were also artists at their craft. Engineers and firemen developed an intimacy with their locomotives, coming to know through sight, sound, and feel the idiosyncrasies of each. The experienced hogger's advice to the young engineer was "run your engine, don't let it run you." Enginemen also needed to know the physical characteristics of the route—the grades, curves, speed restrictions, scheduled stops—as well as the length, weight, and braking behavior of their train, and the amount of switching of cars to be done en route. Every day was different. And, of course, always present were the risks of obstructions on the track, broken driving rods, and other mechanical defects, and even a boiler explosion.

Through much of the nineteenth century, it was common for a locomotive to be assigned to a specific engineer, whose name might even be painted on the cab. Crews took great pride in their locomotives. By generally accepted protocol, the fireman performed routine maintenance tasks above the running board and wiped down the boiler jacket while the engineer lubricated and tended to the running gear below. Some engineers actually accompanied their locomotives to the servicing roundhouse or back shop to ensure that needed adjustments and repairs were made. Perhaps the

most personal relationship an engineer had with his locomotive was with its steam whistle, or "quill." Many an engine and its hogger had a trademark sound, a musical wail, derived from the design of the whistle and the way the engineer controlled steam entering the chambers.

Engineers were normally promoted from the ranks of experienced firemen who, in addition to their duties supplying water and fuel for maintaining steam pressure over the course of the run, shared responsibility with the engineer for watching signals, complying with rules and instructions, giving warnings with the bell and whistle, and monitoring engine and train performance.

As the railroad's influence on the American scene declined, and the electric and diesel-electric locomotive replaced steam in the middle of this century, the job descriptions, and even social status, of the locomotive crew changed as well. Many traditional duties of the fireman, along with much of the romance of railroading, vanished as steam locomotive fires were banked for the last time. Gone were the days when enginemen bonded with their favorite locomotives; the new motive power roamed the system. Electrics and diesels were safer, cleaner, easier, and less costly to operate and maintain. With complex electrical components now replacing the largely mechanical machinery of steam power, the engineer became less directly involved in daily maintenance activities.

THE CONDUCTOR

"Brains," "Captain," "Big Ox" . . . Nicknames, endearments or epithets, they have all been used to describe the railroad conductor. Although part of a team—the train crew—that also included a locomotive engineer and fireman, the conductor and his subordinate trainmen (brakemen, flagmen, switchmen, etc.) worked largely outdoors and physically removed from the engineer. Therefore, good communications and close coordination between all members of the crew were critical.

The conductor was responsible for the safe operation of his train and was the final authority among the crew members for its operation—

a position often contested by engineers in one of the longest-running feuds in railroading. Road conductors handled trains across the main lines and branches of the railroad, working under the generally "in absentia" supervision of a trainmaster and receiving their movement authority from a timetable and train dispatcher. They were governed by a book of operating rules and a myriad of other instructions.

A Southern Railway conductor chats with one of the few passengers riding the *Asheville Special* on a May day in 1975. *Mike Schafer*

A road conductor in passenger service once enjoyed a status in the popular culture second only to the locomotive engineer. Impressively uniformed, and with gold timepiece in hand, he guided passengers to their accommodations, performed the necessary safety inspections and tests, gave a "highball" to the engineer to proceed, collected tickets and fares, handled paperwork associated with the run, and looked after the safety and comfort of his passengers. As "captain" of the train, the conductor maintained discipline over all operating and service personnel aboard, including those of the Pullman and Railway Express companies. He directly supervised operating crew members in such jobs as assistant conductor, trainman, flagman, and baggageman. These positions assisted the conductor; the flagman being specifically

responsible for protection of the train against the approach of other trains when stopped, and the baggageman for handling the checked baggage, mail and express being transported in the baggage car.

Road freight conductors oversaw the safe and timely transport of cargo. A waybill accompanied each shipment describing its origin and destination, the route to be taken, the commodity involved and any special handling instructions. This information, along with other instructions, guided the conductor and his crew in the picking up and setting off of cars at stations or businesses en route.

THE BRAKEMAN

The brakeman had probably the most maligned job in railroading, both in verbal and physical abuse. Often a "boomer," roaming from railroad to railroad in search of work, he has been tagged with such unflattering nicknames as "Pinhead," "Shack Stinger," and "Scissor-Bill." The work of the brakeman has always been among the most dangerous in the industry. In fact, the title derives from its original role in controlling the speed of trains through the use of handbrakes on the cars. Brakemen generally ran along the tops of the moving equipment, jumping from car to car, to reach the brake wheels and "tie 'em down."

Coupling locomotives and cars during the early years of railroading was no less perilous. The link-and-pin-style coupler required the trainman to go between the equipment to make or break the connection. The results were predictable. A brakeman's "seniority" could be estimated from the number of fingers he was missing; his career prematurely ended by the loss of a limb; his life expectancy reduced to the shortest of all railroaders. Not until the late nineteenth century did the widespread use of air brakes and automatic couplers give the brakeman a fighting chance to survive long enough to be promoted to conductor.

The recent removal of the once-familiar caboose from the rear of most freight trains, along with today's widespread use of electronic communications, has greatly changed life and work on the road for train-service employees. Radio communication

Uniforms

The first American conductors and brakemen wore their own suits as uniforms. The only distinction was a leather strap with the word CONDUCTOR or BRAKEMAN spelled out worn on a silk top hat. Following the Civil War, uniforms became a combination of sorts of a Union Army uniform and a gentleman's suit. The garments generally followed the style of men's clothing of the times.

By 1900 the clothes were all made of a substantial wool blue cloth, the coat being a long frock or morning coat with buttons—even in the back—and worn with a regular vest and trousers. The cap was now taking on its classic shape. Essentially a cut-down version of the silk top hat,

the standard trainmen's hat had arrived.

By the mid 1910s, the coats had become shorter. With a high front, short and narrow lapels, and four buttons on the front, the classic trainman's uniform came into being. With as many as 21 total pockets in the coat vest and trousers, it remained the standard of railroading until the post-World War II era.

Some railroads streamlined the uniform to a tailored three-button coat with a military officer or "bus driver" cap. Others opted for a gray uniform. The last change

came in 1969-1970 when the Chicago & North Western and the Illinois Central both went to an unattractive olive green suit that resembled that of an elevator operator. Today there is one railroad, the SouthShore Line between Chicago and South Bend, Indiana, where the train crews still wear the four-button traditional uniform.

RIGHT: Row 1 (left to right): the Pullman Company hat used by its sleeping-car conductors; a traditional cap for the Northern Pacific, used until NP's 1970 merger into Burlington Northern.

Row 2: Erie Railroad trainman's hat, trimmed in silver (conductors wore gold trim); a Santa Fe hat, with AT&SF being first to use the military cap style.

Row 3: Kansas City Southern employed "Rebel Gray" uniforms and caps with the title embroidered on cap band; the cap of a CB&Q "collector," a trainman assigned to suburban or commuter service who assisted the conductor in ticket collection duties. Burlington's uniforms for 1956 were a shade lighter than navy blue. Uniform was worn with a maroon tie.

ABOVE: The crew posing here model the pre-1948 Santa Fe conductor (left, with gold trim) and brakeman (right, with silver trim)—classic uniforms, but was the heavy 14-ounce wool really the right thing for a tour of duty through the desert? *Both renderings, Mitchell A. Markovitz*

THE
FREIGHT
BRAKEMAN

There were usually two Brakemen on every freight train — one on the engine, the other on the caboose. Besides running, jumping, climbing, swinging and hopping they were always on the look-out for hot boxes (overheated wheel journals), defective brake riggings or anything else that could break down which often did.

The Brakemen were not only required to do the switching along their route but were called on to make minor, on-the-road repairs to most any part of the train.

between trainmen on the ground and the engineer has reduced the number of brakemen and switchmen needed for passing hand signals during switching operations.

THE DISPATCHER AND TELEGRAPH OPERATOR/AGENT

The dispatcher controls train and work equipment movements over the railroad, arranging meets between trains and issuing instructions (train orders) and messages regarding conditions affecting safety and efficient operation of the line. Where the workload requires the use of more than one dispatcher at a time, each is given responsibility for a segment of railroad, generally consisting of all or part of a division. Technological advances in communications greatly affected the size of territory a dispatcher could handle, as well as the means by which movement authority and other information was conveyed to train crews. For more than a century beginning in the mid-1850s, the principal ways of doing this were, first, by telegraph and later by telephone using telegraphers (operators) at on-line station depots and towers to relay orders and messages to trains. The dispatchers also instructed operators to set signals and align track switches for the desired routing of the trains. If the station handled passengers and cargo, the operator often served as ticket and freight agent, as well as telegrapher for sending and receiving commercial

155

ABOVE: The Conrail operator at Kanauga, Ohio, readies his train-order hoops for an impending northbound freight out of West Virginia bound for Columbus, Ohio. It's the spring of 1979, and many railroads still relied on operators—working closely with the dispatcher—to govern train movements. This operator has just received orders from a dispatcher in Corning, Ohio, has copied them onto the train-order tissues ("flimsies"), and is now tying them to the train-order hoops. As the train rolls past the station, the locomotive fireman will reach out to catch the upper hoop's train orders while the conductor in the caboose will snatch the lower ones. Not all train-order stations had the luxury of fixed train-order hoops. At many locations, the operator had to hold the hoops (page 159). If the crews somehow missed the hoop, the train would be required to stop to retrieve the orders. *Mike Schafer* RIGHT: A dispatcher on the Belt Railway of Chicago in 1995. CTC (Centralized Traffic Control) panels (rear in photo) were once commonly used to automatically and remotely set signals and passing-siding switches. They are being replaced by television screens and computers. *Brian Solomon*

messages for the public over lines of the railroad or Western Union.

It was to be expected that relations between dispatchers and train crews would often be strained. Crews, anxious to reach their destination and get the rest required before they could be called again, sometimes referred to the dispatcher as the "Detainer" or "Train Delayer." The dispatcher, trying to keep the railroad flowing efficiently, viewed an impatient conductor as a "Brainless Wonder."

Communications and signal enhancements of the last 50 years have virtually obsoleted the job of operator. Whereas at one time a train's routing and progress could be controlled and verified only when it reached and passed a lineside station manned by a telegrapher, today's dispatchers can be in direct and constant contact with train crews via radio. On many routes, they also maintain electronic control of signals and switches for authorizing and routing train movements. One by one, the "brass pounders," along with the signal towers and depots that once dotted the railroad landscape to shelter them, are falling victims to technology.

THE CARMAN

The carman is something of a jack-of-all-trades when it comes to keeping in running order the railroad's freight and passenger rolling stock. They are known in the language of the rails as "car knockers" or "tonks" because of their ever-present hammer used in checking wheels for the dull sound indicating a crack. Armed with gauges for determining equipment compliance with railroad and government standards, plus the tools unique to their craft, these Mechanical Department employees inspect, lubricate, and repair cars and test train airbrakes in the terminal preparatory to releasing a train to the Transportation Department for dispatching over the road. Other mechanical shop crafts ready the road's locomotives for service.

The principal focus of the carmen's attention has always been on a car's running gear; that is, its brakes, wheel and axle assemblies (trucks), and coupling mechanisms. The nature of this work has changed with advances in technology. While the reliability of most car components has improved, the quest for greater carrying capacity per car has often resulted in more complex mechanical systems and a requirement for better trained carmen. In years past, one of the most time-consuming functions of the carman was lubricating axle journal boxes, an activity which has been virtually eliminated with the almost total shift from friction to roller bearings. Although the overall carrying capacity of the nation's railcar fleet has been increasing, the trend toward larger and better utilized equipment has resulted in a steady decline in the number of cars in service and, therefore, fewer brakes, trucks, couplers, and such to inspect and repair. Consequently, the ranks of carmen have shrunk, but not the importance of their continuing role in the safe and efficient operation of trains.

THE TRACKMAN

The trackman has endured perhaps the hardest labor of any railroader. The rails, crossties, tie plates, spikes, fastenings and ballast that comprise the track structure are in continual need of adjustment, repair, or renewal. Historically, these were primarily manual tasks performed by laborers with strong backs and hardened muscles using simple tools of the trade such as the spike maul, pick axe, spike remover, lining bar, and tie tongs. These trackmen were organized into crews or gangs of up to a dozen or more members and assigned to work a specific section of railroad line, perhaps 20 miles in length, under the direction of a section foreman. Two or more adjacent sections were managed by a track supervisor, or roadmaster, who reported to the division engineer.

One common job on the track was to replace and line rails, a heavy task requiring the coordinated efforts of several trackmen moving the rail in unison, often to rhythmic chants or songs. This and other activities of the section gangs requiring choreographed action which gave rise to the appellation "gandy dancer" for this craft.

Most trackwork was performed under traffic, with passing trains posing a serious threat to trackmen on the right-of-way. The workers relied heavily upon the dispatcher to advise train crews of their presence on the track and to control train movements through the area. Trackmen not only worked on the track, but when away from home, they

Ruth Trueblood Eckes, Railroad Telegrapher

World War II brought job opportunities for women on the railroad and one who answered the call was Ruth Trueblood. Responding to an ad in the local paper, this young lady signed on with the railroad for trainees' wages of 30 cents per hour and a promise of a job. Ruth was schooled by the Northern Pacific Railway as a telegraph operator in Morse key and the Philips code, a shorthand version of Morse preferable for use in copying out long messages. At the time, operators filled a key position on the railroad, relaying train orders and information which kept the trains running safely. On busy main lines, the telegraph supplemented the telephone, but on branch lines the telegraph was often the only form of communication available to the railroad. Operators in remote areas lived next to their job, usually in railroad-provided facilities along the line.

Ruth remembers, "I went right to work. This was wartime and the railroads needed bodies desperately to keep the trains moving. The volume of business was incredible, and we moved it all without computers or modern traffic control using just train orders and the telephone or telegraph. I broke in at McCarver Street Station in Tacoma, Washington, a very busy little station on the double-track main line to Portland carrying NP, GN, and UP traffic. I handled train orders and messages and inspected all trains for hotboxes [overheated journals] and dragging equipment seven days a week. We had a novel method of alerting the crews to hotboxes: If the hotbox was near the head end, we'd rub our head and hold our nose; if it was mid train we'd rub our stomach and hold our nose; if it was at the rear, well you can guess what we'd rub!"

Ruth also worked a series of jobs at remote Cascade Range sites on the NP in western Washington State, both on the main line over Stampede Pass and on various branch lines.

Although the railroad spent a significant amount of time training its telegraph operators, it wasted no time explaining the "perks" of living out on the railroad. There were none. Railroaders slept in rough accommodations, ate modest food, and made do with what was available. Ruth recalled, "My first 'solo' telegraph operator's job was at Kanasket, Washington, a remote junction on the main line with the Enumclaw branch. When I arrived I learned that the depot had burned to the ground and that the railroad telegrapher was expected to work out of a converted "outfit" car [a boxcar from work-train service]. The living accommodations were worse—an ancient one-room shack. From there I moved on to Eagle Gorge where, lacking an ice box, I kept the food cold by slinging it in a box under a mountain waterfall."

A job at busy Easton, Washington, on the NP main line brought home the responsibilities and dangers of working around a railroad. Ruth reminisced, "You didn't dare fall asleep on the job. There were too many trains for that. The *North Coast Limited*, No. 2 [Northern Pacific's premier passenger train], would come off the mountain late at night and start going like gangbusters, and I'd have to hoop his orders up to him with copies for the engineer and conductor."

"To hoop up train orders you tied the paper order to a string suspended between what looked like the two legs of a large wishbone at the end of a long handle. Then you dug in your feet about two feet from the track, buttoned up your coat tight so it wouldn't get caught on the engine (we were cautioned against wearing skirts for the same reason), and braced yourself, holding the first hoop up high for the fireman who'd snatch the string and the orders. The headlight of the approaching train was so bright you couldn't see anything behind it. It just kept getting bigger and bigger and the onrushing train sounded like a big wind coming at you—it was eerie, spine tingling! The steam engine would rush by, its wheels trying to suck you in. After the fireman had grabbed the orders, you'd have to bend down quickly, grab a mail bag to throw into the lighted door of the Railway Post Office car (while dodging the mail bag the postal clerks threw out the door), then hold up a second hoop so the conductor could grab his orders. Then she'd be gone, picking up speed around the bend to the east. You'd stand and shake awhile after doing it. I still get chills just thinking about it!"

After a busy 12-year career on the railroad, Ruth left the railroad in 1956 marrying (a railroader, of course; Ed Eckes, a machinist for NP) and settling in Auburn, Washington, to raise a family.

"Hooping up" train orders "on the fly" took dexterity and sometime more than a little courage. The need for both is illustrated in this early 1960s scene at Nelson, Illinois, as a white-hatted operator hands up orders to the fireman of an eastbound Chicago & North Western freight moving nonstop. *Jim Boyd*

often lived in makeshift camps along the right-of-way, or aboard railcars outfitted with kitchen and dormitory facilities. Regardless of where they rested, trackmen had to be prepared to respond on short notice to accidents and weather conditions that had damaged track.

Over time, the introduction of labor-saving machinery and the availability of better transportation to work sites has permitted larger sections of line to be covered by fewer trackmen. Today many track maintenance functions are performed by highly mechanized gangs with skilled machine operators traveling over a division, region, or even the entire system.

PASSENGER TRAIN ON-BOARD SERVICE CREWS

For the century preceding the 1950s, railroads dominated the commercial transportation of passengers. America's eagerness to travel ever-faster and with increasing comfort, plus often intense competition between railroads for this business, prompted constant service improvements. Nowhere was this more evident than in the amenities aboard intercity trains, particularly those operating overnight between major points.

The on-board dining and sleeping-car accommodations introduced in the 1860s were immediately popular and led to a wide array of additional services catering to businessmen, wealthy vacationers, the elderly, women with children, and, eventually, the whole spectrum of travelers.

By the twentieth century, service personnel aboard the nation's finest trains had self-describing titles such as dining-car steward, chef-cook, waiter, Pullman conductor, sleeping-car porter, lounge attendant, chair-car attendant; passenger representative, train secretary, and stewardess-nurse.

In common with most railroad practice through this period, these jobs were usually segregated by gender and race. The vast majority were the domain of males. Stewards, passenger representatives, secretaries, barbers, stewardess-nurses and Pullman conductors generally were white, while the remainder of the dining car, lounge, sleeper and chair car staff were people of color. For a period in this century, Filipino men were frequently employed as Pullman lounge-car attendants. Although there were strong bonds of comradeship among service crew members, they often formed along racial lines.

A hierarchy existed on the trains, perhaps best illustrated by the dining car. The steward was the boss, with responsibilities for any menu changes, ordering and inventorying supplies, greeting and seating passengers, supervising the efficient operation of the car, collecting payment for meals, and preparing the car's accounts. The typical diner had between 36 and 48 seats. The kitchen staff, under the direction of the chef-cook, might have two to four cooks, each with specific

A Santa Fe trackman clears the switches at East Peoria following a central Illinois snowstorm in 1985. *Steve Smedley*

meal preparation. Three to six waiters covered the dining room, plus duties such as pantryman (plating salads, etc.) and room service. Dining-car protocol generally found the waiter with greatest seniority working in the pantry, while the youngest was assigned to tables farthest from the kitchen.

Life on the road often meant long hours on duty, relieved by periods of fitful sleep in dormitory-like quarters. As with all jobs dealing with the public, the greatest challenge was working by the adage, "The customer is always right." However, it was often the most outrageous or aggravating customer who became the subject of stories told, enjoyed, exaggerated upon, and retold again and again around the railroad.

Since 1971, when it assumed responsibility for intercity passenger-train operations in the U.S., Amtrak has attempted to maintain many of the traditions of its predecessor railroads, but with greatly simplified and less labor-intensive on-board services. The job titles are fewer and different, but the objective remains the same: To provide the passenger with a safe and comfortable travel experience.

A stewardess-nurse greets passengers boarding Baltimore & Ohio's *Columbian* in the late 1950s. Stewardess-nurse service was inaugurated in 1937 on B&O's *Shenandoah* between Jersey City and Chicago and later extended to include other trains. Stewardess-nurse service on the B&O ended in 1963. *B&O, William F. Howes Jr. collection*

INDEX